'IBSEN THE ROMANTIC'

Edited by Errol Durbach

IBSEN AND THE THEATRE

'IBSEN THE ROMANTIC'

Analogues of Paradise in the Later Plays

Errol Durbach

The University of Georgia Press
Athens, Georgia

The University of Georgia Press
Athens, Georgia 30602

Typeset and printed in Hong Kong

Library of Congress Cataloging in Publication Data

Durbach, Errol, 1941–
   "Ibsen the romantic."
   Bibliography: p.
   Includes index.
1. Ibsen, Henrik, 1828–1906 — Criticism and interpretation.
2. Romanticism — Norway. I. Title.
PT8895.D78   1982   839.8'226   81-1249
ISBN 0-8203-0554-5   AACR2

Contents

Acknowledgements

I am particularly indebted to the Ibsenite scholars and editors of the past fifteen years whose studies have shaped and guided our critical responses to Ibsen. Where my indebtedness to them is not manifest, I hope it may nevertheless be taken for granted.

I should also like to thank Mr R. Cartlidge, and my colleagues at the University of British Columbia, Dr J. L. Wisenthal and Dr Patricia Merivale, who have generously shared their ideas with me; Mr R. F. Hill of King's College, London, for his helpful comments on the initial stages of this study; and especially my wife, an invaluable common reader.

I am grateful to the editors of *Scandinavian Studies, Mosaic* and *Educational Theatre Journal* for permitting me to incorporate into this study some material which originally appeared in journal articles: 'The Apotheosis of Hedda Gabler', *Scandinavian Studies*, XLIII (1971) 143–59; 'Sacrifice and Absurdity in *The Wild Duck*', *Mosaic*, VII (1974) 99–107; 'Temptation to Err: The Dénouement of *Rosmersholm*', *Educational Theatre Journal*, XXIX (1977) 477–85; 'The *Geschwister-Komplex*: Romantic Attitudes to Brother–Sister Incest in Ibsen, Byron, and Emily Brontë', *Mosaic*, XII (1979) 61–73.

The author and publishers wish to thank the following who have kindly given permission for the use of copyright material: Oxford University Press, for the extracts from *The Oxford Ibsen*, translated and edited by James Walter McFarlane *et al.*; and A. P. Watt Ltd, on behalf of Anne Yeats and Michael Yeats, for the verse from 'The Choice' in the *Collected Poems of W. B. Yeats*.

Note on Translation and Quotation

I intend this book primarily for English readers of Ibsen or for those, like myself, with a rudimentary working knowledge of the original texts. Because part of my argument depends upon a close reading of Ibsen's language, I have, wherever necessary, quoted the original Dano-Norwegian. This will also provide the non-Norwegian reader with a sense of Ibsen's Romantic terminology and its affinities with other traditions of Romanticism. The edition I have used is *Ibsens Samlede Verker* in the Fakkel-Bok edition (Oslo, 1962–8) in three volumes. Quotations from *Brand* and *Peer Gynt* are taken from volume II, and those from the later plays from volume III. Page references are given in parentheses after the quoted passages.

The English quotations are taken from *The Oxford Ibsen* (London, 1960–77) in eight volumes, edited by James Walter McFarlane and translated by Professor McFarlane and others. Again, page references are given in parentheses after the quoted passages.

Occasionally I have offered my own translation of lines or passages of dialogue when it seemed to me that a more literal and less elegant reading was necessary to make a point, or where I wanted to stress the etymology of a particular word, or where it seemed necessary (as in the section on *Rosmersholm*) to distinguish between Ibsen's synonyms. I am unable to provide references for my own translated passages, but I hope the reader will be able to locate their contexts without difficulty. (In most instances, when I have translated a line or passage I have also provided the original.)

1   Introduction: 'Ibsen the Romantic'

The quotation marks around the title of this book and of this Introduction indicate an idea for investigation rather than a position confidently asserted – but they also acknowledge the fact that the topic is already over fifty years old. E. M. Forster's essay 'Ibsen the Romantic' first appeared in 1928, with its image of the dramatist as a 'boy bewitched' (side-whiskers, irritability and all) by a primeval romanticism lurking in the 'strange gnarled region of his heart'. The later plays, writes Forster,

> have a romantic intensity which not only rivals the romantic expansion of their predecessors, but is absolutely unique in literature. . . . his stage throbs with a mysteriousness for which no obvious preparation has been made, with beckonings, tremblings, sudden compressions of the air, and his characters as they wrangle among the oval tables and stoves are watched by an unseen power which slips between their words.[1]

Trolls mutter, white horses charge, ghosts glide, the sea lures, and the dead and damaged objects of our civilisation are refashioned (like those in the Ekdal loft) into a land of romance. And, even if Ibsen's romanticism lacks a source that Forster can easily identify, its primary vehicle, he suggests, must surely have been the mountain scenery of Norway, where Ibsen would have experienced a 'passionate intensity . . . comparable to the early experiences of Wordsworth in the English lakes'.[2]

'Romanticism', as Forster's essay ultimately defines it, is an idea vaguely synonymous with 'poetry', and closely associated (although, admittedly, in a manner difficult to apply to Ibsen) with beautiful human relationships. ('Though he had the romantic temperament', says Forster, 'he found personal intercourse sordid.'[3]) It also includes that familiar world of marvellous

1

'romantic' Gothicism, of faery-lands forlorn, permeated by the
powerful natural forces of fire, water, and avalanche. But what
Forster takes no account of in his definition is Ibsen's habitually
ironic attitude towards these elements of Romanticism: his sense
that faery-lands forlorn may be destructive and regressive myths
(as the Ekdal loft surely turns out to be), and that mountain
experiences may as frequently prove epiphanies of horror as
Wordsworthian revelations of infinitude. As for Norway's landscape, there is more mountain gloom than mountain glory in the
frozen glare of the ice-peaks and glaciers that tower behind the
final agonies of *Ghosts*; and the scenery of sentimental National
Romanticism – that geography of mystical purity and spiritual
refreshment – is demolished as early as *Brand*, where, as James
McFarlane puts it, 'the repudiation of Romanticism's Nature is
abrupt and vehement'.[4] Even in the last plays, where the protagonists once more struggle magnificently up the peaks of promise
towards transfiguration, the region they finally inhabit is the Ice
Church of inhuman aspiration, where death is the only revelation. On the same evidence that Forster adduces for his image of
Ibsen the Romantic one could argue for its antithesis.

  The problem is obvious: there are as many conceptions of
Romanticism as there are critics of Romantic literature, and as
many Romantic Ibsens. When Maurice Valency, for example,
describes the confessional element in Ibsen's drama as the 'special
sort of masochism we call romantic', or the 'romantic impulse' of
Hedda Gabler as 'a disease',[5] it is clear that we are intended to
understand Romanticism as that peculiar form of decadence so
defined by Goethe and detailed by Mario Praz in *The Romantic
Agony*. It would be possible, if not very instructive, to compile an
entire lexicon of 'Romantic' Ibsens to demonstrate the semantic
confusion and the multiplicity of romanticisms, which make any
discussion of the topic perilous. One remains grateful, nevertheless, to those critics who have worked through the tangle of
specifically Norwegian forms of Romanticism to locate Ibsen's
indigenous or local affinities: *Nasjonalromantikken* or National
Romanticism of the early historical drama, which Ibsen was later
to despise as pernicious fictions; *Huldreromantikken* or 'Faery'
Romanticism of folkloric tradition, which Ibsen satirised in Julian
Poulsen, that Bunthorne of sham Romanticism in *St John's
Night;* and *Nyromantikken* or Neo-Romanticism of the 1890s,
typified in Hamsun's article 'Fra det ubevidste Sjæleliv' ('From

the Unconscious Life of the Mind') and already anticipated in Ibsen's psychological studies of Rebekka West and Ellida Wangel.[6] Some of these local romanticisms were undoubtedly a late blooming, in the remote North, of European Romantic themes–Brian Downs points to the Rousseauistic features of National Romanticism in, for example, the celebration of peasant nobility and the image of a pure historical past untainted by the vices of modernity. And it is possible to find in the emergence of an independent Norway in 1814, after her emancipation from four centuries of Danish rule, a late historical paradigm of the political hopes which shaped the Romantic sensibilities of France and England in the age of revolution. The social conditions in Norway, of course, were vastly different. There was no oppressed peasantry, and no industrialism. But the American and French revolutions had already pointed the way for a democratic constitution which would affirm the sovereignty of Norway (despite her political status as a 'gift' to Sweden), and a nation was in the process of being reborn in the spirit of bloodless revolution. Ibsen wrote his first play, *Catiline*, in response to the revolutionary political climate of 1848; and it is possible to chart the course of his political concerns from the fervour of *Catiline* to the tragic failure of liberal idealism in *Rosmersholm*, where the reactionary backlash is most keenly felt, and so project a revaluation of his Romantic hopes analogous to the European response to the collapse of post-revolutionary idealism. It is clear, at any rate, that the phases of European Romanticism are recapitulated in the development of Norwegian cultural history, and that literary influences filtered gradually northwards to inspire a group of writers already responsive to these new currents of feeling: Wergeland, Welhaven and Asbjørnsen in Norway; and Oehlenschläger, Johan Ludvig Heiberg and Henrik Hertz in Denmark. Ibsen, as Brian Downs points out, 'was not a sudden, causeless phenomenon, born in a hyperborean desert with no traceable ancestry, but stood well in the stream of the ethical, religious, political and sociological thought of his time'.[7] This is an aspect of the Romantic Ibsen that I must leave to those more competent to evaluate his role in the various romanticisms that comprise Norwegian literature from the 1830s to the 1860s.

And what of Ibsen the Romantic *dramatist*? It is one of those curiosities of theatrical history that, when Ibsen's *Ghosts* was staged at the Théâtre Libre in Paris, Sarah Bernhardt was also playing Sardou's *Cléopâtre* in the 'romantic' *fin de siècle* style (and applying, it is said, a *real* asp to her bosom). Once again, definitions of Romanticism bifurcate: on the one hand the epitome of decadent exoticism, and on the other the exemplar of those metaphysical concerns which, as Terry Otten argues in his study of the Romantic drama, are the hallmark of the English Romantics. 'Shelley,' he writes, 'perhaps unconsciously, was moving towards a new kind of drama, a drama which by the end of the century was to find full expression in Ibsen's late symbolic dramas.'[8] And what makes the new drama quintessentially 'Romantic', as Otten defines the term, is its refusal to affirm *external* criteria of social morality (as in the Shakespearian mode), and its protagonist's strenuous search after a moral order *within* to counter the cosmic emptiness and the chaos around him. For Shelley and for Byron, as for Ibsen after them, there is no order and no God – except in so far as their protagonists are prepared to conceive of Him. This is a far cry from Forster's vision of Ibsen's romanticism. Ibsen as Romantic *dramatist* is seen in quite another guise: as one standing in direct relationship to European Romanticism, without intervenient local influences, participating in and shaping its mythologies, and finally projecting its spiritual concerns into the images and archetypes of the twentieth century.

This is the Ibsen who emerges in Brian Johnston's recent study as

> a post-Romantic artist who still remained loyal to Romantic aspirations: who, though he saw everywhere the betrayal of revolutionary and Romantic ideals, still held onto the impossible goal of a 'revolution in the spirit of man' . . . a militant Romantic who is subversively smuggling the explosive Romantic powers into the pragmatic bourgeois world that had turned its back upon them.[9]

This image of Ibsen the Romantic once again, it seems to me, takes too little account of the ironic, sceptical, at times counter-Romantic and anti-Romantic temperament which sees all too clearly a bourgeoisie grasping at romantic possibility and, in the very attempt to make it viable, devastating and destroying life itself. What Johnston argues most convincingly, however, is for Ibsen's centrality to the moral intelligence of the late nineteenth century, and his close affinity with Hegel's ambitious programme of Romanticism: nothing less than the redemption of man's alienation from himself and from nature by rediscovering 'the total human spirit within the conditions of the Present'.[10] It is an elaborate and finely detailed argument; and, even if one cannot accept the direct and immediate influence of the late German Romantics on Ibsen, his cultural affinities with Hegel, Schelling, Schiller and Goethe are either a matter of astonishing coincidence, or a consequence of his complete absorption of the ideas, images and spiritual concerns of the *Zeitgeist*. These archetypes of Romantic literature have been brilliantly synthesised, as Johnston notes, by M. H. Abrams in *Natural Supernaturalism;* and merely to compare Abrams's paradigm of the Romantic quest in the poetry and romances of late eighteenth-century Germany to Ibsen's *Peer Gynt* is to recognise Peer's participation in the alienated Romantic hero's search for a recovered sense of pristine unity in himself and in society:

> In Novalis' romances the process of representative human experience is a fall from self-unity and community into division, and from contentment into the longing for redemption, which consists of a recovered unity on a higher level of self-awareness. This process is represented in the plot-form of an educational journey in quest of a feminine other, whose mysterious attraction compels the protagonist to abandon his childhood sweetheart and the simple security of home and family (equated with infancy, the pagan golden age, and the Biblical paradise) to wander through alien lands on a way that rounds imperceptibly back to home and family, but with an access of insight (the product of his experience en route) which enables him to recognize, in the girl he left behind, the elusive female figure who has all along been the object of his longing and his quest. The protagonist's return home thus coincides with the consummation of a union with his beloved bride.[11]

The general narrative framework, the dramatic events, the symbols and metaphors that link Ibsen to Novalis and Goethe are so inescapable that one is inclined to accept, on the basis of this evidence alone, a Teutonic variant of Ibsen the Romantic. Indeed, Peer's explicit reference to Goethe's *Faust* might seem to confirm, unequivocally, Ibsen's conscious reliance upon German

Romanticism for the themes and ideas of his own Faust drama: 'To quote a famous author,' says Peer, '"Das ewig weibliche ziehet uns an!"' (III, 349). Peer has not quite called to mind the original line; but, even if he had, the image of the redemptive woman is most inappropriately conferred upon the carnally seductive Anitra.[12] Nor, as James McFarlane argues, is *das Ewig-Weibliche* embodied, without irony, in the figure of the blind and aged Solveig – Peer's fantastic projection of a female wish-dream to shelter him against the Buttonmoulder, the inescapable reality of death.[13] But, it seems to me, the anti-Romantic or counter-Romantic implications of this Goethean archetype are manifest throughout the body of Ibsen's drama, from Lyngstrand's flaccid vision of eternally waiting womanhood to old Foldal's pathetic belief 'that somewhere out in the wide wide world, far away perhaps, there is to be found the true woman' (VIII, 189). For Ibsen, the Romantic notion of Eternal Womanhood, *das Ewig-Weibliche* – a constellation of abstract ideals which man may strive towards but never possess – ultimately serves only to pervert the reality of sexual relationships and the satisfaction of desire. Faust may be saved by his refusal to yield to the illusions of fulfilment in the world; but Borkman and Rubek, by the same token, are damned for interposing the metaphors of Romantic questing between desire and human experience. And the women in their lives cry out against this essential lovelessness which fashions them into bloodless images of an infinitude beyond attainment. The dramatic structure of *Peer Gynt* may conform to the paradigm of the Romantic quest. But the voice that speaks from within this structure is a dissenting voice, that 'other' Ibsen[14] who both participates in and stands apart from the European tradition towards which he gestures, the Romantic Ibsen and the counter-Romantic.

What I want to examine in the chapters that follow are the tensions between these two Ibsens, the impulses that pass from one to the other, and the paradoxical simultaneity of Romantic and counter-Romantic attitudes which make Ibsen a Romantic of extraordinary individuality, both celebrant and critic of a vision potentially redemptive and potentially ruinous. The Romantic Ibsen I have in mind (and whom I shall discuss in his own terms) is not Forster's poet – which is not to deny the poet in Ibsen, but rather to locate his romanticism in a drama of spiritual distress, in his protagonists' search for consolation in the face of death, and their attempt to rediscover a world of lost Paradisal hopes in the mythology of Romanticism. Redemption from cosmic nothingness, from meaninglessness – this is the nature of the Romantic quest which Ibsen's people share with those of Byron, Stendhal, and Jens Peter Jacobsen. Hugo von Hofmannsthal, writing in 1891, was among the first of Ibsen's critics to link his dramatic concerns with a pervasive European mood; and the composite picture of the Ibsen hero that he sketched in his essay is far closer to my sense of Ibsen the Romantic than Forster's image of the boy bewitched. The people in Ibsen's drama, wrote Hofmannsthal, are possessed by a desperation to restore meaning and style to life, anxious (like Niels Lyhne, Jacobsen's hero) not only to write poetry 'but instead oneself become the stuff of poetry',[15] forever yearning for ancient myths of significance in the modern world and for miracle in a faithless age:

> This mysterious element, which is to come and carry one away and give life some great meaning, gives all things new colour and every world a soul – this thing has several names for these people. Sometimes it is the 'miraculous' for which Nora longs; for Julian and Hedda it is Grecian, the great Bacchanalia, with noble grace and vineleaves in one's hair; or it is the sea with its mysterious allure; or it is a free life on a grand pattern, in America or Paris. All these things are only symbolical names for something 'out there', something 'different'. It is nothing other than Stendhal's yearning search for the 'imprévu', for what is unforeseen, for what is not 'weary, stale, flat and unprofitable' in love and life. It is nothing but the dream-longing of the romantics for the moonlit magic wilderness, for openings in the mountainside, for speaking pictures, for some undreamed-of fairy-tale element in life.[16]

The 'miraculous' for which the Ibsen protagonist yearns, the faery-world forlorn, Hofmannsthal goes on to suggest, is ultimately to be located in the subconscious, in dim memories of a lost and dream-like childhood 'in a kind of enchanted forest from which they emerge insatiably homesick and peculiarly insulated'.[17]

I want, in the chapter that follows, to define even more carefully the nature of that lost world in the plays of Ibsen, the myths and archetypes and attitudes that shape the Romanticism of his protagonists – and the counter-Romantic vision which dramatises their tragic failure to transpose these fictions and symbols of significance into the realities of life.

Notes

1. E. M. Forster, 'Ibsen the Romantic', repr. in James McFarlane (ed.), *Henrik Ibsen: A Critical Anthology* (Harmondsworth, 1970) p. 233.
2. Ibid., p. 234.
3. Ibid., p. 232.
4. James McFarlane, Introduction to *The Oxford Ibsen*, III (London, 1972) 17.
5. Maurice Valency, *The Flower and the Castle* (New York, 1963) pp. 123, 200.
6. See James McFarlane, Introduction to *The Oxford Ibsen*, I (London, 1970); Brian Downs, *Ibsen: The Intellectual Background* (Cambridge, 1946), and *Modern Norwegian Literature 1860–1918* (Cambridge, 1966); and Ronald Popperwell, *Norway* (New York, 1972).
7. Downs, *Ibsen: The Intellectual Background*, p. ix.
8. Terry Otten, *The Deserted Stage: The Search for Dramatic Form in Nineteenth-Century England* (Athens, Ohio, 1972) p. 14.
9. Brian Johnston, *The Ibsen Cycle: The Design of the Plays from 'Pillars of Society' to 'When We Dead Awaken'* (Boston, Mass., 1975) Preface, n.p.
10. Ibid., p. 316.
11. M. H. Abrams, *Natural Supernaturalism: Tradition and Revolution in Romantic Literature* (New York, 1971) p. 246.
12. I am grateful to Dr Patricia Merivale for showing me her paper '*Faust* and *Peer Gynt*: Ironic Inversions'. 'It is useful no longer to wonder if Peer's misquotation . . . could be a slip of Ibsen's memory', she writes. 'It is simply the most explicit clue to Ibsen's deliberate employment of the Faustian structure to invert, ironically, the Faustian theme.'
13. McFarlane, 'Introduction to *The Oxford Ibsen*, III, 29–30.
14. For a detailed discussion of Ibsen's 'otherness', see Inga-Stina Ewbank, 'Ibsen on the English Stage: The Proof of the Pudding is in the Eating', in Errol Durbach (ed.), *Ibsen and the Theatre* (London, 1980).
15. J. P. Jacobsen, *Niels Lyhne* (1880), quoted in Hugo von Hofmannsthal, 'Die Menschen in Ibsens Drama', repr. in McFarlane, *Ibsen: A Critical Anthology*, p. 134.
16. Hugo von Hofmannsthal, op. cit., p. 134.
17. Ibid., p. 135.

2 'The Land without Paradise'

FIGUREN: Husk at *én* med flamme-riset
mannen drev av paradiset!
Porten har han lagt et sluk for;—
over *det* du springer ei!
BRAND: Åpen lot han *lengslens* vei! (II, 123)

THE FIGURE: Remember, *one* with flaming sword
Drove man out from Paradise!
Outside its gate he set a chasm . . .
Over *that* you will never leap!
BRAND: But he left open the path of *longing*! (III, 246)

This passage, which appears towards the end of *Brand*, contains nearly every feature of the spiritual geography, the mythology and the metaphors which characterise Ibsen's vision of man's fallen state: 'paradiset', the dream of Paradise – that image of a perfectly ordered reality, a model of absolute value, timeless and therefore exempt from the law of change; 'et sluk', an abyss – the real world in which man is mired, exiled from Eden, and subject to process and mutability;[1] 'flamme-riset', the rod of flames – icon of punishment, and a reminder that the wages of sin in the fallen world is death; and 'lengslens vei', the path of longing – man's nostalgic yearning for a lost Paradise, the source of the Romantic *Sehnsucht* which permeates Ibsen's world like a threnody of loss. The same note sounds again at the end of *Peer Gynt* when, with the eyes of a dying Moses, Peer gazes on a Promised Land which his own experience has turned to dust and ashes. *Lengslens vei* seems no longer open to this death-infected exile from Eden:

PEER. . . . . I'll clamber up to the highest peak;
I would see the sun rise once again,

9

And stare at the promised land till I'm tired;
Then heap the snow over my head.
They can write above it: Here lies No one;
And afterwards – then – ! Things must go as they will.

CHURCHGOERS [*singing on the forest path*]:
   Blest morning,
   When God's might
Spears earth with burning light:
   We, the inheritors,
   Sing out to heaven's towers
The Kingdom's battle-cry against the night.
PEER [*crouching in fear*]:
Don't look that way! It's all a desert.
Alas, I was dead long before I died.   (III, 418)

These lines will re-echo in John Gabriel Borkman's dying vision of
another vast and inexhaustible kingdom, 'The Kingdom I was
about to take possession of when . . . when I died' (VIII, 231). Like
Peer's *lovede land*, Borkman's *rige* is a wilderness of ice and
freezing winds; but the crucial difference between these two
visions of a ruined and forfeited Eden is that in the later play
those contrapuntal, hymn-like reassurances of a Paradise regained all fall silent: the churchgoers' confident belief in *Gudsriket*, the Kingdom of God; their faith as *arvinger*, heirs to a
living tradition; and the efficacy of *Gudsrikets tungemål,* the
language of God's Kingdom. In Borkman's world there are no
such defences against the night and the failure of promise. The
protagonists of the later plays now yearn for Paradise in a
language which transforms God's *tungemål* into the prose of
secular speech; the kingdom for which they yearn is a mundane
analogue of some dimly remembered *Gudsrike;* but their yearning seems to intensify in proportion to the steadily diminishing
faith that once guaranteed the recovery of Paradise.
   Lengslens vei, the Romantic longing for 'Paradise' – whatever
the specific, variant meanings of that concept – clearly derives
from the mythology of Christian faith and persists, even when
that faith declines, in secular expressions of what George Steiner
has called a 'deep-seated nostalgia for the absolute'.[2] As many
literary historians have argued, the myths of Romanticism and its
characteristic concepts appear, both originally and in their later

manifestations, as 'metareligions' or 'surrogate creeds',[3] 'displaced and reconstituted theology, or else a secularized form of devotional experience'.[4] Marx's dream of a secular Utopia, Freud's vision of a homecoming to death, and Lévi-Strauss's analysis of man's devastation of the last vestiges of Eden are all, in a sense, modern forms of Romanticism; for, as Steiner argues,

> the major mythologies constructed in the West since the early nineteenth century are not only attempts to fill the emptiness left by the decay of Christian theology and Christian dogma. They are themselves a kind of *substitute theology.* They are systems of belief and argument which may be savagely anti-religious, which may postulate a world without God and may deny an afterlife, but whose structure, whose aspirations, whose claims on the believer, are profoundly religious in strategy and in effect.[5]

One version of Ibsen's Romanticism is clearly that of a secular theodicy, a response to man's need for consolation against the certainty of death in a world no longer able to assuage his fears, the need to redeem the consequences of the Fall by a powerful assertion of the imagination, and the need to rediscover godhead in the God-abandoned universe.

I

It is a basic premise in Ibsen's later plays that God is dead. One tends to take this fact for granted, relegating the drama to that general cultural climate defined by Hillis Miller in *The Disappearance of God,* or gesturing vaguely towards Nietzsche's sonorous pronouncement of God's death in *The Joyful Wisdom* of 1882 to account for the habitual failure of faith among Ibsen's protagonists. But, as early as 1866, Brand had already sung the obsequies for the God of a debilitated dispensation – rejecting, as Kierkegaard had before him, 'the impersonation of insipid human kindliness'[6] in the languishing figure of a discredited, post-Enlightenment Christ.

BRAND: .   .   . *I* am going to a funeral.
AGNES: A funeral?

EINAR: Who's being buried?
BRAND: The God you just called *yours*. . . .
　　The God of hacks and time-serving drudges
　　Shall be wrapped in his shroud and laid in his coffin.
　　And in broad daylight. This thing must have an end.
　　It is time, don't you see? He has been ailing
　　These thousand years.　(III, 88)

The voice of God may still be heard in that ironic declaration of
caritas as the avalanche buries Brand. But the central experience
of the play remains His progressive disappearance, implicit in the
substitution of materialism for faith and of bread for belief in the
community, the growing secularism of the Church as a now effete
institution, and, paradoxically, in Brand's own assertion of God's
ministry after burying the 'holy decrepitude' of nominal Christendom. By redefining God in the image of his own intransigent will,
by assuming the mantle of a self-appointed prophet, he stands in
the gravest danger of aspiring towards godhead 'simply to seem
worthy' (in the words of Nietzsche's madman) of filling God's
empty space. He rejects the community as unworthy of grace. He
sacrifices child, wife and mother to the deification of his own
uncompromising nature. And he imposes on humanity an image
of God so relentlessly merciless and cold that his most notable
achievement, as Shaw unkindly puts it, is to have caused 'more
intense suffering by his saintliness than the most talented sinner
could possibly have done with twice his opportunities'.[7]

　　Shaw is unkind because he fails to take account – so much does
he loathe the idealist – of the ambivalence which characterises the
Romantic, or the magnificence of his attempt to restore man 'to
the condition in which he walked with God in the garden'.[8] Brand
fails, because he never stops to inquire whether his call to
spiritual revolution derives from the living God or from some
neurotic inner compulsion. Intending the career of a Kierkegaardian knight of faith, Brand finally enacts the arrogance of a
Nietzschean superman whose God is indistinguishable from the
loveless, discreative impulses of his own personality. And God, so
defined, is as good as dead. *Brand* is as complete a rendering of
the Nietzschean madness and as critical an analysis of the Kierkegaardian position as one could hope to find among the statements
of crisis that characterise the spiritual history of the nineteenth
century. Ibsen did not merely allude to the tradition and its

horrors, which cliché has already dulled for us. He dramatised, in a series of extraordinary variations, the meaning of God's death and its awful implications for those who live in the abyss.

In the plays that follow *Emperor and Galilean*, the voice of God and the voices that once chanted His litanies all fall silent, or echo only as parodies of a remembered liturgy. In the grey Galilean world of *Ghosts* the remnants of Christian doctrine persist only as moribund ideas – 'old defunct theories, all sorts of old defunct beliefs' (v, 384) – which continue to haunt Mrs Alving. God has already given way to duty, and dogma to the power of public opinion. And, when human nature rushes in to fill God's empty spaces, it does so not in the effete Christianity of Manders but in Engstrand's specious manipulation of orthodox systems of morality, rationalised in the moral piety that will eventually persuade the Church into partnership with the brothel-keeper. The Devil speaks the language of the priest, and an entire moral system stands upon the verge of collapse. Christian values have become mere ghosts, old virtues emptied of validity, and unscrupulously exploited by hypocrites who can turn the system into profit. Dressed in the piety of his Sunday suit, Engstrand demonstrates the power that feeds off the last tatters of orthodoxy and reduces it to nonsense. He is the repository of all values perverted, and everything eventually passes to him: the power of priesthood, the Alving money, the Alving name, the Alving daughter. It is Engstrand who triumphantly inherits the fallen world.

In *Ghosts* the parody of *Gudsrikets tungemål* is shocking, ironic. In the final scene of *The Wild Duck*, in the desperate attempt of the onlookers to reconcile the death of Hedvig with a tradition of grief that can contain it, the language of prayer passes beyond parody into black and aching farce:

HJALMAR. . . . [*He clenches his hands and cries to heaven*]:
   Oh, God in high . . . if Thou *art* there! Why hast Thou done this to me?
GINA: Hush, hush, you mustn't say such terrible things. We had no right to keep her, I dare say.
MOLVIK: The child is not dead; it sleeps.
RELLING: Rubblish! . . .
MOLVIK [*stretches out his arms and mutters*]: Praised be the Lord. Earth to earth . . . earth to earth . . .

RELLING [*whispers*]: Shut up, man! You are drunk!   (VI, 240–1)

The priest who presides over these obsequies is defrocked and drunk–but not so drunk as to forget that poignant account in Mark's gospel of the raising to life of Jairus's daughter: '*Barnet er ikke dødt: det sover*' – 'The child is not dead, but asleep. . . . And taking the child by the hand he said to her, "Talitha kum!" which means, "Little girl, I tell you to get up." The little girl got up at once and began to walk about, for she was twelve years old' (Mark 5: 39–43). It is within the perspective of a faith now hopelessly inoperative that Hedvig's absurdly meaningless sacrifice must ultimately be viewed. There is no language, except that of despair, in which to speak of it. And even *that* language is reduced to platitude or pathetic self-indulgence.

It is in *Rosmersholm*, however, that God's disappearance becomes the first term in the protagonists' strenuous moral argument: 'There is no judge over us', Rosmer admits in the spirit of terrible freedom. 'Therefore we must see to it that we judge ourselves' (VI, 379). Existential freedom – man's consciousness of absolute autonomy in the absence of God – imposes upon him the responsibility of exemplary moral action, the imperative to create value where none exists even to the extent of holding a final doom session over the self. But, however their responses are manifested, there is scarcely a major protagonist in any of Ibsen's last plays who does not model his values and behaviour on the assumption of a *deus absconditus* or whose spiritual status is not defined by that awareness. They are either pagan devotees of Dionysos or seekers after the pre-Christian spirit of the ancient Vikings, self-declared apostates or defrocked priests, freethinkers, atheist rebels, or agnostics tormented by their doubt. Hedda dreams of the free spirit, irradiated by the orgastic religion of ancient Greece, living as God amidst the clutter of bourgeois existence. Solness shakes his fist in the face of an apathetic deity who sanctions the senseless deaths of little children, and dedicates himself to a new religion of secular humanism. And Allmers, the self-styled atheist, devotes himself to a momentous existential undertaking, nothing less than the definitive exploration of '*det menneskelige ansvar*' – man's responsibility – under the great stillness of the heavens. But in his dreams he still yearns for the beneficent God who will recreate the malformed world by healing his crippled child, a subconscious clinging to that old habit of mind which cannot easily relinquish the certainty, stability, reassurance and comfort of the Christian dispensation. In many ways Allmers's predicament seems the paradigm of the Romantic dilemma in Ibsen's drama, which, to state it in its simplest and crudest terms, is to be trapped between a traumatic sense of existence as process, change and death in a world devoid of consistent value, and a nostalgic longing for a lost world of static hierarchies where death has no dominion. And in order to resolve this dilemma, the atheist / agnostic / apostate will fashion out of the raw material of existence his analogue of that lost Eden – a symbolic Paradise which promises eternal life, and which he seeks to possess not as *metaphor* but as *fact*.

II

The idea of Paradise as one of the central myths of the Romantic imagination has been illustrated, in its historical variety and complexity, by M. H. Abrams in *Natural Supernaturalism*. The tradition is inaugurated, he suggests, in Wordsworth's revaluation of Milton's theodicy and his redefinition in secular terms of the 'paradise within'. Having lost faith in an apocalypse by revelation, he argues, the Romantics turned to the hope of recovering Paradise by revolution; and, when the French Revolution failed to realise that political Eden in which man would live as the New Adam, the despair and disillusionment yielded a single solution: a revolution in the spirit of man, an apocalypse by imagination or cognition which would restore heroism to the ordinary, and grandeur to the dimensions of everyday experience.[9] This is the substance of Wordsworth's 'high Romantic argument' in which pre-Christian intimations of a golden age or pastoral Elysium, and Miltonic echoes of a lost Christian Paradise, are all subsumed in the conviction that man's imagination can rediscover, in the natural world, an earthly Paradise rooted in the life of the common man:

Paradise, and groves
Elysian, Fortunate Fields – like those of old
Sought in the Atlantic Main – why should they be
A history only of departed things,
Or a mere fiction of what never was?[10]

Man's mind, in harmonious union with nature, makes possible a spiritual redemption from the 'sleep of death'. It rediscovers, in other words, a spiritual value within the otherwise inanimate world of mundane reality with which the self can unite in a great 'consummation'.

The desire for spiritual transformation, for resurrection from the sleep of death into a state of Edenic perfection, finds expression, more or less literally, in nearly all of Ibsen's plays. Its affinity with remembered vestiges of an earlier Christian tradition is particularly evident in Rubek's vision, in *When We Dead Awaken,* of a Paradise regained through the artefacts of the artistic imagination. His great sculptural masterpiece, 'The Day of Resurrection', is the perfect dramatic correlative of the Romantic quest: 'My vision of Resurrection — the loveliest, most beautiful image I could think of — was of a pure young woman, untainted by the world, waking to light and glory, and having nothing ugly or unclean to rid herself of' (VIII, 278). But the 'resurrection' that Rubek desires is possible only *outside* of nature, that unclean and tainted world of the chasm — and only in an immediate reconstitution of the old Paradise in the new without the intervening fall. It may be possible to see a Wordsworthian solution in some aspects of Ibsen's thought; but it is Ibsen's sceptical questioning of that Romantic tradition that ultimately defines his vision. For Ibsen, to discover Paradise as a 'simple produce of the common day'[11] and to find a solution to spiritual death in the radical identity of self and nature, the Romantic protagonist must have had to make two assumptions: that some divine reality must necessarily inhere beneath the surface of phenomenal nature, and that the essential self can discover its analogue in the epiphany of 'natural supernaturalism'.[12] But in Ibsen's plays, as I have suggested, nature is no longer instinct with sympathetic Paradisal affinities. It is a world without value, a desolate reality. The epiphany of light and clarity at the end of *Ghosts,* illuminating a landscape of unremitting harshness, is an emblem of the tragic fact that joy and glory are no longer discoverable in the frozen waste beyond the little world of men. 'Man's discerning intellect', to use Wordsworth's phrase, finds no analogy, in *Ghosts,* with a 'goodly universe';[13] and the Ibsen protagonist who seeks his kingdom in the mountain world of nature encounters only the brute, indifferent force of the avalanche. The self, moreover, in Ibsen's world, has no essential ground of value which finds its counterpart in nature. It is fragmentary, illusory, and it leads those who seek it out to the 'nothingness' at the core of Peer Gynt's onion.

Again, there is a close association between Ibsen's vision of man's lost integrity and that of Blake and the German Romantics, who envisage the Fall from Paradise in images of fragmentation and alienation, and who dream of a state of self-completion and community in some New Jerusalem or *Drittes Reich*. The disintegration of the self, the fragmented social order, Blake's 'fall into Division', Hölderlin's description of society as *disjecta membra*, Hegel's sense of his culture as 'the self-alienated spirit'[14] – all these images of a fall from wholeness, and the promise of a Paradise restored, find articulate expression in the visionary speeches of Brand:

> But there is
> One thing that does prevail and endure –
> That is the uncreated spirit, once redeemed
> From Chaos in the first fresh Spring of time, and still
> Extending bridges of unalterable faith
> From banks of flesh to banks of spirit.
> Now it is hawked from door to door, and cheap . . .
> Thanks to this generation's view of God.
> But out of these dismembered wrecks of soul,
> From these truncated torsos of the spirit,
> From these heads, these hands, there shall arise
> A whole being, so that the Lord
> May recognize his creature Man once more,
> His greatest masterpiece, his heir,
> His Adam, powerful, and tall, and young!   (III, 92–3)

There are echoes, here, of Blake's Universal Man, the first Adam, who falls from 'Perfect Unity' and the 'Universal Brotherhood of Eden'[15] into division and fragmentation, and whose 'Resurrection into Unity' is effected through a redemptive vision of Paradise where integrity is rediscovered. But Brand locates this new Eden within his own psyche – a reflection of his desire, very like Peer Gynt's, to be 'myself entirely', to seek traditional values not outwards or upwards but in the deep recesses of the self, in this way becoming both subject and source of his own redemptive psychology:

Within! Within! That is my call!
That is the way I must venture! That is my path!
One's own inmost heart – *that* is the world,
Newly created, and ripe for God's work.
There shall the vulture of the will be slain.
And *there* shall the new Adam at last be born again.

(114–15)

To restore the 'new Adam' in oneself becomes one of the enduring quests, given the notations and the terms of modern existentialism, of Ibsen's protagonists in the later plays – a strenuous attempt to envision new heaven and new earth, the wholly integrated self, by reordering one's processes of consciousness, by *seeing differently*. 'The eye altering alters all', says Blake.[16] But, if the visionary revelation can redeem man by making him whole again, it can also damn him when he sees obliquely with the scratched left eye of the troll. John Gabriel Borkman, in an ironic echo of Blake's aphorism, justifies his vision of a monstrously distorted reality in the language of a romanticism become perverse: 'Det er øyet som forvandler handlingen', he says. 'Det gjenfødte øye forvandler den gamle handling (III, 550) – 'It is the eye that transforms the deed. The eye, regenerated, transforms the old deed.' The source of Romantic salvation, the eye, now blurs the moral and spiritual vision into a form of astigmatism incapable of distinguishing between the new Adam and the old. Neither Brand nor any other of Ibsen's visionary humanists succeeds in finding the 'Perfect Unity' *within*, nor the 'Universal Brotherhood of Eden' in which the entire social community regains its cohesion.

The external corollary to the search within is a paradise of the harmoniously ordered cultural life, in which the antinomies of existence are reconciled in a new spiritual amalgam – those analogues of the Third Empire that recur in so many of the plays after *Emperor and Galilean*, where the idea is most clearly defined. It is not a quintessentially Ibsenian concept, as it is sometimes assumed to be. There are echoes of Kant, Hegel, Schiller and Blake in its formulation;[17] and Wordsworth's divine–poetic mission, his programme for the regeneration of the human spirit in a democracy of souls, has its origins in a similar revelation of the new egalitarian community. Rosmer's vision, in its general implications, is similarly Wordsworthian – an attempt to transcend the conflict of orthodoxy and liberalism, the forces tearing society apart, in a new nobility of mind and soul until the ripples of his idealism, spreading in ever widening circles, finally incorporate one universal nobleman. Borkman's empire of benevolent socialism, Solness's dedication to human happiness in creating homes for men – these visions imply a variation on the 'Universal Brotherhood of Eden'. But there is no Third Empire in Ibsen where all contradiction is finally resolved in Edenic harmony, or where the attempt to synthesise discordant opposites does not result in their mutual destruction. Nor is the humanist ideal of the regenerated community ever realised within the smaller unit of the family; for the idealist himself inevitably proves incapable of sustaining, in his own fragmented and alienated life, the joy and community he so fervently envisions. The fallen world in Ibsen remains a world of division, a *perpetuum mobile* of conflicting impulses which denies the Romantic dream of a reintegrated Eden.

The analogues of Paradise in Romantic and post-Romantic literature are legion; and, even when poets no longer speak of the classical Elysium or the New Jerusalem or Paradise, their secular variants on the happy prelapsarian place remain authentic replications of the Edenic idea. Similarly in Ibsen, although the literal concepts of *Paradis, lovede land* or *Gudsrike* are almost entirely obscured beneath the colloquial dialogue of the realistic drama, they are nevertheless invoked by ingenious secular equivalents of Paradise: Hedda's vision of a mythical pagan alternative to bourgeois culture, in which men live in freedom as demigods; John Gabriel Borkman's ore-bearing, subterranean kingdom of infinite riches and power; Solness's airborne Kingdom of Orangia; or, more abstract in its conception, Allmers's search for a dimension of human existence forever exempt from the law of change – Eden as a condition of imperishable angelic bliss. These, and many others, are the kingdoms of power and glory which Ibsen's protagonists try to fashion out of the raw material of human experience. But what Ibsen dramatises in these alternative Edens is the fallibility inherent in *all* the Romantic visions of Paradise – that converse of a vital, positive and spiritually redemptive vision of perfect unity. For just as *lengslens vei,* the longing for Paradise, may finally infect the soul with the sort of *Heimweh* that afflicts Ellida Wangel, so Paradise itself may prove an illusion concealing a barren waste, a mirage hovering above the reality of devastation. This is the ambivalence that Northrop Frye detects in the very structure of Romantic symbolism:

The journey within to the happy island garden or the city of light is a perilous quest, equally likely to terminate in the blasted ruins of Byron's *Darkness* or Beddoes's *Subterranean City*. In many Romantic poems, including Keats's nightingale ode, it is suggested that the final identification of and with reality may be or at least include death.'[18]

But the most appalling aspect of the quest for Paradise is that it may lead towards an anti-Eden, a world of static forms, of cold and motionless alternatives to human passion and joy – most certainly an ideal world in being exempt from process, but paradoxically dead in its very deathlessness and incapable of accommodating man as living inhabitant. These are the 'cold pastoral' qualities of Keats's Grecian Urn – an alternative to the world of human limitation and the multiple frustrations of 'breathing human passion', but an Eden forever petrified in frozen gestures of unconsummated love, a world out of nature where nothing lives or moves. If it evokes sensations of beauty, this Paradise also invites a complex of unrequited desires to match the frustrations of the phenomenal world. Byzantium, in Yeats's 'Sailing to Byzantium', is another such Paradise sundered from the realities of process which make us human but render us mortal. The most complete analysis of the fallacies of Paradise appears in Wallace Stevens's 'Sunday Morning', with its image of that deathless state for which his persona yearns, but which is merely another aspect of the death she fears. It is a poem which makes fully articulate what is implicit in nearly all the later plays of Ibsen, where to live in the Paradise of one's own construction is to dwell down among the dead men:

> Is there no change of death in paradise?
> Does ripe fruit never fall? Or do the boughs
> Hang always heavy in that perfect sky,
> Unchanging, yet so like our perishing earth,
> With rivers like our own that seek for seas
> They never find, the same receding shores
> That never touch with inarticulate pang?[19]

The self made whole again, the secular guarantee of immortality, a pseudo-religious defence against the fear of death – however one defines the nature of the Paradisal quest, it is clear from Ibsen's analysis of Romantic psychology that the search may lead directly to a living Hell, and that in the very attempt to fashion an alternative Eden the protagonist may destroy the life around him and consign himself to a living death. For if 'Paradise' is their only possible answer in the Godless universe to the ravages of time and the consequences of the Fall, then it must by its very nature be timeless and immutable – like death itself. It is one of the central ironies in Ibsen that the fear of death impels his protagonists towards the morbidity and deadliness which characterise their kingdom–that frozen no man's land 'which never moves, which never changes, which never grows older, but which remains forever, icy and silent.'[20] The ambivalent Paradise of Ibsen's drama, the double vision which perceives it, and the equivocal nature of his Romanticism finally extend to our perception of his protagonists and our evaluation of their life-missions, quests, and ideals – a gallery of magnificent and mad Romantics, whose Edenic visions are the source at once of their potential redemption and their unregenerate destruction.

III

It is not entirely surprising that Ibsen hardly, if ever, appears in histories of European Romantic or post-Romantic literature – a fate he shares with Byron, and probably for much the same reason: 'Byron I omit altogether,' writes M. H. Abrams in his Preface to *Natural Supernaturalism*, 'not because I think him a lesser poet than the others but because in his greatest work he speaks with an ironic counter-voice and deliberately opens a satirical perspective on the vatic stance of his Romantic contemporaries.'[21] Precisely the same may be said of Ibsen the Romantic; and those definitions of Romanticism, such as Morse Peckham's,[22] which must bend and twist themselves to accommodate the peculiar genius of Byron also make it possible to read Ibsen in a similar light. Byron, in fact, is one of the few English Romantics whom Ibsen knew (in Adolf Strodtmann's German translation); and his enigmatic comments in a letter of 1872 suggest that Byron assumed an importance for him quite disproportionate to Ibsen's acquaintance with his poetry:

I have not read very much of Byron, but I have a feeling that

his works translated into our language would be of great
assistance in freeing our aesthetics from many moral prejudices
– which would be a great gain. . . . It is acknowledged here that
German literature required Byron's assistance to enable it to
reach its present standpoint; and I maintain that we need him
to free us from ours.[23]

What Byron he might have read, and how much, is uncertain;
and I make no claims for influence. But the voice that cries out in
Cain re-echoes also in *Hedda Gabler* and *Rosmersholm* and *Little
Eyolf*, not merely the ironic counter-voice of a Romantic dis-
sident, but the cry of fear in the face of death and the silence of
God – that awareness of what it means to inhabit 'the Land
without Paradise'.
   '*The Land without Paradise*' is the stage-setting for Byron's
Cain, one of his typically abstract locations which replace the
physical landscape of conventional drama with a dramatic image
of man's metaphysical condition. Like the *sluk*, Ibsen's image of
the abyss outside the gate of paradise, Byron's is a world in which
man must die – the fallen world of process, time and change; and
the absurdity of existence under the sentence of death befouls for
Cain, as it does for Hedda or Allmers, the very quality of life
itself:

I live

But to die. And living, see no thing
To make death hateful, save an innate clinging,
A loathsome and yet all invincible
Instinct of life, which I abhor, as I
Despise myself, yet cannot overcome.
And so I live. (*Cain,* i. 109–15)

He yearns for Paradise – which, for him, is a condition of eternal
life – hating his parents who brought death into the world,
estranged from an apathetic God whose morality is merely circumstantial, who can make sin of virtue within a single generation by turning Cain's love for his sister into the flaming rod of
punishment for their children. Above all, since death has not yet
become a human experience in the Land without Paradise,
Cain's fear of what remains mysterious and inexplicable to all
men infects his being all the more intensely:

> Thoughts unspeakable
> Crowd in my breast to burning when I hear
> Of this almighty Death, who is, it seems,
> Inevitable.   (I. 257–60)

There is no consoling faith for him, nothing to counteract man's final obliteration into nothingness.

Ibsen's *sluk* shares some of the purely metaphysical dimensions of Byron's Land without Paradise, but its geographical location is also spatial or, at any rate, rooted in the concrete and particular world of phenomenal reality: the wasteland of charred stumps and withered leaves in which Peer Gynt is haunted by memories · of lost opportunity; the desiccated garden in which Hedda Gabler is trapped and bored; that world of deliquescent organic change, of growth, decay, ineluctable undertows and death which the Allmers inhabit; and even the bourgeois parlours where death enters by doors barred against it – like Borkman's coffin-trap, another frozen pastoral, echoing with the *danse macabre* even while it tries to sustain the illusion of deathlessness. Existence in the *sluk,* bereft of meaning, becomes mere absurd contingency to those who inhabit it. And, tormented by the fear of death, the senseless decay of the body, the meaninglessness of life, Ibsen's people cry out against the futility of all endeavour. Thus Solnes and Allmers:

> And now, looking back, what does it all add up to? In fact, I've built nothing. Nor did I really sacrifice anything for the chance to build. Nothing! Absolutely nothing!   (VII, 439–40)

> There must be some meaning in it. Life, existence, providence – surely they can't be so utterly meaningless.... Perhaps the whole thing is just haphazard. An aimless drifting, like some wrecked and rudderless ship.   (VIII, 67)

Nothing, *nichts, ingenting*: this is the distinctive quality of existence in the Land without Paradise. 'One sticks one's finger into the soil', writes Kierkegaard, 'to tell by the smell in what land one is: I stick my finger into existence – it smells of nothing.'[24]

Death in all its manifestations broods over Ibsen's world – not merely in stunning, climactic suicides and accidents, but as a slow ineffable process expressed sometimes through metaphor, sometimes as an abstract concept, sometimes in symbolic or almost expressionist devices invested with recognisable human form, sometimes as characters in the terminal stages of a debilitating disease: syphilis, tuberculosis, cancer. Hedda's world, for example, her very house, stinks with the odour of death – her dead father surveying the action like a ghost, the autumnal garden decaying beyond the French windows, oppressive reminders of old Aunt Rina dying off-stage, Løvborg's shocking suicidal mistake, and Hedda's inevitable final gesture, which destroys both herself and her unborn child. And even beyond this world of dying aunts (whom Hedda cannot bear to see or visit) there is the operation of another force that subsumes all individual death. In *Hedda Gabler* Ibsen calls it 'history' – organic process, flux, and decay in all its manifestations from the foetus in the Gabler womb to the disappearance of Gablerism from the cultural map of European society. In *Little Eyolf* the same general vision of the Land without Paradise is abstracted into *forvandlingens lov,* the law of change, which sooner or later each character contemplates as a power to which all passion, the body, and life are eventually subject. Each in his own way tries to deny this law or arrest it by symbolic means, for each (with the possible exception of Asta) views change not as dynamic possibility, but as deterioration and decay. To discover an *unchanging* principle in human existence and human relationships is, for them all, to rediscover Paradise:

> RITA: . . . Anyway, everything has to end sometime.
> BORGHEJM: Oh, not everything – I hope. . . .
> RITA: Not everything, did you say?
> BORGHEJM: Yes, I firmly believe that there is at least one thing in this world that has no end.
> RITA: You are doubtless thinking of love . . . and similar things.
> BORGHEJM: I am thinking of anything which is delightful!
> RITA: And which never ends. Yes, let's think of that. And hope for it, all of us. (55)

This sort of yearning, however, is often brutally contradicted by the angels of death who come to remind them of their mortality – such as the Buttonmoulder, waiting for Peer at the next cross-roads; or who, like the Rat Wife and the Stranger from the Sea, embody a conflation of the impulses of sexual love and mortality; or who confront us with the decay of the body not as an abstraction, but as the terrifying reality of sickness and disease, as in the case of Osvald Alving, Dr Rank and Lyngstrand. Ella Rentheim, for example, garbed in black velvet, enters the dark sepulchral world of John Gabriel with the chilling effect of an Ingmar Bergman harbinger of death:

> [... *The room becomes half dark. A moment later there is a knock on the tapestry-lined door at the back.*]
> BORKMAN: Who's that knocking? [*No answer; there is another knock....*] Who is it? Come in!
> [ELLA RENTHEIM, *a lighted candle in her hand, appears in the doorway. She is wearing her black dress, as before.*]
> BORKMAN [*stares at her*]: Who are you? What do you want with me?
> ELLA RENTHEIM [*closes the door and approaches*]: It's me, Borkman.... It is 'your' Ella ... as you used to call me. Once. Many, many years ago.... The years have taken a hard toll of me, Borkman. Don't you think so? ... No longer those dark curls, falling over my shoulders. Remember how you used to love to twist them round your fingers?
> BORKMAN [*quickly*]: That's it! I see now. You have changed your hair style.   (viii, 192)

Borkman's reaction to her appearance modulates from a frightened bewilderment to the pathetic, ludicrous, even strangely amusing response of one who – so carefully immured against both life and death – has now to confront the inevitability of change. He simply denies it. Ella's hair, as Ibsen describes it, is 'silver white' – but he responds only to its style and not its colour; she tells him that she is dying of cancer and cannot last the winter – but he reflects that the winters tend to be rather long in Norway. If the fear of change and death compels him to deny the facts, the imminence of death compels Ella towards another solution:

> Think how infinitely sad it is for me to know I shall be taking leave of all living things, of sun and light and air, without leaving behind me a single person who will think of me with affection and sadness, remember me the way a son remembers a mother he has lost.... When I die, the name of Rentheim dies too. I feel strangled by the very thought. To be obliterated

from existence . . . even to the extent of one's name. . . . Don't
let it happen. Let Erhart bear my name after me! (202–3)

Those who die in Ibsen's *sluk* are inevitably the last of their line,
so that death comes as total extinction. And the thought of so
complete a loss of identity strangles and tortures like the thought
that burns in the breast of Cain. Christian assurances of a
compensatory Heaven, an afterlife which will confer some
ultimate meaning on existence, do not even enter the realm of
Ella Rentheim's contemplation. Her answer to death is defiantly
secular: she will live on in her surrogate child – not in any literal
sense, for he is in fact her sister's son, but in his *perpetuation of
her name* as a living idea. *Names*, in this play, assume magical
connotations of permanence: imperishable essences which survive mortality, symbols of secular redemption which – like John
Gabriel's own pretentious and sonorous name – link the mundane
to the archangelic. In the absence of God, Ibsen's protagonists
must refashion their own conceptions of divinity; and from the
Land without Paradise they must project Edenic denials of the
nothingness which confronts them in the end.

The fear of death is not customarily associated with the
Romantic temperament, which, we have been habituated to
believe, is morbidly *attracted* to the easeful thing rather than
fearfully *repelled* by it. Freud's idea of the 'death wish' has set the
seal on what is now generally accepted as the Romantic's inherent
and instinctive urge towards inertia – as in the case of Werther,
the nineteenth-century Hamlet, Keats, and Hedda Gabler, who
have all been said to manifest the Freudian syndrome in their
search for an alternative to the fallen world. George Steiner puts
it well:

> It is the crowning act in Freud's unbroken attempt to recon-
> cile man to a godless reality to make this reality endurable by
> suggesting a final release from it. . . . Whereas Marx intimates
> an Edenic condition free of necessity and of conflict, Freud
> knows that such freedom would be tantamount to the repose of
> death.[25]

But it is precisely against such an Edenic condition that the Ibsen
protagonist baulks. Even Hedda, the arch-Romantic, is possessed
in equal measure by 'romantic' thoughts of dying beautifully and

an overwhelming, 'unromantic' fear of death itself; and it would be more true to say of Ibsen's people that they are defined by a syndrome significantly different from Freud's – by their *refusal to acknowledge* the awful reality of death, and their search for symbols of permanence to counteract that fear. It is a pattern of behaviour most clearly described by Ernest Becker as the *denial of death:* 'The idea of death', he writes, 'the fear of it, haunts the human animal like nothing else; it is the mainspring of human activity – activity designed largely to avoid the fatality of death, to overcome it by denying in some way that it is the final destiny for man.'[26]

This denial, Becker argues, may assume an heroic protest against fate, a life-enhancing illusion which bursts the boundaries of time into a new dimension of reality; or it may manifest itself as a perversion of life, an inability to grasp death as a reality to be acknowledged and transcended. Brand's allegory of the spiritually dead community clinging to memories of the past recalls precisely such perversity. He tells the tale of a king who will not relinquish the corpse of his lover to the grave, incapable of ever admitting the finality of her death, and

> every day undoing
> The patchwork linen of the shroud,
> Putting his ear against the heart,
> And seizing pitiful crumbs of hope
> That life might come again; imagining
> Life's blood-red roses bloomed again
> Upon that clammy form.   (III, 239)

Unwilling to face death, he ultimately robs himself of life. And his fate is, in many various ways, the paradigm of all those fear-stricken protagonists in Ibsen who in denying death and questing after permanence commit themselves to death-in-life.

Even Allmers, who more than anyone in Ibsen's plays protests his longing to cease upon the midnight, is patently obsessed by the fear of process and the dread of sexuality. When he speaks of his mountain experience in league with death the good companion – 'absolutely without fear' (VIII, 101) – his tone gradually slides into self-indulgent forebodings of mortality which mock their very substance: 'People in my family don't usually live till they are old. . . .' Hermann Weigand, quite correctly, dismisses the whole mountain episode as fabrication, another self-deceiving distortion of fact and feeling: 'In reality he had the worst scare of his life', he writes. 'The hysteria of fright made it appear to him as though death were bodily walking by his side, a gruesome fellow-traveller.'[27] This surely is how death finally appears to Allmers when he comes to claim his child; and it is fear and not fascination that ultimately drives him to the most complex denial of death in Ibsen's drama, to multiple symbols of permanence which assure his special status as a creature somehow exempt from the law of change.

IV

I shall have constantly to return to this triadic pattern in Ibsen's drama – the fear of death, the denial of death, the construction of an elaborate symbol-system to immortalise the self – and, of course, to the paradox which underlies the entire structure and ensures the frustration of the myth of self-perpetuation. As I have suggested, the dominant metaphor of that mythology is the Paradise-kingdom which features so prominently, under a variety of different names – such as Orangia/Appelsinia in *The Master Builder,* or Peer's Gyntiana, which, more consciously than any other of these analogues of Eden, articulates the protagonist's single motivating desire to conquer death:

> The world's outmoded! Now it's the turn
> Of Gyntiana, my new young land!
> Given the capital, it's already done.–
> A golden key to the gate of the ocean!
> A crusade against Death! (iii, 345)

Like Borkman's Kingdom, Gyntiana will conquer death in visions of capital and gold, economic imperialism, and those myths of a commercial Paradise which remain the substance of the modern dream – like Gatsby's, and which, like Gatsby's myth, transforms itself into an image of the ash-pit. But the fallible Paradise, the anti-Eden which ultimately exhibits the very qualities of the condition it seeks to elude, is only *one* variation on this Romantic theme. 'Korstog mot døden' (ii. 184) – the crusade against death – outlines the nature of the primary, obsessive quest in Ibsen, but not the death-defying strategies of his protagonists. A geo-graphically located 'kingdom' is one such device, but there are so many synonyms for Paradise and so many symbols employed in the crusade, that the geographical metaphor becomes too limiting and narrow. In speaking of 'analogues of Paradise' I also have in mind what Jerome Buckley, in a wide-ranging article, has defined as 'Symbols of Eternity: The Victorian Escape from Time'.[28] His detailing of this pervasive post-Romantic theme offers diverse examples of nineteenth-century Edens, establishing in the particular images of writers from Coleridge to Joyce all the major variants which *cohere* in the drama of Ibsen: Rossetti's 'substitute religion' of sexual experience; the Aesthetic belief in the 'power of art to arrest the moment'; William Morris's attempt, in *The Earthly Paradise,* to fashion 'worlds of artifice beyond the reach of change'; the related attempts of Words-worth, Pater and Joyce to 'fulfill the desire for everlastingness, for a continuity beyond both sense and time' in moments of epiphany; and Browning's image of Heaven as a 'perpetual extension of his life's unfulfilled mission'. To these symbols of eternity Ibsen adds the peculiar secular and psychic visions that define his own dramatic characters: the self-immortalising myths of Hedda Gabler and John Gabriel Borkman, the chorus of children pressed into the service of an impossible teleological ideal, and sexual desire divinised by taboo into forms of the imperishable. None of these human realities survives the process of Edenic transformation. The self congeals; the child dies; desire remains eternally frustrated. The importance of Ibsen to the history of Romantic ideas, it seems to me, derives from his relentless reappraisal of Romanticism's attempt to deal with the fears and anxieties of existence, his analysis of the failure of substitute religions to assuage the human wound; and, in so far as his vision is powerfully critical in its diagnosis of the fallacies and fallibilities of Romanticism, its characteristic voice will seem correspondingly despairing. But it is not, for this reason, neces-sarily *anti*-Romantic.

Morse Peckham has called these phases of disillusionment and despair in nineteenth-century literature 'Negative Romanticism' and its alienated and guilt-ridden spokesman the 'Byronic hero' – terms challenged by those for whom Romanticism is an essentially affirmative tradition, and for whom a heroism based upon negation would be anathema. M. H. Abrams, in rejecting the 'counter-Romantic' voice as heretical or renegade, would seem to assume this position. But, however questionable his terms of reference, Morse Peckham does provide the context of ideas and movements to which Ibsen's anomalous romanticism belongs. He argues, moreover, that 'Negative Romanticism' (Carlyle's 'Everlasting No', for example, or Byron's nihilism) is merely a precondition for the positive recovery of meaning in the Godless post-Enlightenment universe.[29] And, however misguided the methods of Ibsen's Romantic questors, their search for value remains the positive corollary of their devastation of *all* value in the attempt. What the plays reveal is the difficulty and the pain of the search for value, the ceaseless probing, the strenuous experimental attempts to grasp the nature of reality, the tragedy of living through the intermediate phases of despair between the loss of Paradise and its rediscovery. Ibsen's romanticism, embodied in the world of his drama, is a process of constructive evolution through which the mind and spirit of man moves: from the collapse of Enlightenment values and the death of God, through vain and self-defeating attempts to insulate the self against absurd contingency, discovering – sporadically and intermittently – a resolution of the Romantic dilemma in what we now recognise as an existential reshaping of man's moral nature and his spiritual wholeness. And, if the vision seems peculiarly 'counter-Romantic', 'negative' or despairing in its analysis of error, it is also guardedly optimistic in its view of man – a challenge to the modern sensibility, whose psychology and symbols remain predominantly Romantic, to formulate constructive responses to traumatic experience without recourse to glib despair. If the 'counter-Romantic' voice instructs by negative example, by irony, there is also that other voice that celebrates joy in the jaws of death, that sees in the law of change not decay but the continuous transformation of the self, that re-establishes value in an empty world by accepting responsibility for one's actions and decisions, and that creates meaning in the void where none existed.

I do not see Ibsen's drama as a *consistent* or *coherent* movement from despair to resolution, or from Negative Romanticism to existentialism; nor do I share Brian Johnston's sense of a programmatic Hegelian development in his plays. The evolution of mind and spirit, bedevilled by incomprehension, occasionally discovering in 'responsibility' or 'joy' a possible way out of its dilemma, now plunging into chaos again when such solutions seem inadequate or inappropriate to the psychic needs of the character – it is this ebb and flow that seems to characterise the rhythm of Ibsen's romanticism. It is not my intention, therefore, to follow any chronological method in discussing the plays – nor, indeed, to offer thoroughly comprehensive analyses in the excellent style of John Northam or Charles Lyons. I have offered here a general model of the Romantic dilemma, the crises of faith which precipitate it, the anxieties which are their consequence, and the metaphors and symbols which link Ibsen's specific vision of the dilemma to the larger context of English and European Romanticism. In the chapters that follow I shall discuss some variants of this general model, taking examples from a number of plays and dealing with them thematically. The central, unifying theme will be the protagonists' 'symbols of eternity', especially those fashioned out of the delicate fabric of existence which, subjected to the psychic need for a perfection and a stability not of this world, disintegrate into tragic images of ruined lives – Paradise bought, in the words of Baudelaire's paradox, at the cost of one's eternal salvation.[30] The anti-Paradise, the *Kindermord*, the perversion of love are some of the major themes that the 'counter-Romantic' voice most poignantly articulates, and which will occupy the major portion of this discussion. And in the final chapter I shall attempt to answer some of those urgent Romantic questionings which Ibsen's people share, more or less consciously, with the woman in Wallace Stevens's 'Sunday Morning':

What is divinity if it can come
Only in silent shadows and in dreams?
Shall she not find in comfort of the sun,
In pungent fruit and bright, green wings, or else
In any balm or beauty of the earth,
Things to be cherished like the thought of heaven? . . .
Shall our blood fail? Or shall it come to be
The blood of paradise? And shall the earth
Seem all of paradise that we shall know?

Notes

1. These two aspects of Ibsen's symbol-system have been discussed in illuminating detail by Charles Lyons in *Henrik Ibsen: The Divided Consciousness* (Carbondale and Edwardsville, Ill., 1972). He sees them primarily as opposing myths of order and the chaos of phenomenal existence (to which all order ultimately reverts), and, like many other critics of Ibsen's mythology, he emphasises the esoteric and peculiar nature of these symbols. 'Ibsen', he writes, 'is concerned with myth, but his concern is with private processes of consciousness, not with racial or communal patterns of action' (p. xiii). I would argue that the Paradise–abyss mythology in Ibsen links the psychological anxieties of the individual to a pervasive and public pattern of action.
2. George Steiner, *Nostalgia for the Absolute* (Toronto, 1974) p. 5.
3. Ibid., p. 2.
4. M. H. Abrams, *Natural Supernaturalism*, p. 65.
5. Steiner, *Nostalgia*, p. 4.
6. From Søren Kierkegaard, *Attack upon 'Christendom'* (1854–5), trs. W. Lowrie (Princeton, NJ, 1944) p. 123.
7. *Shaw and Ibsen: Bernard Shaw's 'The Quintessence of Ibsenism' and Related Writings*, ed. J. L. Wisenthal (Toronto, 1979) p. 133.
8. Ibid., p. 137.
9. Abrams, *Natural Supernaturalism*, ch. 6 (pp. 325–72).
10. William Wordsworth, 'Prospectus for "The Recluse"', ll. 47–51. See Abrams, *Natural Supernaturalism*, p. 467.
11. Wordsworth, 'Prospectus for "The Recluse"', l. 55.
12. Morse Peckham discusses the fallibility of these assumptions as 'Analogism' in *Romanticism: The Culture of the Nineteenth Century* (New York, 1965) pp. 25–6.
13. Wordsworth, 'Prospectus for "The Recluse"', ll. 52–3.
14. See Abrams, *Natural Supernaturalism*, pp. 257–8, 293.
15. Ibid., p. 256.
16. Ibid., p. 375.
17. See ibid., p. 206 for a discussion of Kant's 'higher third stage' – a synthesis of nature and culture.
18. Northrop Frye, 'The Drunken Boat: The Revolutionary Element in Romanticism', in Frye (ed.), *Romanticism Reconsidered* (New York and London, 1963) p. 19.
19. Wallace Stevens, 'Sunday Morning', from *The Palm at the End of the Mind* (New York, 1971) p. 7.
20. Harold Pinter, *No Man's Land* (London, 1975) p. 95.
21. Abrams, *Natural Supernaturalism*, p. 13.
22. See Peckham, *Romanticism*, and 'Toward a Theory of Romanticism', *PMLA*, LXVI (1951) 5–23.
23. *Ibsen: Letters and Speeches*, ed. Evert Sprinchorn (New York, 1964) p. 118.
24. Kierkegaard, quoted in J. Hillis Miller, *The Disappearance of God* (Cambridge, Mass., 1963) p. 9.

25. Steiner, *Nostalgia*, p. 21.
26. Ernest Becker, *The Denial of Death* (New York, 1973) p. ix.
27. Hermann Weigand, *The Modern Ibsen* (New York, 1925) pp. 342, 344.
28. Jerome Buckley, 'Symbols of Eternity: The Victorian Escape from Time', in Warren D. Anderson and Thomas D. Clareson (eds), *Victorian Essays: A Symposium* (Kent, Ohio, 1967) pp. 1–15. The quotations that follow derive from this source.
29. See Peckham, *Romanticism*, and *Beyond the Tragic Vision: The Quest for Identity in the Nineteenth Century* (New York, 1962).
30. Quoted by Abrams, *Natural Supernaturalism*, p. 416. Baudelaire is referring, here, to the artificial paradise induced by drugs.

3 'Paradise Within': Hedda Gabler and John Gabriel Borkman as Types of the Romantic 'Self'

If we cannot conceive of Hedda Gabler posing the highly articulate metaphysical queries of Wallace Stevens's woman in 'Sunday Morning', it is probably beacause we know next to nothing of her psychic life. Hedda's history is predominantly social – a fully dramatised image of a *ci-devant* aristocrat for whom Gablerism is a code of obligations heaped by nobility upon her nature, and who lives in a world where people no longer do 'that sort of thing'. But as a psychological study of sexual distress, the fear of death, and the yearning for some intimation of immortal value, Hedda Gabler is enveloped in almost Pinteresque blankness. A phrase, a gesture, a sense of something left unspoken beneath broken sentences – we clutch at straws to make her whole or, bewildered by the force that drives her, attribute to her actions the motiveless malignity of Iago. More recently, she has been portrayed as a woman in whom the poetry of life runs deep but whose channels of expression have been dammed by the society in which she lives, in whom idealism burns with a hard gem-like flame but which – thwarted by her status in the world – can only burn itself and others in an agony of frustration. But this is to see *Hedda Gabler* as a problem play inducing the audience to seek solutions to essentially secular or political dilemmas: give her a seat on the *Storting* or the directorship of a bank, and she will stop firing her pistols aimlessly at the sky. It is becoming increasingly more difficult to release Hedda from the toils of Women's Liberation and restore her to the predicament from which there can be no liberation in this life. Her agony is not that of a thwarted power-hungry politician. It comes from the tragic

sense, which she shares with Stevens's persona, of 'the dark /
Encroachment of that old catastrophe' – the dreadful fall into a
world of generation, time and death – for which the only remedy
is a form of divinity in a world devoid of gods.

By means of a series of photographic negatives – the dark side
of Hedda's romanticism – Ibsen asks us to extrapolate the image of
her complex inner life, her crucial inability to reconcile immortal
longings with the ugly facts of animal mortality: with beauty that
must fade, with flowers that must die, and with the natural processes of sexuality, childbirth and death. More incarcerating even
than her status in a world of bourgeois men, the whole organic
world becomes her trap. Flowers overwhelm her as she enters the
parlour, and the smell of the late Mrs Falk's dried roses continues
to haunt her like the 'odour of death. Like a bouquet, the day
after a ball' (vii, 212). The withered, yellow leaves remind her
that September has come – a thought that rankles and disturbs:
the year has turned, and she is a month nearer to parturition.[1]
And, with the vehement denials with which Ibsen's other protagonists confront death, Hedda denies the physical reality of her
pregnancy, the ineluctable 'claim' that binds her not only to the
roles of Tesmanism and maternity but also to the bodily functions
of begetting and dying. Aunt Julle can contemplate the sewing of
shrouds and the sewing of nursery garments as aspects of a
natural process; but, for Hedda, nature itself is appalling and
ugly. She will not contemplate its issues, neither her own foetus
nor Aunt Rina's terminal condition: 'No, no, don't ask me. I
don't want to look at sickness and death. I must be free of
everything that's ugly' (239) – 'La meg få være fri for alt det som
stygt er' (iii, 419). It is an extraordinary freedom that Hedda
ultimately demands when life *and* death are instinct with that
ugliness from which she flees. Beauty alone remains – a state of
almost miraculous abstraction from the realities of life, a perfection of style which, paradoxically, only death can finally confer
upon her.

All the images of organic life in *Hedda Gabler*, of flux and
process and generation, are subsumed (as I have already
suggested) in Ibsen's idea of history – that very real academic
discipline, exemplified in the divergent world-views of the two
men who practise it, and in the visions of time past and futurity
made explicit in their theses. Each major figure in the play is
defined 'historically' – his 'historical' sense being the measure of his

grasp upon reality and his ability to cope with the changing world about him; and history, as reality or metaphor or symbol, constitutes the world-view in which their romanticism must be evaluated. 'The Enlightenment', as Morse Peckham points out, 'placed perceptions by putting them into the frame of unchanging nature; Romanticism places them by putting them into the frame of historical process. Reality is neither space nor time; it is the process of history.'[2] At one extreme of the Romantic spectrum of roles and types stands the Byronic hero, lost and confounded in the changing world; at the other stands the historian, the biographer of the spiritual self, whose progress from the failure of Enlightenment certainties, through nihilism and despair, to the recovery of vision details the entire movement of Romantic consciousness.[3] The history of the *world*, as Carlyle was to express it, is the biography of great *men;* and history becomes the experience, to those who can endure it, of phenomenal reality in the process of its happening. The 'Negative Romantic' will either cling to a static vision of the historical past, or view historical process with abhorrence and disdain. Hedda, Jørgen Tesman and Eilert Løvborg are living exemplars of Romanticism arrested in different attitudes of stasis and denial.

In Thomas Mann's novella 'Disorder and Early Sorrow', Dr Cornelius, Professor of Renaissance History, trapped amid the disruptions of modern Germany and the Bohemianism of his family, meditates upon his philosophy of history:

> He knows that history professors do not love history because it is something that comes to pass, but only because it is something that *has* come to pass. . . . The past is immortalized; that is to say, it is dead; and death is the root of all godliness and all abiding significance.[4]

Against the lawless and incoherent present, he idealises the ordered and disciplined past; and his intellectual and political sympathies lie with Philip II – the hero of the Counter-Reformation – and the 'futile struggle of the aristocracy, condemned by God and rejected of man, against the forces of progress and change'.[5] But Dr Cornelius is sufficiently perceptive to recognise the morbidity inherent in his conservatism: its hostility to history in the making, its clinging to death as against life, and, above all, the terrible danger of imposing these stultifying values on his own small daughter – the child of 'history', the incarnation of a living historical present. The structure of the novella is peculiarly Ibsenian–except for the fact that Mann articulates, beautifully and clearly, what remains oblique, implicit and understated in *Hedda Gabler*. Tesman obviously inhabits that historical tense which Muriel Bradbrook calls the 'past perfect',[6] where past and present no longer exist in reciprocal relationship to each other, where history can no longer be modified but only more fully disclosed in isolated, static and comfortably dead images. The domestic industries of Brabant in the Middle Ages are so totally absorbing that Tesman can see neither causality nor destiny as the outcome of historical investigation; and, in stupefied amazement, he learns of the new evaluative, prognostic history practised by his rival for the Chair:

LØVBORG: . . . And this one deals with the future.
TESMAN: With the future! But ye gods, we don't know anything about that!
LØVBORG: No. But there are one or two things to be said about it, all the same. . . . It's in two sections. The first is about the social forces involved, and this other bit . . . that's about the future course of civilization.
TESMAN: Amazing! It just wouldn't enter my head to write about anything like that.   (VII, 216)

Hedda may sneer at his intellectual limitations, but her allegiance, even more tenaciously than Tesman's, is given to an immortalised past – 'the root of all godliness, and all abiding significance' – enshrined in the small inner room off the Tesman parlour, presided over by the portrait of her dead father, invested with the aura of sanctity and the mystery of death. The emblems that define her – the portrait and the pistols – and her visions of style and affluence that middle-class standards render mockingly anachronistic, all look back to an age of chivalry and nobility which Hedda *cannot* relinquish although she *knows* it is dead beyond recovery. To move with the times means accommodation to social change, to accepting her descent into the bourgeoisie. One doesn't do that sort of thing. One denies *this* aspect of history, of change, as one denies all others.

  In contrast, Løvborg's vision of history as a continuum – the 'past imperfect' organically linked to the present and flowing into

the future – would seem to offer a positive Romantic alternative to
the static histories of the others. But, if Romantic history is a
biographical record of spiritual progress, then Løvborg's career in
the drama implies no such positive essence. Muriel Bradbrook
speaks of his manuscript on the future of civilisation as 'conceived
through direct experience of life and by natural energy';[7] but the
Løvborg we see is a man sadly run to seed, whose natural energy
cannot sustain Hedda's vital challenge, and for whom bourgeois
teetotalism is the only alternative to reckless debauchery. It is
impossible to derive his philosophy of history from Ibsen's text.
But he seems, in many ways, a Spenglerian before Spengler[8] – a
prophet of decline, dissolution and collapse, for whom the destiny
of the future is a death of spirit, failure of conviction, and loss of
nerve. This is conjecture, based on Løvborg's despairing experience in the play; but Ibsen's notes on his innovative historical
manuscript corroborate this despair and Løvborg's attempts to
deny the ravages of process in the refuge of alcohol:

> The manuscript that H. L. [Løvborg] leaves behind is con-
> cerned to show that the task of humanity is: Upwards, towards
> the bringer of light. Life on the present social basis is not worth
> living. Therefore imagine yourself away from it. Through
> drink etc. –   (VII, 490)

One cannot, of course, accept the notes instead of the finished
text as an indication of the author's intention; but there is at least
the possibility that Ibsen himself shares something of Spengler's
historical pessimism at the end of *Hedda Gabler* – that vision of a
sublimely discreative society, where the fate of the 'future' depends upon the union of a barren woman and an intellectually
effete scholar:

> Then H. [Løvborg] is brought to his death. And then those two
> sit there with the manuscript they cannot decipher. And the
> aunt sits with them. What an ironical comment on human
> striving towards development and progress.

> There is talk of building railways and roads in the service of
> progress. No, no, that's not it. You have to make room for the
> human spirit to take the great turn. Because that's on the
> wrong road. The human spirit is going in the wrong
> direction.   (Ibid.)

If there is anyone in the play who shares this authorial vision of spiritual evolution, as distinct from 'progress' in the technical sense, it is surely Hedda herself. She may endorse Tesman's view of the abiding significance of a completed past; and her detestation of the social forces shaping the future, her fear of the future itself, may coincide with Løvborg's view that life is no longer worth living. But, ultimately, Hedda's view of history is consistent with her own most intense Romantic longing: to burst out of time, to discover a dimension of spiritual intensity no longer discoverable in the obtuse bourgeois parlour, to live *mythically* in a world beyond historical change and death. Her vision of Paradise has no correlative in the real world of human experience, any more than the 'castles in the air' of which Solness and Hilde dream. It exists only as a function of her psychic longing to inhabit *mythic* history, where life, abstracted from *world* history, assumes the self-generating properties of divinity. It is that 'polar' view of history which, for Spengler, typifies the Classical culture:

> In the world-consciousness of the Hellenes all experience, not merely the personal but the common past, was immediately transmuted into a timeless, immobile, mythically fashioned background for the particular momentary present; thus the history of Alexander the Great began even before his death to be merged by Classical sentiment in the Dionysus legend. . . . For Herodotus and Sophocles, as for Themistocles or a Roman consul, the past is subtilized instantly into an impression that is timeless and changeless, *polar and not periodic* in structure – in the last analysis, of such stuff as myths are made of . . . .[9]

Such Classicism, says Spengler, is the mark of a dying culture – Romanticism looking back piteously to a lost childhood before relinquishing itself to death.[10] But the morbidity of Gablerism is only one aspect of Hedda's 'classical' romanticism. Her mythic language speaks most passionately, in bursts of imagery and radiant visions, of a timeless present where beauty, freedom and ecstasy become the spiritual dimensions of man's divinity. The other side of her 'classical' romanticism envisions the dynamic energies of Dionysos.

> Jeg ser ham for meg. Med vinløv in håret. Het og freidig. . . . Og da, ser du, – da har han fått makten over seg selv igjen. Da er han en fri mann for alle sine dage . . . så kommer Eilert

Løvborg–med vinløv i håret.   (iii, 415)

I can see him before me. With vineleaves in the hair. Glowing with passion [*het*] and fearless [*freidig*].... And then, you see – then he'll exercise his own self-controlling power [*makten over seg selv*] again. Then he'll be a free man for the rest of his days.... That's how Eilert Løvborg will come – with vineleaves in the hair.

It is a vision of erotic intensity, ecstatic freedom, and godlike self-assertion. But no one knows what she's talking about. Her vision of vineleaves is met with blank incomprehension. And Ibsen, resolutely refusing to annotate Hedda's mythic yearning, leaves its central mysteries undefined: a sensation of ecstatic release like a pistol fired in the soul, a burst of light, an epiphany of beauty.

... hvilken befrielse der er i dette med Eilert Løvborg.... Jeg mener, for meg. En befrielse å vite at der dog virkelig kan skje noe frivillig modig i verden. Noe som der faller et skjær av uvilkårlig skjønnhet over.   (431)

What a feeling of release [*befrielse*] there is in what has happened to Eilert Løvborg.... For me, I mean. A feeling of release to know that there is still place in the world for something courageous [*modig*], done of one's own free will [*frivillig*]. Something enveloped in the radiance [*skjær*] of instantaneous [*uvilkårlig*] beauty.

Her response to Løvborg's imagined apotheosis thrills with the almost inarticulate, vaguely erotic sensation of a spiritual Elysium rescued from the mundane bourgeois world.

Hedda's esoteric visions of pagan divinity clearly belong to that private life which has no dramatic history, no exposition beyond its own Romantic resonance. But behind the play itself, and beneath Hedda's scattered images, there lies the elaborately articulated Dionysiac mythology of *Emperor and Galilean*; and, even beyond that, the interpretation of Classical myth by the German mythopoetic philosophers of the age. 'Vineleaves in the hair' and the imagery of ecstasy and freedom, beauty and power, are the fragmentary poetic notations of a dialectic in which Dionysos embodies the dynamic energies which fire the anarchic impulses

of existence. Nietzsche's *Birth of Tragedy* (1872) radiates powerfully behind Hedda's glimpses of the Dionysiac principle in human life, the recovery of an ecstatic reality which either destroys
man utterly or redeems him through mystical experience:

> Now the slave emerges as a freeman. . . . Each of his gestures
> betokens enchantment; through him sounds a supernatural
> power, the same power which makes the animals speak and the
> earth render up milk and honey. He feels himself to be godlike
> and strides with the same elation and ecstasy as the gods he has
> seen in his dreams. No longer the *artist,* he has himself become
> a *work of art*. . . . In order to comprehend this total emancipa-
> tion of all the symbolic powers one must have reached the same
> measure of freedom those powers themselves were making
> manifest; which is to say that the votary of Dionysos could not
> be understood except by his own kind.[11]

Hedda's 'vineleaves' ultimately defy rational analysis. *Her* kind
will understand them well enough. That nobody in the play does
so is the measure of man's spiritual debility in the Tesman world.
And Hedda's own failure to discover the god within, to transform
herself into a work of art, is the measure of her betrayal of the
dream of mythic history.

Trapped in the world of begetting and dying, incarcerated in
her own Gablerism and again within the confines of the bourgeois
parlour, Hedda's desperate need to break free of her repressions
and her human limitations finds expression in acts of violence and
fantasies of destruction: the threat of setting fire to the hair of her
rival for Løvborg's soul, her demonic ripping and burning of their
'child', her firing of pistols at moments of terrible tension, her
bursts of wild dance music on the piano. But, despite these
powerful impulses, she remains dissociated from the god and
incapable of acting on his inspiration. She is a Dionysos-*manqué*,
a 'coward' – unable, above all, to find in her own self-consuming
sexuality that ecstatic Viking paradise that Hjørdis offers *her*
lover in an earlier play: 'Out of this life, Sigurd! I will set you on
the throne of heaven, and I will sit by your side!' (II, 90). Anarchic
passion neither finds nor seeks liberation – too fearful, perhaps, of
confronting its own reality, or too repressed by the iron demands
of the Gablerian sexual code. Although bound to Løvborg by
what he calls 'kameratskap i livsbegjært', 'livskravet' (III, 412) – an

alliance in their passion, their lust for life (the sexuality is explicit in these phrases) – she refuses to gratify her hunger promiscuously however powerful the physical attraction. If one is a Gabler one desists from 'that sort of thing'. One preserves one's chastity inviolate – at pistol point, if necessary. And one finds release only by indulging vicariously in the erotic confessions of one's lover. Dionysos, the orgastic god, is no match for Apollo in Hedda's psychic universe.

If Dionysos symbolises the dynamic energies of life, then Nietzsche's Apollo is the principle of static ordering, aesthetic formation and disciplined control of such chaotic dissonance. Apollo is dramatised in *Hedda Gabler* through the traditions of Gablerism itself: its restrictive morality, its imperious awareness of the 'done thing', its self-control, its sense of style which imposes decorous civility upon passionate disorder. And General Gabler's luminous presence, brooding godlike over the action of the play, is a constant reminder to Hedda of what she is, and of the standards and obligations of her lineage. She remains, throughout, Hedda Gabler – the father's daughter – impressing that image of herself on a world incapable of sustaining or understanding the values of the 'past perfect' by which she lives. What is equally evident, however, is Hedda's own reluctance to sustain the positive values of her tradition by making them exemplary in the vulgar middle-class world. As she is a defective Dionysos, so is she a defective Apollo – oppressed by her environment, limited by its limitations, and writhing under the compromises she has made. Gablerism, in the circumstances, becomes a mere protective facade – useless in itself, except as a claim for special status or a weapon for humiliating the less sophisticated: 'Well, what manner of behaviour is that, anyway, flinging her hat just anywhere in the drawing room! It's not done' (vii, 183). Apollo seems, at first, little more than a code of decorous drawing-room manners, an aspect of Romanticism at its most undemocratic.

There are times, however, when Hedda's Apollonian language does move beyond mere snobbery to define the values and principles of her caste: courage, self-control, strength of will, and style – the perfect beauty of a finely performed action. None of these ideas is invested with the visionary intensity of 'vineleaves in the hair', nor are they consciously rooted in the poetic archetypes of classical mythology–with one possible exception. In a play full of paradox and travesties of godhead, it is grotesquely appropriate that a variation on the Apollonian principle should present itself in the person of the red-haired prostitute Mlle Diana, whose name is as cunningly suggestive as the 'vineleaves' of the play's substratum of myth. Brack calls her 'en veldig jegerinne – for herrene' (III, 421) – 'a mighty huntress – of men': a witticism, but a highly ironic one. Diana/Artemis, twin-sister of Apollo, goddess of the chase and chastity, appears in the modern world as a demythologised, parodic inversion of sexual purity – the inevitable fate of godhead in a condition of spiritual decline. This mock Diana presides over a society whose sexuality is defined variously by the adulterous importunities of Brack, Løvborg's debauchery, and her own vulgar prostitution. Apollo, it would seem, has no more place in the bourgeois parlour than Dionysos. Hedda may redeem something of Artemis's fallen divinity in her own indomitable chastity, but it does her little good; and she can lay no other claim to Apollonian principles. She speaks of courage, but she is a coward. She admires the will to action, but she cannot act herself. All that remains to her is a sense of style – the Apollonian defined as a ruthless anti-bourgeois Romanticism: an assertion of a special and superior selfhood, alienated from the social rabble by virtue of its defining difference, and insisting on that difference as an attribute of spiritual election. Aristocrat, hedonist, Bohemian are all variants of this aspect of the Romantic self. Against the mediocrity of bourgeois respectability, they emphasise their 'otherness' in acts of rebellion, extreme eccentricity, or by their shocking and marvellous inimitability. To do 'the sort of thing' beyond the comprehension of ordinary mortals, or to dissociate oneself from the 'sort of thing' that ordinary mortals do, is to ascribe to the self a mythic status which defies nature, mortal limitations, and – perhaps, in the final analysis – death itself.[12] This is the assumption of the Romantic virtuoso – Nijinsky, Paganini, Bernhardt, Liszt – whose virtuosity so exceeds all human capacity that the credulous attribute it to either diabolism or divinity. Morse Peckham defines this paradigm of Romantic virtuosity as one who

> symbolizes the uniqueness of the Self as the source of value by transforming the role into a source of unimagined splendor, order, power, and beauty. . . . The essence of the Virtuoso, then, is the symbolization of the inadequacy of society to meet the demands of the Self, and this inadequacy the Virtuoso

reveals by superhuman control and release of energy in an activity which, to the socially adapted, can only be pointless.[13]

Or, in Brack's words which ring the curtain down on *Hedda Gabler*, 'Men, gud seg forbarme, – slikt noe *gjør* man da ikke!' – 'But, merciful God – one just doesn't *do* that sort of thing!'

But Hedda's virtuosity is achieved only in her extraordinary death. In life, her least admirable qualities are those of a *pretentious* virtuoso – a woman who appropriates to herself a unique and private status from which to oppose the *embourgeoisement* of the socially inferior world, but whose values of 'self' are so compromised by fear, cowardice, contradictory impulses, and an inability to *enact* her visions of divinity that she must seek out an *alter ego* to live her life for her. The ambivalence is central to her personality: Hedda is the only one in her society who can confront its deadliness of spirit, who seeks for enduring value – but, at the same time, she is tragically disqualified from pursuing her quest. Her entire career, in fact, is a series of implicit responses to the questions and their temporary resolutions posited in Stevens's 'Sunday Morning' – that modern rephrasing of the romantic's anguished demand for consolation in the face of death. She cannot, like Stevens's persona, give her bounty to the dead or find divinity in the silent shadows of Christian faith. She can find no comfort in the sun or in the beauty of earth, which, mutable and impermanent, denies all thought of heaven. 'Divinity', says the poet, 'must live within herself' –

All pleasures and all pains, remembering
The bough of summer and the winter branch.
These are the measures destined for her soul

– but there can be no divinity in human feeling when pleasure has been consistently repressed and pain avoided, where the eternal values of the self find no reflection in the changing natural world. All is transient, fleeting – except in her ability to find *another* form of divinity within, to discover God in man, an incarnation of the absolute in the relative,

Until our blood, commingling, virginal,
With heaven, brought such requital to desire
The very hinds discerned it, in a star.

Shall our blood fail? Or shall it come to be
The blood of paradise?

If divinity cannot come to life in Hedda, then she must create
godhead by the power of daemonic inspiration. If *her* blood fails,
then she must find Paradise in the blood of a surrogate self by
fashioning him into a god. There is both magnificence and madness in making Løvborg bring such inhuman requital to her
Romantic desire.

As she had once half-satisfied her sexual craving, at second-
hand, through Løvborg's bouts of sensuality, so Hedda now seeks
to enact through his agency the most urgent desires of the self to
burst into mythic history. She will transform him into her own
yearning for Dionysos, experiencing her anarchic impulses
through the destiny of her once-Bohemian lover. She will redeem
him from the prosaically middle-class Thea, whose major
achievement has been to convert the Bohemian into a respectable
and abstinent academic, stifling his vitality in the process. 'Der er
livsmotet og livstrossen som hun har knekket i meg', he cries (III,
424) – 'She's broken my spirit, my courage to meet life's challenge.'
Hedda, to save herself, must restore his debilitated energies to
their former vigour, inspire him towards the heightened consciousness of his orgiastic past, and, beyond that, to the absolute
freedom of the Dionysiac. In her imagination, she invests
Løvborg with the iconographic attributes of the god – the
vineleaves in the hair – tempting him to magnificence, impelling
him to communion with Dionysos through the liberating power of
drink, then sending him away to Brack's stag-party as if to some
mystic bacchanal. The solid nineteenth-century world-picture,
with all its domestic clutter, becomes suddenly luminous with
spiritual possibility for Hedda; and divinity becomes a potential
in a society which seems to have lost contact with its primal
myths. But there is a great gap, as Nietzsche himself pointed out,
between the Dionysiac Greek and the Dionysiac barbarian,
between divine frenzy and alcoholic maundering – and Løvborg
fails most pitifully to bridge it. The orgastic God is not a
debauchee. Dionysos is betrayed by his sordid, drunken brawling
in the red-haired whore's 'boudoir', and the dream of Hedda's
demigod returning from the bacchanal with vineleaves in his hair
dies forever. The forces of modern vulgarity prove impervious to
the romantic ideal, and Løvborg's inadequacy merely testifies to

the limits of ordinary human capacity. Men cannot live as gods in some eternally orgastic Elysium. Ecstasy is momentary, not enduring. And in imposing an immortal design on frail humanity Hedda merely confirms its insufficiencies. So begins the *Götterdämmerung*.

But still Hedda will not relinquish her vision. Løvborg returns humiliated and despairing – not for having failed Hedda, but rather for destroying Thea's soul by losing their manuscript–'child' in a brothel. Nothing remains for him now but 'to put an end to it all. The sooner the better' (VII, 246) – and in his impulse to suicide Hedda suddenly discovers a means of redemption for her fallen demigod. He must die for *her* sake, not Thea's. Even if she had been unsuccessful in bringing Dionysos to life in him, there still remains the hope of living through Løvborg the courage and willed control of Gablerism, asserting its virtuosity in an otherwise drab and indifferent world. She can still inspire him to die in splendour so that the freedom gained through an exemplary death may triumph over her environment; and she gives him one of the Gabler pistols, confident that the anarchic, destructive action will be transformed into a gesture of noble beauty, shocking the bourgeoisie into confronting those values without which life is not worth living:

> HEDDA: Eilert Løvborg . . . listen to me . . . . Couldn't you let it happen . . . beautifully?
> LØVBORG: Beautifully? [*Smiles.*] Crowned with vine leaves, as you used to imagine?
> HEDDA: Oh no. I don't believe in those vine leaves any more. But beautifully all the same! Just for this once!   (249–50)

Self-immolation for Hedda the Romantic, as for Werther, is no defeat. It is the supreme enactment of style, form imposed upon the chaos of experience, a symbol of the self in its moment of absolute assertion. The triumph of virtuosity is the ultimate liberation of selfhood from the ugliness of process. And beauty is its justification – beauty which has little to do with aesthetics in the ordinary sense of the word. For the 'thing beautifully done' is quite distinct from the middle-class notion of a 'beautiful death' – like old Aunt Rina's. It is the perfect ordering of experience, meticulously stylised, the Romantic's hara-kiri in which the weapon and the symbolic gesture must dramatise the idealism which necessitates such sacrifice. One dies, paradoxically, to defy death itself and the processes of dissolution and decay. Like Cleopatra, Hedda sees suicide as the great deed

> that ends all other deeds;
> Which shackles accidents and bolts up change;
> Which sleeps, and never palates more the dung,
> The beggar's nurse and Caesar's. (*Antony and Cleopatra*, v. ii. 5–8)[14]

But Løvborg's death does not triumph in beauty over accident, change or dung. It merely affirms the horror of life's ugliness and the man's own incorrigible insufficiencies. He dies, by mistake, in a scuffle with the red-haired prostitute, drawn back to the brothel in his search for Thea's 'child'. And, with salacious satisfaction, Judge Brack disabuses Hedda about the imagined splendour of his brutal death. He was shot neither in the head nor the heart: 'Nei, – det traff ham i underlivet', he tells her (III, 432). This is the point at which translation falters: how to mention the unmentionable, to give euphemistic nuance to the sort of thing one doesn't say in the bourgeois parlour. 'When Brack tells Hedda where Løvborg has shot himself,' writes Michael Meyer, in a note on his translation, 'he must make it clear to her that the bullet has destroyed his sexual organs otherwise Hedda's reactions make no sense. To translate this as "belly" or "bowels" is again to miss the point, yet Brack must not use the phrase "sexual organs" directly; he is far too subtle a campaigner to speak so bluntly to a lady. What he says is: "In the – stomach. The – lower part." '[15] Hedda's appalled reaction, however, makes it clear that she has understood all too well. Beauty has turned to an ugliness almost inconceivable. Gablerism has become a ridiculous travesty of Apollonian virtuosity. And the orgastic God, destroying the physical emblem of his manhood, leaves the sexual sphere to Brack's sordid sensuality – 'the only cock in the yard'. In a revelation of overwhelming irony and disgust, Hedda acknowledges a completion of the *Götterdämmerung*: 'Det også! Å det latterlige og det lave, det legger seg som en forbannelse over alt *det* jeg bare rører ved' (III, 432) – 'That too! Oh, I have only to touch something – and mockery and filth spread like a curse over it all.' If 'filth' is too strong for 'det lave', the cry should nevertheless connote whatever is vile, base, and ugly: the horror of

process, the accursed fallen state, the 'dirt of life' which Hedda,
with tragic ineptness, has desperately tried to hold at bay.

ᴠ One fact, however, surely becomes clear to Hedda: selfhood
cannot be delegated. If the self is the source of its own esoteric
values, then it must make them viable without vicarious projection. Hedda must become her own Dionysos, her own Apollo,
reasserting their value even in a society which consistently deni-
grates their spiritual implications. She must gear herself for this
assumption of godhead – the Dionysiac struggle for freedom
through an orgastic action which, in the order and beauty of its
execution, permits the contemplation of suffering and ecstasy
through the willed control of Apollo. As soon as she hears the ugly
details of Løvborg's accident, Hedda knows she must die. There
can be no evasion now. She *must* die, not to escape the consequences of her involvement with Løvborg – she vehemently
rejects Brack's ingratiating offer to hush things up – nor merely to
snuff out an existence of insufferable ennui. She must die to
redeem the world of spiritual possibility from Løvborg's failure,
to restore honour to the Gabler pistol, and to assert herself in an
act of exemplary beauty. Dying is an art for Hedda. Her self
becomes the poem. It is an act calmly accepted as inevitable,
meticulously prepared for, executed in a gesture both real and
symbolic. Her intention remains unstated. She merely removes
the remaining pistol from her writing-desk and carries it into the
Gabler shrine for use at the appropriate moment.

Hedda must die by the pistol, just as Antony must die by the
sword and Cleopatra by the serpent – the instruments of death
crystallising the identity of each protagonist and the values which
give substance to each self: Hedda's romantic aristocracy,
Antony's Roman honour, Cleopatra's magical fascination. But,
if the pistol is the emblem of Hedda's nobility, the inheritance of
her chivalric code, it is also emblematic of her multiple frustrations – of the passion repressed beneath decorum, vitality driven to
destruction by 'the done thing'. It is the perfect symbolic correlative of her defective personality, an amalgam of contradictory
Dionysiac and Apollonian impulses. Debased by Løvborg and
traduced by Hedda as a means of aimlessly relieving her tensions,
the pistol must become an instrument of achievement, the
symbolic means to ecstatic freedom through an act of courageous
self-discipline. For only in death can Apollo and Dionysos be
finally reconciled. All that is needed now is the perfection of will

and the challenge to self-definition. And it is the insidious Brack, in all his threatening vulgarity, who intensifies Hedda's determination to elude such ugliness. 'Heller dø!' – 'Rather death!' – she cries, than the loss of her already compromised freedom to Brack's sexual coercion, or the subjection of her pitifully limited autonomy to *his* will and desire. All her clearly articulated values – *mot, kraft, vilje, skjønnhet* – become *his* gift, *his* to dispense with. And all her deepest fears of sexuality, of the dirt of life, and the submission of her self to another's demands, become incarnate in Brack, who, cynically convinced of the bourgeois tendency to capitulate sooner or later to the inevitable, sneers at Hedda's aristocratic pretensions: 'Slikt noe *sier* man. Men man *gjør* det ikke' (433) – 'It's the sort of thing one *says*. But one doesn't *do* it.' This is the critical challenge. For the first time in her life, and the last, Hedda must *act*. The Gabler tradition must become exemplary or crumble. Freedom must be celebrated ecstatically, or slavery accepted. She must ultimately become her self, or lose it altogether. Hedda withdraws into the privacy of the Gabler sanctuary and bursts into a wild dance melody on the piano, unleashing momentarily the furious energies which she guards so closely, triumphantly proclaiming that other side of her nature even in this house of mourning. The music, the dithyrambic frenzy, the rhythms of ecstasy provide the perfect accompaniment to the mysteries of Dionysos – and a few seconds later she shoots herself, in the temple, beautifully, heroically, in the grand style, all her anarchic energy channelled into this single act of will.

She is finally, for the only time in the play, 'Hedda Gabler'. Like the Duchess of Malfi, who, in the end, has nothing to assert but *herself,* so Hedda proclaims, through symbolic gesture, the essence of what it means *to be who she is*. Not since *Brand* and *Peer Gynt* have names become so important to Ibsen as in the last five plays, which, with the exception of *When We Dead Awaken,* all emphasise the individuality – both real and symbolic – of the central protagonist, and the significance of *naming*. 'Eyolf' is obviously an extremely complex meaning, with 'big' and 'little' implications, imposed by Allmers on the living reality of his child and his half-sister. But 'John Gabriel Borkman' and 'Hedda Gabler' are meanings to be incarnated and enacted by the self-realising, self-actualising protagonist – meanings invested with all the immortal implications of a paradise within: the name as god, the self as divine. 'Hedda Gabler' on the tongue of other people is an ironic denial of the essential Hedda. Aunt Julle speaks the name with acquisitive glee, Løvborg as a rebuke to the married woman, Brack with proprietorial possessiveness. And, even when Hedda dies in a final consummation of the self, the ironies persist. She does not pass, for the chorus of bystanders, into mythic history where the self, however illusory, asserts its time-lessness in an eternity of acknowledged spiritual value. Like Phèdre, she dies in the presence of her great ancestor, restoring to his tradition all its tarnished glory; but Phèdre's gesture of cosmic restoration –

Et la mort, à mes yeux dérobant la clarté,
Rend au jour, qu'ils souillaient, toute sa pureté[16]

– has no place in bourgeois society, where the concept of a tragic *gloire,* a private standard of integrity for which one dies, is merely pointless or incomprehensible. In a sense, the tragic heroine passes, by virtue of her extraordinary assertion of value, into a form of mythic history. But, in *Hedda Gabler,* there is no longer a community to register significance or perceive the peculiar nature of Hedda's *gloire.* This is a consequence, undoubtedly, of the incorrigible spiritual insufficiency of the bourgeoisie with their 'Fancy that!' in the face of tragedy. But it must also be a consequence of the self-cancelling, self-defeating *paradis artificiel* of Romantic selfhood.

So far, my partisanship will surely have been evident – a tendency to accept Hedda at her own valuation, and to see terminal events from an exclusive point of view. One is almost compelled into this position by the vision and the anguish that underlie her yearning for Paradise; and *not* to acknowledge the spiritual impulse that drives her is to reduce Hedda's motives to a malignant bitchery, or to take sides against her in the uncom-fortable and pusillanimous company of Tesman and Brack. But, for all the demands made upon our own capacities to respond to the positive elements in Hedda's romanticism, Ibsen's crucial ambivalence remains. John Northam, the most persuasive of all apologists for the heroic Hedda, puts the case succinctly:

To die for a certainty that depends entirely upon the promptings of one's isolated essential self demands a kind of courage.

But the courage, the vision, the poetry are never allowed to cancel out the absurdity, the destructiveness and the triviality.[17]

These are the qualifications which have ultimately to be accounted for. And, in so doing, it seems to me that one encounters not merely a Romantic tragedy but the tragedy of Romanticism itself: man's infinite spiritual aspiration pushed destructively beyond man's capacity to sustain it – the negation of life in the strenuous attempt to affirm it.

Of all the people in their society, only Hedda and Løvborg can envision life lived intensely in defiance of the sleep of death around them. It is significant, in a play so permeated with the odour of death, that its central poetic core should cling to the idea of life in all its possible permutations and associations with power, sensuality, and appetite: *livet, livsmotet, livstrossen, livsbegjært, livskravet, livsgildet.* And yet, so torn between the need for life and the dread of living, Hedda can celebrate *livskravet* only in the act of relinquishing it. This is what is most beautiful, she believes, in Løvborg's death: 'Det at han hadde kraft og vilje til å bryte opp fra livsgildet' (III, 431) – 'That he had the power and the will to tear himself away from the celebration of life.' And her own most triumphant celebration is negated by the form of its assertion. Ensnared by paradox, the Romantic quest for enduring vitality finds its apotheosis in the permanence of death. For infinitude is not a human dimension which men inhabit as gods, but a metaphor of one's yearning; and to obscure the distinctions between life and poetry, to demand that mortal men *live* the timeless moment in reality, is to destroy in the name of spiritual perfection – as Hedda destroys Løvborg, as the self cancels the self. Hedda's Romantic insistence upon *becoming* the poem, creating selfhood as a source of imperishable value, obscures the fine distinction that Wallace Stevens makes between godhead and mortal approximation – 'Not as a god, but *as a god might be*.'[18] In one sense, she may be said to have mastered contingency by perfecting the self and projecting it as a symbol in the act of death. But the dilemma remains: the supreme Romantic stylist, as Morse Peckham puts it, may *symbolise* the self:

But how was one to *be* the Self? It had separated itself from history, for it had separated itself from all but one aspect of human life, but to the Romantic, sooner or later, history must be encountered, for history is reality.[19]

And not the mythic history to which Hedda aspires, but that concept measured by the living reality of process, generation, growth. Hedda in finally asserting her self also sunders that self, in a grotesquely literal manner, from history in its most organic, most palpable form. Her unborn child dies with her – the living counterpart of the symbolic 'child' which she burns in a fit of jealousy and triumph at the end of Act III. The future history of civilisation perishes twice in Ibsen's play. And in this act of perverse negation, Hedda's Romantic selfhood stands condemned in its barrenness.

II

If 'Dionysos' is the central metaphorical expression of Hedda's Romantic individualism, the myth that initially defines John Gabriel Borkman is even more accessible as a major archetype of European Romanticism – an image from recent history of a fallen man–god who, in the early nineteenth century, gave living substance to the idea of a transcendent, unlimited selfhood. 'Do you know how I sometimes feel?' asks Borman. 'I feel like a Napoleon who has been maimed in his first battle' (VIII, 186). And, like Napoleon, he stands in imposing majesty, with one hand thrust into the front of his coat, in the great drawing room with its heavy tapestries and its Empire furniture, waiting for the emissaries from the outside world to acknowledge his indispensable, superhuman genius. It is too easy to reject John Gabriel Borkman as a vivified cartoon of megalomania – the sort of image that the modern sensibility has become accustomed to in the pages of *Punch* or the *New Yorker*. The irony *is* there, of course; but it is an irony finely placed within the complex tonalities of post-Napoleonic attitudes towards a failed Romantic dream. The aspiration is implicit in its very collapse; and the image of Borkman must accommodate not only the egocentric madness but also what Inga-Stina Ewbank has called 'the two antipoles of the glorious but also deadly vision of Borkman'.[20] Romantic and counter-Romantic, visionary magnificence and parodic deflation, spiritual questing and moral censure: these interpenetrating

views of Napoleonism shape the elusive tone of the play and its
tragic–ironic evocation of the aftermath of Romantic failure in a
world where the deposition of Napoleon and the triumph of
middle-class materialism placed heavy limitations, once again, on
the infinite capacities of the human spirit. Borkman's Napoleonic
evaluation of himself, to place it in a Romantic context, is very
clearly Byronic – that tragic image of the wounded eagle, defeated
in the very act of imposing itself upon the disordered energies of
experience, yet still commanding admiration for the super-
humanity of its aspiration:

> Conqueror and Captive of the Earth art thou!
> She trembles at thee still, and thy wild name
> Was ne'er more bruited in men's minds than now
> That thou art nothing, save the jest of Fame,
> Who wooed thee once, thy Vassal, and became
> The flatterer of thy fierceness – till thou wert
> A God unto thyself; nor less the same
> To the astounded kingdoms all inert,
> Who deemed thee for a time whate'er thou didst assert.[21]

The counter-Romantic corollary, implicit even in Borkman's most
visionary rhapsodies, exposes such Napoleonic *Übermenschlikheit*
and its murderous consequences in tones of Dostoievskian moral
irony. Raskolnikov and Borkman share the common belief (and a
common exemplar in Napoleon) that

> an 'extraordinary' man has the right . . . that is not an official
> right, but an inner right to decide in his own conscience to
> overstep . . . certain obstacles, and only in some cases is it
> essential for the practical fulfilment of his idea (sometimes,
> perhaps, of benefit to the whole of humanity).

To which a friend of Raskolnikov's replies, 'Oh, come, don't we
all think ourselves Napoleons now in Russia? . . . Perhaps it was
one of these future Napoleons who did for Alyona Ivanovna last
week?'[22] These are the antipoles, Byronic and Dostoievskian,
between which the gradations of Borkman's romanticism are
ranged, and in terms of which we must judge his splendid and
catastrophic attempt to be a god unto himself.

There are three aspects of Borkman's Romantic self-creation, three versions of Napoleonism, each carefully demarcated in the play and its narrative exposition. The first of these is seen entirely in retrospect, and may possibly be coloured by what James McFarlane calls Borkman's 'self-administered mythopoeic therapy':[23] the Napoleon of mercantile imperialism who will create on earth his dream of pseudo-religious capitalist humanism. He meets his Waterloo at the hands of Hinkel; and in his arrest, arraignment, and imprisonment he experiences not merely a Napoleonic maiming, but a hideous fall from paradisal aspiration into the abyss: 'Og jeg i avgrunnen'; 'Og enda så styrtet han meg i avgrunnen igjen' (III, 539, 554) – 'And I fell into the abyss'; 'Then he pushed me into the abyss again.' It is from the horror of the abyss – with all that the metaphor implies of failure, process and collapse – that Borkman devises his elaborate stratagems for denying reality and death. This second phase is dedicated to the perfection and justification of Napoleonic egocentricity, a troll-like dream of utter self-sufficiency in which, like Hedda Gabler, John Gabriel Borkman invests his name with mythopoeic qualities of 'extraordinary' value. The solipsistic self, again, projects a symbol of itself that defies mortality. Then, in a series of devastating blows, each entry into his Empire drawing room, hermetically sealed against the forces of life, impresses upon him the fallibility of his design and the illusion of self-styled godhead. It is Gunhild who finally draws blood in the Gyntian revelation that he has been dead before his death; and with a fatal vehemence he flings himself into an ultimate assertion of self – not as a symbol but as an act of being, not as a metaphor of power and glory poetically conceived but as a kingdom to be possessed by triumphant entry. Napoleon finally enters, in frozen isolation, his *paradis artificiel* of death.

But Borkman is not the only Romantic in the play. The most pathetic of all its visionaries is old Vilhelm Foldal who clings, like a decrepit Peer Gynt, to the myth of *das Ewig-Weibliche* as an ultimate redemptive value: 'It is a noble and uplifting thought that somewhere out in the wide wide world, far away perhaps, there is to be found the true woman' (VIII, 189). And, with a ruthlessness typical of the way in which each smashes the other's dreams, Borkman dismisses this projection of value onto an ethereal womanhood with scorn. 'In the last resort,' he comments later to Ella, 'one woman can always be replaced by another'

(198). What distinguishes Borkman's romanticism from Foldal's is a resolute rejection of *any* alliance – and especially the sexual – which compromises his solipsistic ideal. For each protagonist, in Ibsen's structure, is a mirror in which the other's romanticism is reflected, distorted or edged into focus until the visionary 'claim' and the visionary 'mission' – *krav* and *misjon* – with their competing and conflicting egocentricities, finally envelop everyone in a single, obsessive desire. 'All the dreams of this play', writes Charles Lyons, 'are dreams of possession and innocence . . . of expiation and regeneration.'[24] But beyond and encompassing these dreams lies that impassioned quest for personal immortality in the Valley of the Shadow, for symbols of permanence – monuments, names, redeemers – in the face of foulness, failure and death. With almost monomaniacal determination, each envisions a kingdom to be possessed in solitary splendour: 'All this I would have created . . . created alone', 'I alone shall be his mother! I alone!', 'Only me', 'So out into the storm alone!' (VIII, 186, 204, 207, 220). 'Bare jeg alene.' 'Alene' – the word shrills throughout the play in declarations of adamant self-sufficiency, each assertion of self negating the others' claim to special status while ironically condemning them – as Mrs Borkman condemns her husband – in the name of her own egocentric deficiency: 'You have never loved anything outside yourself', she cries, ' – that's the truth of the matter' (209). The other truth of the matter, implied but never fully spoken, is that what lies outside the 'extraordinary' self is death-infected, perishable. And no one gives his bounty to the dying.

Ella Rentheim's mortal sickness turns all the unspeakable fears of the other protagonists into a dramatic confrontation with death as a grim reality – the physical mirror of the metaphysical dread that haunts the lives of them all. And, like John Gabriel's, her love denies whatever lives and breathes in the world beyond herself: 'Over the years it has become more and more difficult – and in the end quite impossible – for me to love any living thing: human, animal or plant' (193) – 'alt hva som levende rører seg' (III, 545), 'everything that lives and moves'. She accuses Borkman, with the viciousness typical of all the accusations in the play, of murdering her compassion, killing her capacity to love and her susceptibility, and creating darkness and barrenness in her psychic life and in the world. It is a charge that borders, as John Gabriel says, upon dementia; for, however culpable he might have been in denying her sexuality, Ella's *Angst* and her lovelessness clearly have their roots in the Romantic's fear of process – the organic world that moves and breathes beyond her. What she most resents is Borkman's having denied her a defence against change and death, of having cheated her of a child – for she regards the child, with the insistence of so many of Ibsen's other protagonists, as an assurance of personal immortality, an idea miraculously exempt in its symbolic value from process. This is why she has returned. She has come to claim her child from Borkman – not in its living reality, but in its most abstract, psychic sense: the child as *name*, the guarantee of her 'Rentheim' identity perpetuated in her surrogate son. What she loves in Erhart is his promise of a form of posthumous immortality – 'And when I am dead, Erhart Rentheim will live on after me!' (VIII, 203) – and what she really wants of Borkman is that he relinquish *his own name* in her favour. This is the sole aim of her hysterical scene, the only restitution she requires for the settling of old accounts. She trades in symbols, and imagines that Borkman shares her sense of the magical bonding in names and the perpetuation of identity in dynastic naming. It is typical of the Napoleonic temperament that Borkman scorns her stratagem in a statement of absolute self-sufficiency: 'I am man enough to bear my name alone' (ibid.). He has really given up no part of his immortality in relinquishing his son; for the Borkmaniac self is not immortalised through its projection into someone else. Foldal may find redemption in Eternal Womanhood, and Ella in symbolic naming. But John Gabriel Borkman, in isolation, will be his own imperishable essence. He will bear his name *alone*.

It is clear from the moment of her entry that Ella's real antagonist is not John Gabriel but her twin sister, Gunhild; and that in the complex system of real, surrogate and symbolic motherhoods it is Gunhild's projection of a life's mission onto Erhart that must be most strenuously challenged. Hers is very like the connection Ibsen explores in *Ghosts* between Mrs Alving and Osvald, where the child becomes an instrument to exorcise the father's sins, and where the mother – too haunted by her own psychic ghosts to cast off her mind-forged manacles – moulds her son into a personal liberator and redeemer. What distinguishes Gunhild from Mrs Alving is the consciousness of her mission, the intensity of its vision, and its obsessive neurotic edge. If Ella trades in symbols, Gunhild reveals herself in flashes of poetry which envision experience as a collapse from glory into darkness and filth – the abyss, in which one yearns for purity and light, and for assurances of salvation from the consequences of the fall. 'Men så ramlet det da også sammen', she says of her husband's failure of godlike power. 'All ting. Hele herligheten till slutt'. (III, 523) – 'And so the whole thing caved in. Everything. All the splendour ended.' Name, honour, fortune, life – all lie in the ruination from which Erhart must redeem her: 'En, som skal tvette *rent* alt det som – som banksjefen har tilsmustet' (ibid.) – 'One who will *cleanse* and *purify* everything which he – which the Chairman of the Bank has besmirched.' There are strong biblical echoes in her sense of defilement, in the vaguely sexual connotations of being soiled, and in her cry for *renhet*, with its associations of chastity and cleanness. For Gunhild, the mines which John Gabriel invests with a Romantic spirit-life become an analogue of existence in the abyss, *grubelivet*, with its suggestions of pit-like darkness, from which Erhart 'i renhet og høyhet og lys' (551) – 'in purity and exaltation and light' – will redeem Borkman's trespasses against her. His radiance must obliterate the dark shadow cast by his father over their lives. Her dream, as Lyons suggests, is that of transforming the living reality of her son into a form of fixed and unchanging innocence;[25] and her visionary image of Christ the redeemer has its counterpart in her image of the child as a *monument* raised above his father's grave: a grove of living plants obscuring forever the memory of his shameful life. Monument and tree – the inorganic symbol and its living vehicle – are as ironically contradictory as the radiant messianic avenger and Erhart's actual senuality, which denies the vision of ascetic purity. Erhart, as his aunt wistfully remarks earlier in the play, has *grown up*; and the two sisters seem to impose a static symbolism upon the least appropriate incarnation of their dreams – Gunhild with a possessiveness far more dangerous to her sanity than Ella's. For her dream of Erhart is a tenuous defence against despair – and in extremities, as Ella knows, she would stop at nothing to save herself, even at her son's expense. Behind Gunhild's vision there lies an hysterical claim upon her child which must eliminate all other attempts to secure redemption through his agency. 'Og jeg alene vil være hans mor! Jeg alene!' (III, 547) – 'And I alone will be his mother! I alone'. And, when, at the end of Act III, her dream disintegrates, she experiences the loss of Erhart as terrible damage to her psychic 'motherhood':

'Barnløs' (556) – 'Childless'. It is a cry of utter damnation. Ella, in
a gesture of renunciation which belies her inability to love, gives
up her claim on Erhart, commends him to life and happiness,
and yields up her last symbolic defence against death. Only John
Gabriel, despite the failure of his offer of kinship to his son,
remains unscathed by his departure. He alone needs no Christlike
saviour, no agent of salvation. 'So what do you mean to do,
Father?' Erhart asks, just before rejecting him. And, in a manner
typical of Borkman's self-insulation against all dependency, he
replies, 'Oppreise meg selv, vil jeg' (553) – '*Redeem myself*, that's
what I'll do.' He will be his own messiah.

Madman? Criminal? Mystic? John Gabriel Borkman, argues
Wilson Knight, is all three – but, above all, an inheritor of post-
Napoleonic spiritual power, which now devolves upon the figure
of the financier. He is a man whose psychic energies await
recognition – 'a communal symbol of nineteenth-century industrialism in creative transition and a man striving towards
superman'.[26] For James McFarlane, on the other hand, he is a
grandiose sham, a superman *imaginaire*, obsessed with power
and wealth for their own sake and merely dignifying a sordid and
botched embezzlement with mythic fantasies of heroic and social
pretension. His analogue is not Wagner's Wotan, but Bernick,
the mercantile hypocrite of *Pillars of the Community*.[27] It is
difficult, however, to maintain any completely consistent view of
Borkman. His vision is compelling even in its destructiveness; and
its analogues go back to Peeropolis and Gyntiana – the commercial
empire where the dream of power is ultimately the power over
death – and forward to the existential dream of the modern
period, where power is the means to essential selfhood. Ibsen,
writing of Brand's priestly calling and the religious structure of
the play's central 'problem', clearly indicates the irrelevance of
the *specific* circumstances and profession of his protagonist: 'I
would have been quite capable of making the same syllogism just
as well about a sculptor or a politician as about a priest' (III, 441).
Or, he might have added, a financier. It is precisely the point
made by Rupert Forster, John Whiting's soldier of selfhood in
Marching Song, whose impassioned quest belies the notion that
the psychology of Romanticism is now obsolete. Like Borkman,
he must discover the Napoleonic self by imposing its imprint on
the external world:

The night before that last battle I still believed that I could reach a point of achievement never before known to man. The way I chose was conquest by war. Some men need an art to fulfil themselves. Saints need a religion. I had to pursue a triumph of arms. The greatest the world had ever known. By that I believed I could become myself, the man I was intended to be.[28]

Artist, saint and soldier are all implicit in Borkman's own 'calling' — not to pursue a triumph of arms, but to place his Napoleonism at the service of mankind by becoming the messiah of a new humanist dispensation, by asserting the self in a mercantile conquest which is also a Gyntian crusade against death. 'John Gabriel Borkman' conjoins the worldly power of English commercial imperialism with archangelic connotations of the Resurrection. Napoleon and Christ coincide in the Romantic temperament.

Because so much of Borkman's ideology is retrospective, it is difficult to free it from the spurious and the suspect. One works by inference and implication to evaluate the substance of a dream which failed sixteen years before the play begins, but which still rankles in the memory of a man now near to death. Perhaps it is the very proximity of death that colours and distorts the pristine vision, for 'mythopoeic therapy' in Ibsen is invariably administered to invest the self with charms against mortality and time. 'Ja du, tiden går,' Borkman says to Foldal, 'årene går; livet, – uh nei – det tør jeg ikke tenke på!' (III, 537) – 'Yes, you see . . . time passes; the years pass; life, – ah, no – I dare not think of it.' It is a thought that immediately evokes Borkman's Napoleonic self-comparison and his rhapsodic vision of an empire created in lone splendour:

I could have made millions! All those mines I could have controlled! The enormous mineral deposits! The water power! The quarries! The trade links . . . the shipping lines in every part of the globe! All this I would have created . . . created alone. (VIII, 186)

For any comparable sense of material immortality or the expansion of the self into universal domination one must turn to the opening pages of *Dombey and Son*. But Borkman needs no son as partner in his enterprise. Nor a lover. For no one must compromise his solipsism. No one must share his calling:

> I had the power! And the indomitable sense of ambition! All those millions lay there, imprisoned, over the whole land, deep in the mountains, and called to me! Cried out to me for release! But nobody else heard it. Only me.   (VIII, 207)

His is a special, unique calling, a summons by the spirit-world, by motives higher than acquisitive possession and higher than sexual desire, by inexorable necessity – 'den tvingende nødvendighet' (III, 543) – and by his consciousness of a pseudo-religious mission to 'build myself an empire, and thereby create prosperity for thousands and thousands of others ... the power to create human happiness all around me' (VIII, 198, 209). We may, of course, choose to discount the benevolent capitalism that under-lies the vision – Borkman's treatment of his friends and family does not, after all, affirm his commitment to human joy. But the *tone* of his protestation is a familiar expression of dire need. It re-echoes Brand's missionary fervour, Rosmer's new religion of spiritual nobility, or Solness's humanistic dedication to building homes for people to rejoice in. The crucial ambivalence in all these visions, their central paradox, is the dream of the unhappy and alienated man to create what Borkman calls 'forbundsliv hele jorden rundt' (III, 562) – 'a global sense of human community', a Blakean 'Universal Brotherhood of Eden'. In the absence of God, man's immediate responsibility is to his fellow men, to fill the emptiness with human meaning, however he chooses to define his particular form of secular religion. Borkman, argues James McFarlane, has recategorised his greed and personal ambition as an agency of social redemption; but this view belies the 'spilt religion'[29] that powers his Romantic dream of a reintegrated world. The dream fails, as it must, on two accounts. Like Solness, Brand and Allmers, Borkman cannot make his substitute faith viable because his own humanity is so crucially defective, because his conception of himself as redeemer is merely an aspect of that personal insufficiency. The great failure of all self-appointed prophets in Ibsen is always, on the most private and individual level, the inability to enact their projects as living realities in friendship, marriage or in familial relationships with children, parents and siblings. The immediate human need – and especially the demand of sexuality – ultimately belies the Edenic humanism and reduces it to nothingness. This much is obvious. But beneath the spurious humanism of these redeemers lies the ineluctable operation of the Romantic paradox: the search for a deathless paradise which, ironically, merely reduplicates the static forms of death-in-life. Borkman is already dead. His mercantile ideal of wealth divorced from bulk and extrapolated to its Romantic essence in the spirit of the ore envisions a paradise where life itself – love, sexuality and reality – becomes rock-hard, ice-cold, ironlike and inorganic. The song of the ore tolls like a midnight bell; and its music is the *danse macabre*.

Borkman is correct in at least one claim to extraordinariness. The other humanists who so catastrophically fail to enact the tenets of their secular faith – Rosmer, Rebekka, Solness, Allmers – all acknowledge, to their credit, an awareness of free-floating guilt for an often unspecified and repressed offence crying out for retribution; and in their guilt begin the first stirrings of moral conscience, the first movement towards atonement for a mur-dered woman or a child cruelly denied. Borkman alone remains morally unregenerate. The second phase of his Romantic self-hood is given up entirely to the fabrication of stratagems for coping with his fall from Paradise, and with the guilt that normally attends the multiple betrayals of faith, love and trust. His Byronic Napoleonism is both self-definition and self-justification: 'Menneskene skjønner ikke at jeg *måtte* det fordi jeg var meg selv, – fordi jeg var John Gabriel Borkman, – og ikke noen annen' (III, 549) – 'People do not understand that I *had* to do what I did, because I am my self, – because I am John Gabriel Borkman, – and no one else.' Like Hedda Gabler, he has *become* his name; and having failed to impose that self upon the world, the self now draws the entire world into its own sphere with relentless centripetal force. Borkman displays, not as allegory but as a function of Romantic psychopathology, the 'for- og i-seg-væren' of the Gyntian self (II, 171) – 'the for- and within-yourself-existence', the 'I-that-I-amness' which is the hallmark of the Troll's self-sufficiency. 'I sacrificed love and power and glory / For the sake of remaining my own true self,' says Peer (III, 407); and out of this offence John Gabriel Borkman creates a system of values which establishes his pre-eminence among the other nineteenth-century studies of *Selbheit, Ichheit, das insichseiende Fursichsein* and 'the dark idolatory of self'.[30] He is a paradigm of the alienated self – that 'sordid solitary thing ... / Feeling himself, his own low self the whole'[31] – an incarnation of that fragmentary, fallen state which, for Shelley and Blake and Coleridge, is the ultimate experience of evil. This is what the dream of *forbundsliv* has become in Borkman's empire. But he denies the evil. Characteristically, Borkman's egocentricity sees all value through the scratched left eye of the Troll, inverting ugliness into beauty, filth into purity – or, in his case, madness into sanity: 'Vær da aldri så gal å tvile på Dem selv!' (III, 535) – 'Never be so mad as to doubt yourself!' And when the eye, altering its angle of vision, transforms the old deed, then the criminal can acquit himself of crime, absolve himself of guilt and hold the world to blame for its failure of perception. His rationale will be Raskolnikov's – 'but extraordinary men have a right to commit any crime and to transgress the law in any way, just because they are extraordinary';[32] and, if history records no cases of self-absolution from anti-social deeds, it is because the extraordinary man transcends the limitations of legal precedent:

> BORKMAN: Only ordinary people need precedents.
> FOLDAL: The law doesn't recognize such distinctions.
> BORKMAN [*with deliberate harshness*]: You are no poet, Vilhelm.   (VIII, 190)

The remark is primarily intended to devastate the poetaster, but it also suggests that 'John Gabriel Borkman' is really a self-begotten image, born of his own poetic imagination, and that nothing dare exist beyond it except by his toleration.

'Du og han kommer inn under det jeg mener når jeg sier meg selv' (549) – 'You and Erhart', he says to his wife, 'are included in my general meaning when I refer to "myself".' People exist only in so far as he can fashion them into aspects of his selfhood. Frida Foldal, for example, is no more to him than an allegory of his own expulsion from society – the exceptional musician excluded from the dance – and his sympathy for her is indistinguishable from his pity for himself. Foldal, similarly, is treated as a glass in which his own genius is reflected; and, when he refuses to mirror the self-deception, John Gabriel gets rid of him. This *Ichschmerz*, Lilian Furst argues, lies at the heart of the Romantic hero's tragedy: 'His egotism is such as to pervert all his feelings inwards on to himself till everything and everyone is evaluated only in relationship to that precious self, the focus of his entire energy.'[33]

But Borkman stands slightly apart from the cult figures of Romantic individualism – Werther, René, Octave, Manfred – for *his* tragedy is to be unwittingly dependent upon the active collaboration of others in the life-lie of total self-sufficiency. However loudly and often he may protest his Napoleonism, his self remains as tenuous and vulnerable a structure as any of those symbols of eternity nurtured by the other romantics in the play. It can exist only 'out of Nature', cosseted from reality, and protected against injury or deflation by a careful selection of the 'mirrors' which reinforce identity. This surely is one reason why Gunhild is never admitted into the Napoleonic presence: she, more than anyone, knows the weakness in Borkman's defences, the pathetic man behind the myth.

> FRU BORKMAN [*ler hanlig*]: Så *det* behøver du da allikevel å innprentes utenfra?
> BORKMAN [*i svulmende harme*]: Ja, når hele verden hveser i kor at jeg er en uoppreiselig mann, så kan der komme stunder over meg da jeg selv er nær ved å tro det. [*Hever hodet.*] Men så stiger min innerste, seirende bevissthet opp igjen. Og *den* frikjenner meg!   (III, 550)

> MRS BORKMAN [*laughing contemptuously*]: So it is still necessary, after all, for help from the outside world to bolster you up?
> BORKMAN [*with rising anger*]: Yes, when the whole world hisses in unison that I'm a man beyond redemption, there are times when I come close to believing it myself. [*Raises his head.*] But then my innermost, undaunted conviction asserts itself again. And *that*'s what acquits me!

What happens during the two-hour traffic of the play is a traumatic shaking of that undaunted conviction of sixteen years' duration by mirrors that suddenly refuse to reflect his Napoleonism, by accusations that challenge self-acquittal, and by truths that draw blood. The formal structure of Acts II and III is a protracted *sparagmos,* a collapse of Borkman's defensive Romanticism forcing the besieged self to confront its nothingness and reconstitute itself by engaging with the world.

Having incarcerated himself against reality and death – those forces which threaten his divinity – Borkman is driven to elaborate evasions of the obvious, denying that the select few who enter through his door are mirror-images that mock his self-im-mortalising dream. Foldal is *not* one of the exceptional few. His mediocrity parodies, in its reflection, Borkman's Romantic pose and forces him to acknowledge the truth behind the shared deception. Their petulant quarrel reveals the cracks in Borkman's structure; and, when death enters in the person of Ella Rentheim, he can accommodate the horror only by negating her suffering. Hammerblow on hammerblow, the whole thing totters. The failure of the dream, the speaking of truths that have festered in silence for years, the twin Furies of retribution – all conspire to force Borkman's deadliness upon him until, from the vanity of arrogant self-acquittal, he veers to the other extreme of 'knugende selvanklage' (549) – 'shattering self-condemnation': 'I've now gone and wasted eight precious years of my life up there! The day I was released I should have stepped straight out into reality – into the iron-hard, dreamless world of reality!' (vIII, 208).

There is a surprisingly dynamic reordering of Romantic experience in a play which seems, on the surface, so frozen in its attitudes. Borkman radically recasts the contents of his mind when he abandons the dream for reality, and when he reacts against Gunhild's malicious vision of his corpselike state by dedicating his energies to life: 'Not yet! I have been close . . . so very close to death. But now I am revived. I am well again. Life still lies ahead. I can see it . . . this new life . . . bright and sparkling . . . beckoning to me' (210). And, in a spontaneous gesture of affection and kinship, he is able to break down the walls of solipsism by reaching out to his son – not with the rabid tenacity of those who dream of Erhart as redeemer, but as his ally in a world devoid of illusions where men must redeem themselves through effort and atonement:

> No man can find redemption for his failure in another man's achievements. That's nothing but an empty dream, a story you've been given to believe. . . . All these years I have tried to keep myself going on dreams and hopes. But I can't be content with that. And now I'm finished with dreams. . . . It is only by his own present and his own future that a man can atone for his past. Through work . . . unrelenting work for all those things which in my youth I felt made life worthwhile . . . and which

now seem a thousand times more valuable still. Erhart – will
you join me and help me in this new life?   (214)

It is not quite clear yet what those values are that make life
worthwhile for Borkman; but this is an extraordinary readjust-
ment to the world of human contact and the ties of family for so
alien a man to make. It might have been his saving grace. But
life, for Erhart, is synonymous with pleasure – not with work or
redemptive missions or ministrations to the dying. His own
Romantic hedonism impels him southwards in the company of
two women (lest one should pall), confirming his father's cynical
assumption that, if the worst comes to the worst, one woman can
always be replaced by another. So Ella Rentheim loses her name,
Gunhild her redeemer, and John Gabriel Borkman his only
chance of a living *forbundsliv* through commitment and alliance.
Nothing remains for him but to brave the storm of life *alone*.

But there are dangerous implications even in Borkman's
abandonment of dreams for reality, deathly alienation for life.
And it becomes clear, in the final phase of his Romantic quest,
that dynamic change may lead a man of his temperament into
ever-deepening regions of psychic disturbance. For the reality
which Borkman rediscovers is ominously 'jernhårde' (III 549) –
iron-hard – immutable, static, and finally synonymous with existence in the mine-world of ore and stone; and his vague sense of
life-values, 'alt det som i ungdommen sto for meg som selve livet'
(553) – 'everything which in my youth represented life for me' – is
projected in a system of symbols interposed between the self and
its experience of life. His equations are inevitable: 'dette nye,
lysende liv, som gjærer og venter' (550) – 'this new, radiant life,
turbulent and waiting to be lived' – is envisioned in forms that
congeal human feeling and petrify sexuality in a deathless subterranean Paradise. For Borkman's desire, as Lyons describes it,
'is the possession and control of energy, energy held in the
metaphor of the unworked mines, and the desire is clearly a
desire to encompass phenomenal experience in such a way that it
will be held in some kind of stasis.'[34] Unable (as Ella claims *she* is)
to love man, animal or plant, John Gabriel Borkman gives his
bounty to the inorganic mineral 'life' which beckons to him from
his iron-hard Kingdom. And in a final descent to madness he
yields (as Erhart does) to the ineluctable lure of powerful erotic

forces, discovering in his son's craving for sensuality and life the clue to his own course of action. Mrs Wilton, carnal and mutable in her passions, is the human analogue of those eternal powers that draw Borkman towards the mines: erotic flesh juxtaposed with the erotic call of the mineral-life, the sensual body with the sensuality of imperishable spirit.

Of all the declarations of love in Ibsen's plays, Borkman's cry to the ore-bearing strata beneath the layers of ice and snow is the most impassioned and intense. On the sardonic assumption that dead men are paradoxically immune from mortality, he enters physically into the infinitude of his dream Kingdom, 'dype, endeløse, uuttømmelige' (III. 562) – 'deep, without-end, inexhaustible'; and the ice-laden winds that blow from the deathless regions become a 'livsluft' (ibid.), a breath of life from the spirits of the mine:

> . . . I sense their presence – those captive millions. I feel the veins of metal reaching out their twisting, sinuous, beckoning arms to me. . . . But let me whisper to you, here in the stillness of the night. I love you: you who lie in a trance of death in the darkness and the deep. I love you! You and your life-seeking treasures and all your bright retinue of power and glory. I love you, love you, love you.   (VIII, 231)

Borkman's symbols of immortality elude translation: 'skinndøde' and 'livskrevende' – 'an imitation of death' and 'an anticipation of life'. These are the qualities of his subterranean Kingdom which look forward to those phantasmagoric spirit-states in Beckett's plays, where existence becomes a form of minimal consciousness suspended between deathlike trance and prenatal animation, and where the only condition that finally eludes death is deathliness itself. Borkman strives for this condition *in life,* enacting Irene's tragic paradox in Ibsen's last play that when the dead awaken their only revelation is that they have never lived. Borkman never attains to such devastating self-awareness; and Ella's prophecy that he will never enter his cold, dark Kingdom overlooks the fact that he has always inhabited it, *alone* if not triumphantly. In his last gasping phrases, Borkman still speaks of his Paradisal mine-world as *Gudsriket* – 'the kingdom . . . and the power . . . and the glory' – but he does not realise that one who actually enters into the cold regions of his fantasy must suffer its congealing, petrifying influence. The only embrace from those alluring and enticing arms that John Gabriel Borkman is allowed to feel is the touch of the 'ishånd' and the 'malmhånd' (III, 563) – the ice-hand on the heart, and the iron-hand which finally hauls him into the kingdom of death.

In the language of *Gudsriket*, which he has converted to his own secular vision, Borkman may be said to die of 'astonishment of heart'[35] – the medical symptoms of heart-attack and the metaphysical ideas blending, as Inga-Stina Ewbank puts it, into a hallucinatory reality where the heart can petrify and freeze.[36] This is the dead-end of the Romantic quest, one of many such variations in Ibsen's drama where the literal movement into an inhuman Ice Church, free of change and mortality, merely confirms the failure of Paradise in the protagonist's self-immolating death. The spiritual geography of heights and depths, mountain and mine, the glorious Kingdom and the abyss is so insistent a pattern in Ibsen as to suggest a private mythic system with its own esoteric frame of reference and its recondite symbolism. *John Gabriel Borkman*'s inverted Ice Church may certainly have its genesis in Ibsen's poem 'Bergmanden', with its splendid subterranean treasures and diamond studded veins of gold, beckoning from the chasm's darkness with the promise of 'fred og ørk fra evighed' – 'peace and isolation from eternity'.[37] But, within the larger context of European Romantic archetypes, both the poem and the play share (by chance, I imagine, rather than by influence) in a body of ideas and images where the introverted self, withdrawing from reality and human contact, enters a subterranean Paradise of its own visionary creation. There is a brief history of this archetype in Lilian Furst's *Romanticism in Perspective*, where she discusses the German Romantics – Novalis's *Heinrich von Ofterdingen*, Tieck's *Der Runenberg* and E. T. A. Hoffmann's *Die Bergwerke zu Falun*, in which the hero, wandering through a mineshaft, envisions an Eden in imagery of inorganic, mineral life: 'paradiesischen Gefilde der herrlichsten Metallbäume and Pflanzen, an denen wie Früchte, Blüten und Blumen feuerstrahlende Steine hingen'[38] – 'Fields of Paradise, on whose marvellous metallic trees and plants hung fruit, buds, and blossoms of radiant precious stones'. The vision persists, as Lilian Furst points out, to the Symbolists and neo-Romantics at the end of the nineteenth century. It is an aspect of Ibsen's elusive genius that he should seem at one and the same time the central exponent of a public tradition made intensely private and also the most stringent moral critic of such a *paradis artificiel* of Romantic selfhood.

The *dénouement* of *John Gabriel Borkman,* however, moves beyond a merely bleak counter-Romantic vision of alienation bordering on madness. The final gesture of the play, like the holding out of hands that concludes *Little Eyolf,* offers a tenuous possibility of hope to those desiccated creatures whose movement towards human contact may melt the frost of *hjertekulde* – the heart's-coldness of solitude and alienation. Reduced to shadows by their *hjertekulde* and by John Gabriel's, Gunhild and Ella can finally take each other's hands and acknowledge their love for the dead Borkman. Avoiding glib extremes of hope and despair, Ibsen ends this coldest of plays with gestures of minimal compassion, with the sisters' diffident acknowledgement of their shared condition, and with a groping towards reconciliation after a lifetime's hatred. At last they break through the solipsism that has shaped their lives; and, even if they are beyond redemption from the living death, at least they will not die alone.

I have been suggesting that in *Hedda Gabler* and *John Gabriel Borkman* the Romantic quest for freedom from process and death finally leads the protagonist to locate eternity and infinitude not in some external symbol, but *in propria persona* – in the self-immortalising, self-divinising temperament of the poet-virtuoso and the Napoleonic superman. At the same time, however, it is impossible to abstract the self as symbol from the various other symbol-systems in Ibsen: the fantastic kingdom, the child-redeemer, the lover-as-god and Eternal Womanhood as a paradigm of static and sexless perfection. These are the analogues of Paradise that I shall discuss in the chapters that follow.

Notes

1. The line is delivered '*atter urolig*' (III, 391) – with great anxiety. There is the sub-textual suggestion, as Janet Suzman has indicated, that Hedda is counting the months of her pregnancy. See '*Hedda Gabler*: The Play in Performance', in Durbach, *Ibsen and the Theatre,* p. 89.
2. Peckham, *Romanticism,* p. 24.
3. As exemplars of Romantic historicism, Peckham points to Michelet, Ranke, Froude and especially Carlyle, whose spiritual progress from 'The

Everlasting No' to 'The Everlasting Yea' in *Sartor Resartus* recapitulates the historical pattern in a related literary form.

4. Thomas Mann, 'Disorder and Early Sorrow', in Lionel Trilling (ed.), *The Experience of Literature* (New York, 1967) p. 690.

5. Ibid., p. 694.

6. Muriel Bradbrook, 'Ibsen and the Past Imperfect', in Daniel Haakonsen (ed.), *Contemporary Approaches to Ibsen*, II, (Oslo, 1971) 7–24.

7. Ibid., p. 23.

8. The opening sentences of Spengler's *The Decline of the West* have an ironically Løvborgian ring to them: 'In this book is attempted for the first time the venture of predetermining history, of following the still untravelled stages in the destiny of a Culture. . . .' Quoted in Richard Ellmann and Charles Feidelson (eds.), *The Modern Tradition* (New York, 1965) p. 485.

9. Ibid., p. 489.

10. Ibid., p. 491.

11. Friedrich Nietzsche, *'The Birth of Tragedy'* and *'The Genealogy of Morals'*, trs. Francis Golffing (New York, 1956), pp. 23–4, 28.

12. I am grateful to Mr R. Cartlidge for this suggestion.

13. Peckham, *Romanticism*, pp. 21, 22.

14. Cf. Lyons, *Ibsen: The Divided Consciousness*, p. 160: 'The only means of gaining a sense of form which is free from dissolution or change is to create some sense of form out of death. . . . to fix the self within a comprehensive vision of reality is to remove the self from the flux of phenomenal existence – to die and escape consciousness and the phenomena which feed it.'

15. *Hedda Gabler*, trs. Michael Meyer (London, 1962) p. 117.

16. Jean Racine, *Phèdre*, Il. 1643–4.

17. John Northam, *Ibsen: A Critical Study* (Cambridge, 1973) p. 184.

18. Stevens, 'Sunday Morning'. Emphasis added.

19. Peckham, *Romanticism*, p. 32.

20. Inga-Stina Ewbank, 'Ibsen and "The Far More Difficult Art" of Prose', in Haakonsen, *Contemporary Approaches to Ibsen*, II, 82.

21. Lord Byron, *Childe Harold's Pilgrimage*, III. xxxvii.

22. Feodor Dostoievski *Crime and Punishment*, trs. Constance Garnett (London, 1967) pp. 230, 235–6.

23. James McFarlane, Introduction to *The Oxford Ibsen*, VIII (London, 1977) 25.

24. Charles Lyons 'The Function of Dream and Reality in *John Gabriel Borkman*', *Scandinavian Studies*, XLV (1973) 304, 293.

25. Ibid., p. 302.

26. G. Wilson Knight, *Ibsen* (Edinburgh and London, 1962) p. 96.

27. McFarlane, Introduction to *The Oxford Ibsen*, VIII, 25–7.

28. In *New English Dramatists: 5* (Penguin, 1967) p. 214.

29. Cf. T. E. Hulme: 'Romanticism, then, and this is the best definition I can give of it, is spilt religion' – in Herbert Read (ed.) *Speculations* (London, 1936) p. 118.

30. See Abrams, *Natural Supernaturalism*, pp. 295–6. The phrases are those of Boehme, Schelling, Hegel and Shelley.

31. Ibid., p. 266. The lines come from Coleridge's 'Religious Musings'.

32. Dostoievski, *Crime and Punishment,* p. 230.
33. Lilian Furst, *Romanticism in Perspective* (London, 1969) p. 99.
34. Lyons, in *Scandinavian Studies,* xLv, 295.
35. Deuteronomy, 28:28.
36. Ewbank, in Haakonsen, *Contemporary Approaches to Ibsen,* ii, 80.
37. The poem and its translation are included in Appendix ii of *The Oxford Ibsen,* viii, 339–40.
38. Quoted in Furst, *Romanticism in Perspective,* p. 94.

4 'Children of Paradise': Alf, Hedvig and Eyolf as 'Conceptions of Immortality'

Ibsen's gloomy genius would seem, in my account of it so far, to inhere almost exclusively in the anguished cry of the awakened dead against the loss of life's creative possibilities – rather like the blind ascribing values to colours never seen. This is typical. Osvald cries out for life's gladness, Hedda for life's passion, Rebekka for life's joy: but, in a dramatic world that so ruthlessly represses sexuality and that can envision 'life' only in ecstatic dreams, there seems no living substance to these visions. But the gloom of the late Ibsen is not by any means impervious to life at its most dramatically real and vital. Irene, awakening from the dead, knows precisely the cause of Rubek's living death, just as she knows the nature of her own self-annihilating collaboration in their denial of life. Together, as artist and muse, they have created the perfect symbol of transcendent innocence – the resurrected soul awakening from the toils of mortality into eternal life. They call it their 'child' – a cold and marmoreal celebration of immortality, pure spirit freed from all entanglement with the ugliness and the dirt of existence, and immaculate in every aspect of its conception. Sexual desire has been sacrificed to the artwork's sublimity, and passion has been repressed lest it desecrate the purity of the vision. But no child is ever conceived without the reality of physical desire, and Rubek's folly in negating the passionate source of his inspiration recoils upon him as an act of self-destruction. *He* can no longer create. *She* is barren beyond recovery. Both have sacrificed the reality of life – sexuality and joy and children – to its symbolic analogue in imperishable form. 'I should have borne children', cries Irene. 'Many children. Real

children. Not the kind that are preserved in tombs. That should
have been my calling' (VIII, 280). There is nothing ambiguous in
her definition of the life she has never lived. And Ibsen underscores her anguish with his most poignant, most lyrical evocation
of living process in the later drama: a group of small children,
singing and playing, weaves in and out of the action in Act II of
When We Dead Awaken in a dance which, like life, flows chaoti-
cally and formlessly in random, ceaselessly moving patterns. Maja
is merely irritated by the 'noise' and the 'antics'. Rubek, ever the
artist, tries to discover harmony in the awkwardness of their
movements – as if reducing the children to figures in a frieze by
controlling them as art. Only Irene responds to them, as they
respond to her, with the range of feeling that living children
inspire:

> *The playing children have already caught sight of her and have*
> *gone running to meet her. Now she is surrounded by the crowd*
> *of children; some of them appear happy and trusting, others*
> *are shy and fearful.* (273)

There is no clearer image in Ibsen of the meaning of human
fulfilment forever forfeited to the Romantic dream.

When We Dead Awaken juxtaposes, in an almost perfect
schema, two distinct visions of the child: the living reality which
resists all attempts to impose symbolic value upon it, and its
inorganic analogue which petrifies the imperfections of nature
– ceaseless change and growth – in static forms invested with
pseudo-religious intimations of immortality. There is, as I have
suggested, a variation on this pattern in *Hedda Gabler* where
Hedda's unborn foetus and the Thea Løvborg 'child' – unseen
reality and fabricated symbol – juxtapose a vision of history as
generation against history as abstract process, futurity as the
biological child against futurity as a memorial to genius. Hedda
destroys both children in a wanton, annihilating gesture. Irene's
frustrated motherhood finds expression in equally appalling
visions of child-murder, but her fantasies of destruction are
directed only against the cold symbolic 'children' of imperishable
art, those inhuman ideals which destroy vitality and frustrate the
birth of living children:

> IRENE: I should have killed that child.
> RUBEK: Killed it, you say!

IRENE [*whispering*]: Killed it . . . before I left you. Smashed it.
Smashed it to pieces . . . . Since then I've killed it countless
times. By day and night. Killed it in hatred, in vengeance, in
torment. (254)

Even in *Hedda Gabler* the real and the symbolic children never
impinge upon each other. However lurid the fantasy of
Kindermord, Hedda knows that Thea's child is, after all, only a
book; and the death of her own unborn child, however heinous, is
incidental to her own suicide and not deliberately calculated.
The real horror at the heart of Ibsen's world comes about when
the carefully juxtaposed visions of the 'child' suddenly collide –
when the living child is made to bear the burden of an impossible
symbolic value or when the conflation of the mortal child, with all
its pitiful human defects, and the immortal and perfect design of
the Romantic succeeds only in destroying life in all its vulnerability and defencelessness. Brand's dying child, the incipiently
blind Hedvig, the crippled Eyolf are all, as it were, the chorus of
children in *When We Dead Awaken* momentarily isolated as
individual images of a delicate and fragile life, obviously disqualified by their very imperfections from the symbolic function
imposed upon them. The impulse to create a 'Resurrection
Day' – whatever the variant meanings that derive from Rubek's
statue/child – finds expression in the transcendentalism of all
those who seek their own redemption through the agency of the
child. The syndrome will already have become apparent in my
discussion of *John Gabriel Borkman,* where Gunhild and Ella
force Erhart into the symbolic roles of saviour and earthly
redeemer. But Erhart is the single exception to the fate of Ibsen's
children. He is old enough to assert himself and thus escape the
consequences of enacting 'Resurrection Day' as a living reality,
and the consequences of a *Kindermord* far more appalling than
Irene's fantasy of smashing her statue/child. In *Brand, The Wild
Duck* and *Little Eyolf*, it is the living child who dies – not its
symbolic analogue. The Romantic dream of resurrection into
immortal life finally destroys the only life which, in the world of
these plays, has any meaning for the protagonists.

In no other dramatist (with the possible exception of Euripides)
has the death of children so engrossed the vision and the
mythology of the drama as in Ibsen. The list is daunting: children
real, symbolic or metaphorical; children as yet unborn, infants,

youths, adolescents or young men; children stillborn, suicidal, sacrificed, murdered, congenitally defective, debauched, burned or drowned. Muriel Bradbrook was among the first to comment on this near-obsessive theme, detecting in it the Romantic's problem of literary creation in a state of forfeited innocence: 'What had been murdered was the childlike part of himself – the fresh and unreflecting sensuous vitality which feeds the poet. . . . Ibsen, like Rubek, had become "first and foremost an artist".'[1] James Kerans, eschewing Romantic in favour of Freudian psychology, has provided an extremely complex and elaborate psychoanalytic theory *apropos* of *Little Eyolf* – the basic premise psychoanalitic theory *apropos* of *Little Eyolf*–the basic premise being that the *Kingermord* is essentially an event in the sub-conscious life of the hero, analogous to the earliest sexual trauma in the parent–child relationship.[2] And James Hurt, in turn eschewing the Oedipus Complex in favour of the existential theories of R. D. Laing, argues for a double *Kindermord* structure in which the children must be understood as images of the protagonists' divided selves – ego-projections whose deaths mark traumatic crises of selfhood.[3] There are several other theories,[4] and it is with some trepidation that I add yet another to an already lengthy and controversial list. It seems to me, however, that no comprehensive or monolithic theory can successfully account for the diversity of the *Kindermord* themes in, say, King Skule's desire to murder Haakon's royal 'brain child' in *The Pretenders* (II, 299), Hedda's incineration of Thea's 'soul child', and Hedvig's suicide–sacrifice. Some child-deaths, however, clearly reveal a common element; and in confining my discussion to the fates of Alf, Hedvig and little Eyolf I want to suggest their significance within a recognisable and familiar Romantic tradition. Hedvig in particular – Ibsen's most delicately defined image of childhood – should find a place among the children of Blake and Wordsworth and Dickens in that tradition of Romantic protest where the vulnerable child stands at the dangerous point of impact between pristine innocence and adult experience. It is the death of this Romantic child – from the self-immolation of Dickens's Paul Dombey to the self-destructing children in the stories of James and Lawrence and the plays of Whiting[5] – that constitutes the most ferocious indictment of a society that eliminates its future by negating all the child represents: spirit, innocence, joy, authentic selfhood, life itself. And Hedvig, it seems to me, is a pivotal study in the development of this tradition from its Romantic origins to the modern existential implications of the *Kindermord*.

What all three children have in common, however, is an affinity with another aspect of the *Kindermord* – pseudo-theological rather than social in its implications. They are all, by symbolic definition in the plays, child-saviours, miraculous or wonderful in the functions they must perform, whose deaths are looked upon as sacrificial rather than accidental or suicidal. The roles imposed upon them, by implication or association, suggest the 'Resurrection Day' incarnate – the redemption of the family through the agency of this exceptional child. This is the point at which the·Romantic idea of the Paradisal child fuses with that vein of Christian transcendentalism epitomised in Søren Kierkegaard's *Fear and Trembling,* a brooding deliberation on the sacrifice of Isaac in which Romanticism is transformed into a doctrine of absurd belief. Kierkegaard is nowhere more Romantic than in his formulation of a 'teleological suspension of the ethical': the subordination of everything that makes man human and moral and compassionate, as in Abraham's love for his child, in the name of some transcendental imperative or abstraction – God, or the absolute, or (in Gregers Werle's pseudo-religious language) 'den ideale fordring', the claim of the ideal. 'That it was hostile to life', writes Brian Downs, 'was a circumstance that did not vex the ex-theologian with his eyes fixed on the eternal and absolute.'[6] But, for Ibsen, the denial of the living child in the name of some abstract *telos* restates, in terms of the *Kindermord,* the most tragic operation of the Romantic paradox: the death of the human agent of the quest for immortality, and the failure of the humanism which the latter-day Abraham claims as the basis for his secular vision.

The first of these Romantic traditions – the child as innocence and joy, over whom 'Immortality / Broods like the Day'[7] – is most fully discussed in Peter Coveney's *Poor Monkey.*[8] It is an image which persists, as Coveney argues, from Blake and Wordsworth, for whom

A child, more than all other gifts
That earth can offer to declining man,
Brings hope with it, and forward looking thoughts[9]

to the modern, post-war writers for whom the child remained a
creative symbol, 'a focal point of contact between the growing
human consciousness and the "experience" of an alien world,
about which they could concentrate their disquiet, and, impor-
tantly, their hopes for human salvation'.[10] Wordsworth's 'Ode:
Intimations of Immortality from Recollections of Early Childhood' is, of course, a crucial statement of this tradition and a
moving tribute to the Romantic imagination which can rediscover, in visionary gleams and flashes, something analogous to an
epiphany of Paradise. In Hopkins the symbolism is even more
overtly Christian – the poet, as it were, redeeming the consequences of the Fall by seeing with the eye of recovered childhood
innocence 'a strain of the earth's sweet being in the beginning / In
Eden garden'.[11] By recovering the vision of the child, men become
as children once again and enter the Kingdom of Heaven. In his
jottings and notes for *The Wild Duck* Ibsen makes roughly the
same equation between the imagination of the child and the loss,
to the sophisticated adult, of delight and inventiveness and play:

> In becoming civilized, man undergoes the same change as
> when a child grows up. Instinct weakens, but powers of logical
> thought are developed. Adults have lost the ability to play with
> dolls.   (VI, 430)

But the 'ability to play with dolls', as might be expected in Ibsen,
has an ominous counter-Romantic application to those hopeless
creatures in *The Wild Duck* who do precisely that. For the adult
to *see* as a child is not, by any means, to behave childishly. It is
with the 'primal sympathy' and 'the philosophic mind' of the
adult that Wordsworth participates imaginatively in the
children's sporting on the shores of the immortal sea – just as
'genius', for Baudelaire, is '*childhood recovered* at will, childhood
now endowed, in order to express itself, with the powers of
manhood'.[12] As Peter Coveney constantly points out, the positive
symbol of the Romantic child has a dangerously regressive corollary – a sentimental escape, through childhood, into immaturity,
self-pity, and nostalgia for the lost golden paradise of infancy.
This, I think, is the crucial distinction between, for example,
Dylan Thomas's self-indulgent *memory* of a childish Eden in
'Fern Hill' and Wordsworth's *intimations* of immortality in the
'Ode'. And the same distinction is central to the visions, images

and dramatic enactment of 'childhood' in *The Wild Duck.*

'One way of looking at *The Wild Duck*', writes James McFarlane, 'is to see it as a dramatic commentary on the shock of growing up' (VI, 6). Another way of looking at the play is to see it as a comment on the *refusal* to grow up, a nostalgic regression into the green world of childish innocence where the past is redeemed, and where one re-enacts one's youth in a world of artificially reconstituted natural forms. Robert Raphael quite correctly regards the attic-world of the Ekdals as a 'metaphor for the Christian paradise', providing them 'just like heaven, with a world of pure value, a realm of nearly perfect orientation'.[13] What is lacking in this account, however, is the irony of this *paradis artificiel* – that tendency, so pervasive among Ibsen's Romantics, to blur distinctions between the metaphorical and the literal, to confuse an intimation of immortality with immortality as a recoverable Paradise of one's second childhood. Old Ekdal, moving through the rubbish of the attic in search of bears, *inhabits* the lost world of Höidal as a fact, totally insulated against reality and hopelessly sunken in illusion: 'He's collected up four or five withered old Christmas trees,' says Relling, who fosters the lie in the old man, 'and there's no difference for him between them and the whole tremendous living forest of Höidal' (VI, 226). Hedvig never falls into this error. Like the Romantic child of Wordsworth's 'Ode', she is the true poet in the play, the 'Eye among the blind, / That, deaf and silent, read'st the eternal deep.' For, paradoxically, despite her growing blindness, she sees more clearly than anyone in the play, discovering in the world of the attic an expansion of her limited experience of life, a 'green world' of imaginative possibility rather than the pathetic forest of the adults. It is a storehouse of treasures and books, a microcosm of the greater world, the 'briny deep' of the creative mind. And she is able to sustain a delicate balance between fact and fantasy, reality and metaphor. 'Playing with dolls' does not blind her to the inanimate nature of the form that, from time to time, the imagination invests with life. It is this balance that every other adult in the household lacks; and it is Gregers Werle who fatally dislocates it in Hedvig, abstracting from the literal nature of the wild duck and the attic to create a system of allegorical meanings which violates life in the mistaken quest for some transcendental ideal. To him, the attic is an ocean of corruption, the entanglement of lies in which the maimed Ekdal spirit seeks refuge from truth – and, gradually, he begins to undermine the child's clear perception of her world:

> HEDVIG: . . . it always strikes me that the whole room and everything in it should be called 'the briny deep'. But that's just silly.
> GREGERS: No, you mustn't say that.
> HEDVIG: Yes, of course, because it's really only a loft.
> GREGERS [*looking hard at her*]: Are you so certain?
> HEDVIG [*astonished*]: That it's a loft?
> GREGERS: Yes. Do you know for sure?
> [HEDVIG *looks at him, open-mouthed and silent. . . .*]   (VI, 183)

The child's growing bewilderment echoes like a *Leitmotiv* throughout the drama: 'I think he meant something else'; 'But all the time it was just as though he meant something different from what he was saying'; 'I think this is all very strange'; 'everything seems so strange now' (172, 198, 199). And, when her imaginative vision of experience is finally broken down into adult patterns of schematic thought, she too falls into the error of confusing allegory with reality, metaphor with fact. She shoots herself in a hideously literal enactment of the 'teleological suspension of the ethical'.

If old Ekdal is one image of regressive, counter-Romantic childhood, held in perspective by Hedvig's creative vision, then Hjalmar is another and even less appealing portrait of the childish adult. Lazy, irresponsible, greedy, petulant, attention-seeking – all the attributes of a badly pampered child are disastrously viewed by Gregers as evidence of a naïve and unspoiled nature, the innocence of a man–child mired in the fallen world of dirt and deceit. 'Han har alle sine dage vært en mann med barnesinn'; 'han med sitt store troskyldige barnesinn midt i bedraget' (III, 268, 299) – 'He has always been a man with a child's soul'; 'he, with his great innocent nature, his child's soul, in the midst of deception'. *Barnesinn* – 'innocence', etymologically defined as the mind/soul/sensibility of the child – is most beautifully dramatised in Hedvig and most shockingly parodied in Hjalmar, a striking instance of the double-focus, Romantic and counter-Romantic, of Ibsen's ironic vision. Again, no one sees this value in the child. She's at an awkward age, they admit, negotiating the rite of passage between childhood and adulthood when the child is most vulnerable to 'alt det som galt er' (259) – to the madness and confusion of the adult world. The height of *galskap* in the play is Gregers's project for the redemption of Hjalmar's *barnesinn* by seeking to create the conditions of radiant prelapsarian innocence in his life, 'en hel ny livsførelse' (258) – 'an entirely new mode of existence' – in which the child' soul regains its purity. This is what Hedvig dies to achieve – the radiant child sacrified to adult childishness.

Except for John Whiting's adolescent boy in *No Why* who in an eloquent silence asserts his integrity at the cost of his life, there are few other children in drama whose death is as painful as Hedvig's. Ruskin's formula for lucrative Victorian fiction – 'When at a loss, kill a child'–is impertinent, as Shaw maintained,[14] to the shock of Ibsen's child-deaths, which, even in drawing upon a Romantic tradition, expunge all sentimentality from the genre. Hedvig dies in a world which cannot appreciate the significance of her life nor understand the implications of her suicide. But the tradition is clearly evoked: with the death of the Romantic child, innocence and integrity pass from the world, and those who remain lose forever those intimations of immortality to which they had been blind. The other tradition I have in mind is concerned far less with the child as a living presence than with the Romantic visions of the parent, with 'immortality' as a symbol rather than a vision of spiritual possibility. Peter Coveney, whose concerns are with the image of childhood rather than the psychology of parenthood, does not include this tradition in his intellectual history of Romantic children, and there is no readily available framework of reference. But a fine example of what I have in mind occurs in Yeats's 'Among School Children' – surely a companion piece to Wordsworth's 'Ode': both poems profound ontological speculations on the place of childhood in adult experience, yet each defining its intimations of immortality in significantly different ways. Yeats's image of the child, in the final analysis, is remarkably similar to Ibsen's dancing and singing troupe of children in *When We Dead Awaken*: an image of life as organic growth and movement, 'blossoming or dancing', where childhood is inextricable from adulthood as parts of the whole process of *becoming,* and where the only reality is the process itself. For it is the process that is eternal, not the human individual, who must move ineluctably towards death. But this is precisely what the parent will not see in the child: that it was born

to die, subject to the forces of becoming which are the forces also
of life:

> What youthful mother, a shape upon her lap . . .
> Would think her son, did she but see that shape
> With sixty or more winters on its head,
> A compensation for the pang of his birth,
> Or the uncertainty of his setting forth?[15]

It is not even a *child* that she sees on the lap, but a *shape* – raw
material for the symbolic imagination to mould into forms
exempt from death, age, and winter on the head. In the mother's
reverie, the child's image is worshipped as a Platonic 'presence',
'self-born' rather than mortal in its conception, and therefore
symbolising 'all heavenly glory'. This shape upon the lap, in the
iconography of Romanticism, has become an analogue of
Paradise.

Ibsen, as I have suggested, may have derived this potentially
damaging image of the child from Kierkegaard. But the idea is
also typically nineteenth-century, and closely associated with
the failure of faith in more orthodox intimations of immortality.
The child, in other words, has become a substitute religion; and
to call a man's paternity in question may be to deprive him of
'heavenly glory' in its only meaningful form. This is the idea at
the very heart of Strindberg's *The Father,* the most articulate
statement of the symbol in the drama of the period: 'For me, as I
don't believe in a life to come, this child was my life after death,
my conception of immortality – the only one perhaps that's valid.
If you take her away, you cut my life short.'[16] The Romantic child
has moved beyond the symbolism of imagination and sensibility,
original innocence, or the means by which the sympathetic adult
recovers spiritual vision. As a 'conception of immortality' the
child has become the parent's means of eluding time and death,
psychological security against the meaninglessness and absurdity
of life, and a pseudo-religious emblem of personal redemption.
Perhaps we all see our children in more or less similar terms – the
vision may be endemic to parenthood. But it is only in the plays of
Ibsen that the consequences of enforcing the symbolism *literally*
are followed to their logical conclusion in the *Kindermord.*

II

Early in the action of *Brand* there is a terrible account of a crazed father who kills his starving child in an act of appalling compassion. There are no Romantic resonances to the action, no Kierkegaardian suggestions of sacrifice. It is the sort of human incident which makes moral condemnation impertinent, but which Brand himself judges as a 'wild and hellish crime' and an act of 'mindless violence upon a dying child' (III, 109). It is against this *Kindermord,* with all its complex ethical and emotive issues, that Ibsen counterposes the death of Brand's small child and implicitly questions the distinctions between murder and 'sacrifice', or between direct and indirect violence inflicted on a dying child. Brand, dedicated to world-redemption by an extraordinary exertion of the subjective will, demands of himself and his community the sacrifice of 'All' that stands between mortal man and Paradise. But 'All', as James McFarlane points out,[17] has an escalating value which finally abandons conventional units of measurement for an inflated vision – a *Sehnsucht* – beyond all possibility of human fulfilment,

> Which beckons us towards the realms
> Of dreams and wonders; which towers
> Over us like Heaven ablaze with stars. . . .   (206)

All that stands in the way of his Romantic yearning, all earthly temptations, must be expunged in the name of the ideal; and in the willed suppression of his humanity, Brand estranges himself from everyone, denying the moral and emotional ties that bind a man to his mother, child and wife, and repressing all compassion as a form of insipid compromise with the claim of the ideal. If the dearly loved child tempts him to deny his mission, then the child must be sacrificed in the indomitable spirit of God sacrificing His Son or, by typological analogy, as Abraham dared to sacrifice Isaac. God's test of man's capacity for grace, with its redemptive justification, is one of the primary themes of the third act of the play, where Brand must choose to leave the sunless valley of his calling – or remain, and allow his consumptive child to die:

AGNES: One thing God cannot demand of us!
BRAND: But if he did? The Lord can test me

As he tested Abraham.   (137–8)

BRAND: Men hvis han torde? Herren tør
hva 'Isaachs redsel' torde før.   (II, 50)

In the original, the emphasis is placed not on Abraham's test but
on the risk, the horror and the dread of sacrificing Isaac. And,
although Brand at first baulks at the thought of Alf's death, his
decision by the end of the act has the ominous implications of an
accomplished sacrifice dignified as a type of the Crucifixion. Love
of the child is merely a failure of the will; and in the name of his
deified ideal he sets about demolishing the idol which he believes
his love for Alf to have become. God, he claims, has called him
once again – 'Was I not / A priest before I was a father?' (III, 154)
– and Agnes, in accepting Brand's hard decision, at last
relinquishes her child to the sacrificial imperative:

> [*lifting the child high in her arms*]
> God on high! The sacrifice thou cravest
> I dare raise up towards thy Heaven!
> Lead me through the terrors of this world!   (155)

In casting Alf in the Isaac role, Brand's Kierkegaardian
scenario imputes to the child a marvellous identity. For Isaac is no
ordinary son. He is the miraculous child, born of his father's
extreme old age and his mother's barrenness, an incarnation of
God's promise to Abraham of the nation's posterity, and a type of
the saviour. From his sacrifice springs the principle of man's
redemption. This is the special symbolic status that Kierkegaard
sees in the Isaac of *Fear and Trembling*:

> There have been many fathers who thought that with the death
> of their child they have lost the thing they loved most in the
> world, have been deprived of all hope in the future: yet surely
> there has never been a child of promise in the sense that Isaac
> was such a child for Abraham.[18]

Yet such a child must be relinquished! Torn between amazement
at Abraham's obedience to God's inscrutable demand and the
tormenting pragmatism of the moral conscience, Kierkegaard
poses one of the central oppositions in *Brand* – the distinction
between the two forms of child-death that I have detailed:

The ethical expression of Abraham's action is that he wished to murder Isaac: the religious expression is that he wished to sacrifice him: and it is precisely here, in the contradiction of the two expressions of his desire, that lies dread, which may well rob one of one's sleep.   (34)

Abraham's motive is clearly 'absurd'; and the only justification for God's irrational command must be an equally irrational belief in the paradox which can transform murder into a holy action and restore the child to the father – 'a paradox which no thought can encompass because faith begins where thought leaves off' (74). Abraham's absurdity, in other words, is a demonstration of a more-than-human faith. For, in terms of universal ethics, he offends against the law of nature which axiomatically assumes that a father will cherish his son more than his own life; and Abraham's action can be understood only if one acquiesces in the suspension of man's instincts and his morality in favour of some external law that transcends both:

> Here there can be no question of ethics in the sense of morality. In so far as the universal was present, it was concealed in Isaac, hidden, as one might say, in his loins and was compelled to cry out through Isaac's mouth: Do not do this, you annihilate everything.
> Then why did Abraham do this?   (84)

He did it, Kierkegaard concludes, 'for God's sake', trusting in 'absurdity' – in the belief that all things are possible to God; and his faith in the saving power of the absurd ultimately absolves him from the charge of *Kindermord*. 'He believed by virtue of the absurd. . . . In his infinite resignation he gave up everything and then he regained everything by virtue of the absurd' (43, 52).

There is, of course, another and more contemporary sense in which the sacrificial imperative appears *absurd*; and I imagine that Ibsen's sympathies lie with the outraged moral humanism of Edward Bond rather than with Kierkegaard's discussion of sacrifice as a redemptive sacrament. 'The idea that a God could kill his son because it was demanded by some external law and order', says Bond, 'is absolute nonsense. I mean God is moral if He measures up to my standards.'[19] For Ibsen, as for Bond, there can be no prior law to sanction a violation of man's humanity, no

argument of faith to justify the transformation of a heinous act
into an act of salvation. Brand's scenario is crucially defective in
that, although finding seemingly appropriate players for the
Abraham and Isaac roles, it is never quite clear from whom he
derives his mandate. Is his God the ultimately beneficent God of
Abraham, or a manifestation of Brand's own Romantic compulsion? Does he suffer as God's appointed martyr or does he act as
the agent of a self-created idea? The God to whom Brand plays
Abraham, as I have already suggested, is ultimately an aspect of
his own intense desire to recreate the world–God fashioned out of
moral disgust, out of the trauma of an unhappy childhood, and
out of the will that opposes compromise. And when Abraham
mistakes his own deified ideal for the voice of God, and when a
child is sacrificed to the teleological demands of the Romantic
temperament, then Isaac dies in vain and the world becomes
'absurd' in a sense quite antithetical to Kierkegaard's theology.

In 1843 Kierkegaard could still affirm the sanctity of child-
sacrifice and justify Abraham's faith – but only in fear and
trembling, and at great and terrible risk. Brand assumes the risk,
and fails. In asserting 'God' he empties the world of godliness.
And the same paradox ensnares Gregers Werle, Allmers and
Rubek, whose teleological principles (however inadequately or
obscurely conceived) are clearly God-substitutes or pseudo-
religions: 'the claim of the ideal', 'human responsibility', or
'resurrection'. In each case, the strenuous attempt to assert value
merely devastates the world by killing a child, and there is no
redemptive phase to the sacrificial myth which might sanctify
their deaths. They perish in a void, victims of that very attempt to
fill the void with meaning; and the dread which robs the moral
conscience of its sleep – the sense of a contradiction between the
ethical and religious expression of Abraham's action – constitutes
the central experience of the plays. To rephrase the paradox at
the heart of Ibsen's counter-Romantic vision, one could say that,
in asserting a Kierkegaardian form of absurdity, Ibsen's transcendentalists succeed only in creating the 'absurd' conditions of
modern existential anxiety.

To imply that Ibsen is somehow a progenitor of the Theatre of
the Absurd is not, I think, to impose tendentiously a fashionable
modern vision upon unlikely material. The double vision that
shapes his irony, the coincidence of Romantic and counter-
Romantic impulses, also extends to the tension between absurdity

as a more-than-human faith and absurdity as *galskap*: the absurdity of Abraham and the absurdity of Sisyphus. Between them, these two heroes of the absurd establish a spectrum of spiritual states from the Christian existentialism of the 1840s to the agnostic existentialism of the 1940s, each defining by virtue of his experience a radical change in the meaning of 'absurdity'. And Ibsen's plays, it seems to me, are a crucial index of that change in linguistic meaning – an indication of the persistence into the twentieth century of the Romantic dilemma of the nineteenth. 'Perhaps the whole thing is just haphazard. An aimless drifting, like some wrecked and rudderless ship' (VIII, 67). 'If *you* are right and *I* am wrong, life will no longer be worth living' (VI, 242). Senselessness, despair and futility have become the central, damaging experience of both Allmers and Gregers Werle, which, to borrow Camus's definition of absurdity, is the post-Romantic sense of a final and irrevocable banishment from Paradise:

> What, then, is that incalculable feeling that deprives the mind of sleep necessary to life? A world that can be explained even with bad reasons is a familiar world. But, on the other hand, in a universe suddenly divested of illusions and lights, man feels an alien, a stranger. His exile is without remedy since he is deprived of the memory of a lost home or the hope of a promised land.[20]

This is the predicament which the protagonists are left to cope with at the end of *The Wild Duck* and *Little Eyolf.* For it is the death of the child that finally robs them of their lights and illusions of an eternal life achieved only through the sacrifice of life itself.

Georg Brandes may have claimed for Ibsen the distinction of being Kierkegaard's poet, but the extent of Ibsen's conscious use of Kierkegaardian ideas remains highly speculative. 'I have in any case read very little of S.K.,' Ibsen wrote to a friend, 'and understood even less' (III, 443). This may or may not be so. If Ibsen can be said to work from within the Kierkegaardian premises, it is surely 'Isaachs redsel' – the human anguish, and the perilously narrow distinction between faith and self-deception – that must have engaged his attention: Kierkegaard's nightmare vision of meaninglessness waiting to assail the defective Abraham, and the failure of conviction which can turn sacrifice into murder. The knight of faith who regains his child by virtue of the absurd is not lightly to be imitated. The false knight, on the other hand, is a man incapable of seeing his own deficiencies, a self-deluding fraud and cheap tragedian whose ideals are merely devices for masking his moral and psychological failure. He acts not in fear and trembling, but in arrogance. And, in ascribing divine prerogative to himself, he selfishly undertakes his own salvation under pretext of a scheme for world-redemption. The figure is a familiar one in the history of Romanticism: the transcendentalist, incapable of believing the basic tenets of his faith, and yet desperate for consolation against death and redemption from his fallen state. Even those who had abandoned Christianity in the era of revolution, as J. B. Halstead has pointed out, needed to believe in divinity – or in some analogue of the divine; and they tended, he writes,

> to retain the forms and language of their religious heritage, especially the Messianic belief that their time – lacking, in its disunity and egoism, the ties of faith – was big with the next great development for mankind, the step beyond Christianity, into new forms of community and association.[21]

There is no doubting the purity of motive in Wordsworth's evangelism, for example, or in his vision of a partnership with Coleridge:

> joint-labourers in a work
> (Should Providence such grace to us vouchsafe)
> Of [men's] Redemption, surely yet to come.
> Prophets of Nature, we to them will speak
> A lasting inspiration. . . .[22]

But to *inspire*, to enable man through the exercise of his own imagination to discover the analogy of self in the divinity of nature, is vastly different from the *enforced* redemptive schemes of Ibsen's prophets. Mary McCarthy's comment on Gregers Werle puts the point precisely: he is one of those messianic, interfering 'paranoid prophets' whose allusive language and schematic thought is a thinly disguised form of 'God-identification, in which the symbolist imposes on the concrete, created world his own private design and lays open to question the most primary facts of existence'.[23] The 'murderer' of the Romantic child in Ibsen is the Romantic transcendentalist − of whom Brand is a noble if misguided exemplar, and Gregers Werle the secular and contemporary counterpart. All the symptoms of the Brand syndrome, undignified by the heroic temperament, are revealed at their most dangerous in Gregers: the neurotic basis of the idealistic impulse, the proselytising zeal which is a selfish form of therapy to assuage the guilty conscience, and the catastrophic failure to locate transcendental value in a corresponding human reality.

III

Gregers's sense of the fallen world, of which the Ekdal household is a living paradigm, expresses itself in the by-now familiar imagery of nausea, disgust and dirt − a distortion of reality into perverse symbolic meanings. Old Werle speaks in metaphors of those human failures who 'plunge into the depths' and never rise to rehabilitate themselves; and Old Ekdal later elaborates on the literal phenomena from which the metaphor derives: the instinct of wild ducks, when wounded, to plunge into the depths of the sea, entangle themselves in weeds and 'fandenskap' − the devil's own mess − and so perish. Gregers, typically, ignores distinctions between metaphor and fact, extrapolates from the literal meaning of 'sea-depths' to envision an image of the abyss in which man is mired in devilry, and then adds his own offensive tropes to an already grotesquely inappropriate analogue of the Ekdal household: 'en forgiftet sump', 'en snikende sott' 'sumpluft' and 'stank' (III, 249, 252) − a poisoned swamp, an insidious plague and a stinking bog. He smells corruption everywhere, as if carrying with him the tainted atmosphere of Höidal with 'det fæle svarte verket' (250) − its disgusting and filthy works. Ironically, however, it is Gregers who always seems to generate those very conditions which nauseate him. *His* room stinks, filled with the smoke and muck of an ineptly doused fire. Gina, with some justification, calls him a pig; and Relling identifies him as the carrier of a plague which will eventually infect the whole household far more insidiously than the corruption of their fallen natures.

Gregers must save mankind from its condition − that is his mission, already begun (with no success) among the labourers at Höidal. Whether his claim of the ideal originated in a social conscience, or as a personal compulsion, remains obscure. His redemption of the Ekdals, however, assumes the most dangerous aspects of an obsession, a form of self-administered therapy to assuage his guilty conscience, to save Hjalmar from the evil manipulative control of Old Werle, and transform the fallen world of lies and illusion into an effulgence of truth and reality. In a gesture of moral reparation he will make good the sins of his father and restore innocence and purity to life. He puts the worst possible light on his father's charitable treatment of the Ekdals – infected, as Old Werle suspects, with his dead mother's exaggerated sense of betrayal and her hysterical suspicions of infidelity. 'Jeg er ikke overspent' (228) – 'I am not neurotic', he snaps at his father in the very process of incriminating him in the foulness he sees enveloping the life of his friend; and he gives vent to the same vehemently denied condition in a perverse interpretation of some extremely ambiguous facts. Like so many of the inhabitants of this dark and obscure world, Gregers is blind. He sees, as Ibsen implies, only with the clouded and impaired vision of his mother. And this psychic deficiency is enough to disqualify him as the light-bearer and redeemer to a benighted and fallen humanity.

In no other Ibsen play does the delicate fabric of life, the reality upon which the transcendentalist operates, recede so far into the nebulous and the equivocal. In searching for truth, Gregers exhumes the past with a relentlessness typical of Ibsen's conventional plot-structures – but all he reveals is ambiguity, a world devoid of absolutes, which angels might well fear to interpret. The tone of the play is immediately established by the subdued lighting of the opening scene and the small-talk of the servants, where each attempt to elicit information is deflected into qualified conjecture or non-committal possibility: 'Fan' vet', 'Kanskje det' (219) – 'The devil only knows'. 'Well, maybe.' That is as far as it goes. To take it any further is to tread on thin ice. Old Werle may (or may not) have ruined his partner, may (or may not) have betrayed his wife while she lived, may (or may not) have foisted a discarded mistress onto a gullible young man. Evidence points with equal conviction to opposing points of view, and proof becomes both impertinent and hazardous to substantiate. 'The desire for verification is understandable', says Harold Pinter of those who demand unequivocal meanings in experience, 'but cannot always be satisfied. There are no hard distinctions between what is real and what is unreal, nor between what is true and what is false. The thing is not necessarily either true or false; it can be both true and false.'[24] This view of life as a complex of possibilities, where reality and truth have no absolute value apart from the context in which they function, and where men make reality work by accepting all value, all conventions and all relationships as creative illusions – this, it seems to me, is what Ibsen meant by the 'life-lie' or, more aptly, 'det stimulerende prinsipp' (III, 269) – the principle of inspiration and stimulation in life. With his crass appropriation of narrow truths and his reduction of all evidence to a preconceived notion of evil, Gregers smashes through the delicate webs of accommodation and the thin-spun skeins of life only to reveal – with appalling consequences – the 'lie' that holds the whole fabric together. It is, of course, the child, life itself in all its mystery, who finally stands exposed to the smashing and the paring away of protective illusion. At the heart of the equivocal universe there is only Hedvig, conferring the illusion of 'family' upon a union which may (or may not) conform to a legitimate definition of the family unit. Like the mysterious woman in Pirandello's *Right You Are If You Think So*, her identity in the Ekdal household may (or may not) be ambiguous; but, in so far as they believe her to be their child, she sustains the illusion of a happy marriage more creatively and vitally than the various other 'lies' which fantasticate reality out of all existence.

Perhaps Hedvig was born in wedlock, perhaps not. Old Werle's complicity in arranging Hjalmar's marriage for dubious reasons may be mere neurotic surmise. The devil only knows, for both Old Werle and Hjalmar, on equally feasible grounds, may be Hedvig's blood-father. Her incipient blindness is inconclusive evidence either way: there is blindness in the medical histories of both families. And Gina is bound to admit, with alarming candour, when pressed to name the father of her child: 'I don't know.' What does it matter, after all? What is the relevance of *proof* to the reality of their lives? To search it out, in the name of some ideal, is madness. Hedvig retains, to the end, her mystery as one of literature's 'unknowable' children, one who – like Euripides's Ion – sustains a marriage through creative illusion. Creusa, in the *Ion*, needs to believe that her illegitimate son was sired by a God; her husband needs to be told that the child is his; and Apollo permits both to believe whatever truth or lie is necessary to their psychological well-being. In *Who's Afraid of*

Virginia Woolf?, on the other hand, the American Dream
child – invented to confer value upon a barren marriage – merely
dissipates that value by degrading it. That Euripides's God should
cherish the child as a 'stimulating principle' and that Albee
should require its death in order to restore the lie-infected society
to health, are factors pointing to a crucial distinction between the
two versions of the 'life-lie': that which nourishes the spirit on
illusory value and that which aggravates a condition of spiritual
ill, that which elevates an imaginative truth above mere pragmatic fact and that which perverts truth by a neurotic withdrawal
into dream and fantasy. Gregers cannot make the distinction –
nor, for that matter, can Relling, who encourages appallingly
regressive behaviour in the name of stimulation. But, of the two,
Gregers is clearly the more dangerous in confusing mere veracity
with truth, and corruption with an illusion that honours a
workable human reality. By infecting Hjalmar with his own
disastrous confusion, by destroying the illusion of family, he
precipitates the most outrageous action in the play – Hjalmar's
petulant rejection of Hedvig as a bastard and none of his. The
antithesis of this barbarism is Old Werle's discreet acceptance of
his possible paternity by providing for Hedvig in a deed of gift. It
is a wise father in the world of *The Wild Duck* who knows his own
child; but, in the absence of all certainty, it is the man who
acknowledges the probability who affirms life.

Brutally indifferent to the subtleties of experience and fatally
incapable of judging people, Gregers hastens to indict his father
as evil incarnate – thus ascribing to himself the role of man's
redeemer from the foulness and deceit of Old Werle's creating.
Convinced that Hjalmar's home is built upon a pernicious lie, and
mistaking Hjalmar himself as an innocent eligible for the
kingdom of the ideal, he imagines that by reconstituting Paradise
he will enable the Ekdals to exist in an epiphany of revealed
truth. He bursts into the domestic idyll of their home – by no
means an 'ideal' marriage, but one invested with much tenderness
and underscored by the harmonies of Hjalmar's flute – and the
consequences of his intrusion are the destruction of the family in
the name of redemption, and the death of the child on the
pretext of sacrifice. With a grotesque application of an allegorical
idea, he enacts the function of the hunting-dog who rescues the
wild duck from its entanglement in corruption (failing, typically,
to realise the danger implicit in the allegory: the amazingly clever

dog cripples the bird for life). He dedicates his life to this mission of redemption; and his language, accordingly, modulates from execration against the fall to visions of transcendent sublimity in which the consequences of the fall are reversed through revelation, confrontation and self-analysis. A crude version of psychiatry is here invested with a series of pseudo-religious imperatives. After infecting Hjalmar with the cant phrases of idealism and the image of his marriage as a swamp of deceit, the truth-telling analyst merely devastates where he hopes to cure. His view of reality utterly fails to transform his subject's bitter experience into sublimity, 'en høyere innvielse av det store oppgjør' (III, 259) – 'an exalted consecration arising from momentous confrontation'. It is an extraordinary language that he speaks: a linguistic conflation of psychoanalyst and priest in the figure of the transcendentalist desperately searching in the secular life for the sacramental values of a lost tradition:

Så stort et oppgjør, – et oppgjør, som en hel ny livsførelse skal grunnes på, – en livsførelse, et samliv, i sannhet og uten all fortielse – . . . . For der er da vel ikke noe i verden som kan lignes med *det* å ha tilgivelse for en feilende og løfte henne opp til seg i kjærlighet. (258–9)

Such a momentous confrontation – a confrontation on which an entirely new way of living can be founded, – a way of living, a life together, in truth and without any concealment –. . . . For there is surely nothing else in the world which can compare with *this*: to grant forgiveness to one who has gone astray, and to raise her up to your side in love.

The end of Gregers's great redemptive mission is, as he puts it, 'grunnlegger et sant ekteskap' (259) – to lay the foundations of a 'true' marriage. But he is blind to the irony, which Hjalmar draws to his attention, that the exemplar and paradigm of such a union is the match between his father and Mrs Sørby. In fact, Gregers's strenuous attempt to create the conditions for a Paradisal marriage for the Ekdals is rendered ridiculous by the potential for just such a marriage in the 'fallen' world of Old Werle – one based upon compassion, complete honesty, mutual confidence and trust. And, in trying to enforce these values – unnecessarily – on Hjalmar, Gregers undermines the very structure he seeks to fortify. Not only is Hjalmar poor material for Gregers's therapy, but the 'lies' and the 'corruption' which the gullible Hjalmar accepts as gospel truth must inevitably lead to a radical questioning of Hedvig's legitimacy, if Gregers's insinuations are pushed to their final conclusion. The events of Act IV lead relentlessly to that moment when Hjalmar will leap to his outrageous assumption about the child's *right* to live under *his* roof.

It is a simple step from Hjalmar's rejection of the over-symbolised duck as the evil Old Werle has imposed upon his life to the rejection of Hedvig as Werle's bastard child; and the consequences of accepting Gregers's crude analogies follow with catastrophic inevitability. The purblind eyes, the deed of gift, the dark suggestion of Gina's relationship with Werle, which she later corroborates – all the equivocal evidence, distorted by the literal application to life of an inept symbol system, provokes the histrionic self-pitying cry of the self-styled cuckold: 'Jeg har ikke noe barn!' (265), 'I have no child' – as if illegitimacy had the power to eliminate the quality of a deeply affectionate relationship, as if fourteen years of father–daughter bonding could be obviated by a biological nicety. He thrusts the grief-stricken child away from him as the fraud that makes his house uninhabitable, the lie that has brought his home down in ruins, and he stalks out of the room even as Hedvig clings to him. 'Se på barnet, Ekdal! Se på barnet!' (ibid), Gina cries after him – 'Look at the child, look at the child.' But no one in Ibsen ever looks at the *child,* at the living, suffering reality. They see only symbols and emblems and analogies. Or, like Gregers, they see child redeemers who, in some obscure ritual of sacrifice, can effect the hoped-for transfiguration of fallen mankind. The master-stroke of Gregers's pseudo-religion is to impose upon the child's despair a solution to the family's dilemma, an absurd Kierkegaardian proof requiring a violation of the child's humanity to save the ruined household. She must now kill what most she loves.

> GREGERS: Supposing you offered to sacrifice the wild duck for *his* sake?
> HEDVIG: The wild duck!
> GREGERS: Suppose you were ready to sacrifice for him the most precious thing you had in the world?
> HEDVIG: Do you think *that* would help?
> GREGERS: Try it, Hedvig. (VI, 221)

The wild duck. It would be tempting to say nothing at all about this most discussed of creatures and so recognise it for what it is – an object lesson gratuitous symbolising and the most outstanding instance in Ibsen of the counter-Romantic error: the failure to correlate literal and referential concepts with their abstract and non-referential analogues. The wild duck, as Hedvig insists, is no more than that: 'a *real* wild bird' (182), a child's pet defined in careful ornithological detail. Ibsen, at the height of his power as a symbolist, assigns no portentous symbolic value whatever to the duck. He merely presents it as the vehicle for the ridiculous duck-symbolism of Gregers, for whom all surface reality is a system of transcendental referents. Language, symbolism and the ambiguity of images are the very elements of tragedy in this play, as they are in *Othello,* where to assign a symbolic value to a domestic object (such as a handkerchief) and then pursue a course of action on the assumption that the symbolic and the real are identical is to destroy the world. Semantic confusion, the terrible gulf between two versions of the same image, occurs whenever Hedvig and Gregers speak to each other – as when they both refer to the attic in sea metaphors with radically different implications. And so it is with the duck. There exists between Hedvig and her pet a delicate, sympathetic affinity – as a child might project onto her doll her own most intimate sense of her condition. The loneliness, the isolation, the essentially 'unknowable' and secret identity of the child are the qualities she sees in her pet. But to Gregers, the duck symbolises the Ekdals' maimed condition and their state of servile compromise to the illusions which deprive them of light and truth. That the reality does not sustain the abstract value imposed upon it is irrelevant to Gregers, and he begins gradually to infect the child's perception of her world. Hedvig, as Mary McCarthy suggests, is ultimately the victim of a language she cannot understand:

> She has been led by the Higher Critics around her to look for the real reality under the surface of language – that is, to schematize her life as she lives it. . . . Everything has conspired to make Hedvig distrust the *ordinary* way of looking at things.[25]

Hysterical at Hjalmar's rejection of her, Hedvig glimpses vaguely the half-truths of existence that conspire against her – obscure

fears of bastardy, a sense of antagonism against her as an inter-
loper in her father's house – circumstances which, under Gregers's
tutelage, will persuade her towards a symbolic correlation of her
own despised condition with that of the wild duck. The very idea
of sacrifice has now become ominously ambiguous.

It is difficult to infer, with any degree of certainty, exactly what
Gregers means by 'sacrifice' or how he imagines that Hedvig's
gesture will set the world to rights. Perhaps, in his folly, he
imagines that shooting the duck will annihilate the spirit of
failure and corruption of which it is the symbolic analogue. But,
more to the point, there is some ill-defined conviction that a myth
of salvation may be set in operation by the sacrifice of a cherished
being to some obscure *telos*. In rebuking Hedvig for thinking
better of killing the duck, his language reverts to the transcendentalism of Kierkegaardian theology: 'Jeg kan se på Dem at
det ikke er fullbrakt' (III, 269) – 'I can see on your face that it has
not been accomplished.' As both Ansten Anstensen and John
Northam point out, the phrase 'det er fullbrakt' is a direct
quotation from John 19:30, a translation into Norwegian of
Christ's *consummatum est*. Gregers's intentions become somewhat less obsure if no less preposterous; and with fanatical
insistence he tries to break down Hedvig's reluctance to enact his
scenario of redemption, overwhelming her with pseudo-religious
imperatives to manifest 'det sanne, glade, modige offersinn' (III.
270) – the true, joyful, courageous spirit of sacrifice. And, when
the shot eventually rings out, Gregers, in ecstatic anticipation of
the redeeming miracle, instructs the Ekdals in the significance of
the ritual. Gina weeps, and Hjalmar responds to the notion of the
child's sacrifice in strains of sentimental forgiveness and visions of
a new life – which all seem to affirm the efficacy of Gregers's
sacrificial myth: 'Jeg viste det,' he says, 'gjennem barnet ville
opprettelsen skje' (275) – 'I knew it; it is through the child that
redemption will come to pass.' He might be speaking of the
Christ-child or the Isaac of the Kierkegaardian parable. The *real*
child lies dead in the attic, rejected again and again by her
father, until finally driven to her sacrificial death-in-love to
restore his affection and the harmony of the family. For her, as
for the other deluded Romantics in Ibsen's world, there are no
longer boundaries between the literal and the metaphorical,
between the real and the symbolic. Hedvig performs in *fact* what
for Gregers has been a *parable*. But the myth of Isaac has been

tragically inverted. It is the child who now assumes the place of the sacrificial animal, while the Abraham for whom this propitiatory offering is made strikes a series of declamatory poses which makes nonsense of the child's gesture.

The final moments of the play are given over entirely to absurdity – not the positive Kierkegaardian absurdity which Gregers claims to have achieved, but its anti-type: *galskap*. Old Ekdal makes his appearance in full military regalia, a comic–pathetic actor of his alcoholic life-lie, whose illusions are impervious to all attempts at symbolic therapy. Tragi-comic pandemonium breaks loose when the child is discovered; and then there follows the farce of her obsequies presided over by a drunken priest and his congregants, all seeking refuge from the implications of this grotesque mistake in the clichés of maudlin religiosity. The most desperate defence against *galskap*, however, is Gregers's insistence on the child's death as a sacrament, against all evidence to the contrary: 'Hedvig has not died in vain', he proclaims, mistaking Hjalmar's sentimental remorse for the recovery of a noble dignity. 'Give him nine months,' Relling replies, 'and little Hedvig will be nothing more than the theme of a pretty little party piece' (vi, 241). And the sort of performance he envisions recalls the most embarrassing scenes in the literature of Romantic childhood: the deaths of little Nell and little Paul and all the other innocents 'so untimely torn from a loving father's heart' (242). This is the ultimate indignity that may be heaped on Hedvig, the final refusal to *look at the child*; and Gregers, shifting from one extreme of absurdity to the other, sees the possibility of all life as a *galskap* no longer worth living. In Ingmar Bergman's production of the play, Gregers yields to this vision of cosmic nihilism by slipping Hedvig's pistol into his pocket – the thirteenth man at table fulfilling his destiny in the ultimate absurdity of suicide. But what Gregers fails to grasp is the antidote to futility implicit in the vision of the play: the realisation that there are no absolute and immutable values, no transcendental essences prior to the existence of complex and delicate human realities. 'Liberty', Ibsen wrote in his jottings, 'consists in giving the individual the right to liberate himself, each according to his personal needs' (431). The genius of *The Wild Duck*, it seems to me, is that it clarifies more articulately than almost any other play of the period one of the central impulses of European Romanticism – the attempt to introduce value into the world by saving it in the name of some ideal authority. More than this, it compels a wonderful sense of the frailty and beauty of life and its vulnerability to the dangers of the redemptive impulse. And it implies a solution to the Romantic dilemma of redis-covering value which, with modern hindsight, anticipates the basic premises of existential thought.

There is, as I have already suggested, a strong evangelical impulse in Romantic literature. The assumption of the poet-prophet, acting on the divine authority of his own will, is that the self may be redeemed from meaninglessness by generating meaning in the world. This, as Morse Peckham puts it, is the heroic and world-redemptive stage of Romanticism[26] – which finds its most sublime expression in Wordsworth as nature's prophet, and its most pernicious in the prophets of fascism, for whom German Romanticism is still held accountable and of whom Gregers is the prototype (however well-meaning in his intentions). For the transcendental hero who must redeem the world pri-marily to save himself reduces all men to raw material for his own therapeutic uses. 'If I'm to go on living', Gregers tells his father, 'I must find something to cure my sick conscience' (VI, 196). Redemption, it follows, has become an aspect of individual pathology to assuage one's guilt for the evil of the world; and in the name of saving others, the transcendentalist proposes a remedy fashioned out of his own sickness. It is not enough to cure himself. Value is not generated in isolation. 'I must indeed look for something beyond myself', Gregers confesses to Relling (225). And it is precisely here that his scheme fails. For to redeem others by imposing one's will upon them, no matter how disinterested the motive, is to violate the very concept of selfhood and individuality and liberty for which one strives. In this way, as Peckham suggests, the very ground of Romanticism is undercut by the negative implications of transcendentalism. For,

> to impose one's will upon others, even for the sake of redeeming them and the world, even for the sake of revealing value to them, is to treat them as mere instruments for realizing the will, to treat them as objects, to treat them, in short, as society treats the alienated Romantic.[27]

There can be no ideal solutions to the human predicament in the world of *The Wild Duck,* no teleological absolutes to sanction the suspension of man's ethical nature. The individual self, each according to his need, must find the 'stimulating principle' which restores value to the world and affirms the nature of that selfhood. In the final analysis, and despite the stringent counter-Romanticism of the play's tone and vision, Ibsen asserts in *The Wild Duck* the ultimate conviction of Romanticism: 'that a metaphysic with its derived value-system cannot be absolute, that the only absolute, at best, is the *drive* to a metaphysic, the *drive* to order and value, never to a particular order or a particular set of values'.[28] Peckham's description of the Romantic position might also serve to define, at its most stimulating and creative, Ibsen's idea of the 'life-lie' – that antidote to cosmic meaninglessness and futility which we recognise, in the twentieth century, as the existential hero's response to absurdity.

IV

The role of the child in *The Wild Duck* is defined, as I have suggested, by a 'double-family' configuration, with Hjalmar and Old Werle as the ambiguous points in the father–mother–child nexus. In the even more complex triangularities of *Little Eyolf* there are at least three familial configurations, each linked to a related sexual patterning;[29] and these interconnections make it extremely difficult to isolate the child as a Romantic emblem distinct from the various sexual analogues of Eden. 'Eyolf' as both name and Allmers's intensely private symbol-system clearly includes both child *and* sister as 'little' and 'big' aspects of the same idea; and it is clear that Asta – the putative half-sister – becomes for Allmers the sexual corollary to the child as redeemer, ideal and apotheosis. There is, in other words, a conflation of paradisal analogues and substitute religions in which the symbolism of the Romantic child and that of the Romantic lover coincide in the idea of 'Eyolf'. The most compelling of the various triangular structures in *Little Eyolf* is that which opposes the conventional family, bound by blood and sexuality and body, with the symbolic family, bound by spirit and the heart's mystical affinities. And 'Eyolf', in each of these literal or surrogate family structures, clearly means something very different to the parent-figures in the groupings. As the real child of a legally defined marriage, the offspring of Rita's body and the issue of the Allmers's mortal sexuality, little Eyolf is seen by them as a maimed emblem of their marriage. But, as the surrogate or adoptive child of Asta's heart, the product of an incest fantasy, little Eyolf begins to assume for Allmers all the immortal attributes of the Ideal spiritual family. This aspect of Romantic child-symbolism is so inextricable from the sexual themes in the play that I must, of necessity, limit my discussion in this chapter to Eyolf's affinities with Hedvig, and deal with the symbolism of *little* 'Eyolf' in the context of the *big* 'Eyolf' symbol and the complex ideas in Romantic incest-patterns.

The third triangle – the most tenuous of all the surrogate family structures – is one which, quite literally, *looks at the child* and sees him for what he is: a pathetic little boy in need of special care, whose crippling disability cannot be denied and who must therefore be reconciled to his condition. Borghejm, an occasional visitor to the house and all but engaged to Asta, clearly relates to the child *in loco parentis*. He is, as James McFarlane suggests,[30] a type of adoptive father to Eyolf, who, with Asta, completes a triangular relationship which mirrors the rejection and the ineffectual reality of the literal family, and the fallible symbolism of that other spiritual grouping. Eyolf's misfortune is that he has the wrong parents. Rita dresses him grotesquely in a soldier's suit, allowing him to indulge in the hopes of boyish activity which the crutch cruelly belies. The consequences of actually *seeing* his predicament are too shattering for both his parents, and so neither can help him to accept its inevitability. It would seem, from the child's few brief remarks, that he has been encouraged to regard his lameness as a temporary thing. 'Don't you think I'll soon be well enough to go along with you?' he asks his father. 'I think it would be so marvellous if I could come climbing in the mountains' (VIII, 43). And Allmers says absolutely nothing to disabuse him of this pathetic ambition. *Theoretically*, his attitude towards the child's education and psychological adjustment to his handicap are admirable:

> I want to help him to achieve a harmonious relationship between what he desires and what lies within his reach. That is not how he approaches things now. All he longs for are things which must remain forever beyond his reach. I want to create within him a sense of happiness. (53)

But he does nothing of the sort. His actual intentions, it soon transpires, are far more abstract and far more ominous. It is Borghejm who encourages the child to practise archery, as the most suitable activity for him, and who will teach him to swim; and it is Asta who lavishes affection and concern on him. His real mother hates him as an intrusion on her possessive claims to Allmers's undivided attention; and his father, for whom he is a constant reminder of the guilt-engendering consequences of sexual desire, ironically forces the pitifully disqualified boy into the service of an impossible and perverse transcendentalism.

It is painfully ironic that Allmers, so obsessed with process and death, with the fear of the body and sexuality, should be constantly confronted with this phobia in the presence of little Eyolf. As always in Ibsen, the child as a 'conception of immortality' bears evidence in the very defects of the body of mortality, change, and the frailty of the human condition which belies the symbolism. The twisted leg and the crutch are inescapable reminders of their neglecting Eyolf in the throes of passion – emblems of what Allmers believes to be the retributive consequences of sex. And in their guilt and self-recrimination they see the child as an eternal rebuke whose gaze they dare not meet and who must be thrust away, unless they can devise some stratagem for ignoring the obvious. Allmers, like the other Ibsenian transcendentalists, is skilled in such evasion. Desperate to deny the laws of change and retribution, he transforms the living embodiment of these forces into an immortal conception whose mission will be to redeem the fallen world of sexuality and death. Like Gregers, he fashions a teleological ideal out of his own deep neurotic disturbance; and in the name of this ideal he suspends all human and ethical responsibility to his wife, his sister and – most damagingly – to the *real* little Eyolf. For 'Eyolf', the *symbolic* child, is no more than an evasionary technique in whose name the conscience, racked by guilt, denies any commitment to another human being and in which the psyche, terrified of death, seeks refuge in a transcendentalism radically divorced from reality.

An atheist, overwhelmed by the sense of cosmic 'nothingness' and anxious to fill God's empty space with human meaning, Allmers dedicates himself (even more consciously than Gregers) to the neo-religion of secular humanism. In his yearning, he dreams of a God who will recreate the malformed world by healing the crippled; and by day he thinks about his great contribution to existential philosophy, his tome on 'Man's Responsibility'. Like

Hjalmar's great photographic invention, however, this book is the worst kind of 'life-lie' – an apologia for rationalising his insufficiency which reduces one of the primary ethics of liberal salvation to effete lip-service. 'Responsibility' has clearly lost all value for Allmers; and the ideal, unsupported by living experience or by the force of ethical decision, degenerates into frivolity. It is hardly worth writing about. 'What's best in one goes into thinking', he says. 'What gets down on paper doesn't count for much' (43). And so he thinks long into the night on man's responsibility, quite indifferent (as he seems to have been ever since Eyolf's accident) to those marital responsibilites which are his wife's *raison d'être*. But his most dangerous evasion of human responsibility lies in his grandiose renunciation of the humanist undertaking in favour of his son – his latest 'project' – who will be made to incarnate the pseudo-religious idealism of the stillborn manuscript. Prompted by an ambiguous confrontation with death in the mountains, he hurries home to the family, imbued with the dubious enthusiasm of a new life's-mission scarcely distinguishable from the escapist propensities of the first. This is what he announces to his wife: 'Eyolf skal være den fullferdige i vår slekt. Og jeg vil sette mitt nye livsverk i *det* å gjøre ham til den fullferdige' (III. 492–3) – 'Eyolf shall achieve the consummation of the family line. And my new life's work shall be that of bringing him to that consummation' (VIII. 54).

Fullferdig may not be entirely synonymous with the *fullbrakt* of John 19:30. But James McFarlane, in echoing the *consummatum est*, catches precisely the religious tone in which Allmers expresses his secular beliefs. Its echo is heard whenever he envisions Eyolf as a surrogate for his own unrealised ideals: 'I want to encourage growth in all the budding ambitions he holds within himself – so that they put forth blossom and bring forth fruit' (53). The child will not only become an apotheosis, a symbol of ultimate meaning, an answer to time and death; he will also redeem his father's failure, as Christ redeems mankind. Of his unwritten manuscript, Allmers remarks, 'Men tro du meg, – der kommer en bakefter som vil gjøre det bedre' (III, 487) – an almost direct quotation, as John Northam points out, of John the Baptist's anticipation of Christ in Mark 1:7: 'There cometh one mightier than I after me.'[31] Within the triangular structure of the real family, it seems that the only way the mother can cope with her guilt is to wish the child dead; and the only way the father can cope with *his* is to symbolise the child out of life. It is only after Eyolf's death that Rita can see her offence against the child, and force Allmers to confront his perverse motives in moulding the living boy into what, with devastating accuracy, she calls a 'vidunderbarn' (505) – literally, a 'miraculous child', a *Wunderkind*. 'Because', she says, 'you were consumed by a lack of faith in yourself. Because you had begun to have doubts about this great mission you were giving your life to. . . . And this is why you wanted to make a child prodigy out of poor little Eyolf' (viii, 79). Eyolf the child, the human reality, is denied many times before his drowning; and hindsight lends an ironic relevance to the mutterings of the Rat Wife, for whom death is the ultimate gift of compassion to those little creatures rejected and persecuted by the gnawing of conscience.

Eyolf's death, however, remains difficult to account for. Rita's *wishing* the child dead has no direct causal connection with the actual drowning; and Allmers's 'teleological suspension of the ethical' is a form of essentially passive aggression – unlike the cruelty and confusion inflicted by the adult world on Hedvig. The child is not 'murdered' by a Brand-like exercise of the uncompromising will, but neither is he sacrificed by Ibsen as part of a redemptive myth to save the Allmerses. 'Eyolf', writes Orley Holtan, 'dies that others might live more abundantly.'[32] But to see the child as a sacrificial scapegoat is to see him as a symbol – and this merely perpetuates the very habit of mind against which Ibsen is seen to protest. Eyolf's drowning, in any case, does not relieve a suffering humanity of sin and guilt. If anything, it unleashes an intensified consciousness of retribution incapable of exorcism even by the half-hearted expedient of suicide. Haunted by the child's reproachful eyes and the rhythmic insistence of the cry at the quayside – 'The crutch is floating' – the Allmerses find themselves incarcerated in a union of remorse more desperate than before. The immediate effect of Eyolf's death on Allmers is to knock away his own peculiar crutch – his spurious life's-mission, his pretentious humanism and the symbols which screen him against the horrors of process – and confront him with reality in all its desolation. The primary significance of Eyolf's death, it seems to me, is that it is totally without any significance, totally without the sort of profound meaning that Allmers demands to find in it. It is *absurd*. And Allmers's attempt to rationalise the drowning in transcendental terms merely impresses upon him the cosmic pointlessness of the thing. Deprived by their atheism of any consoling faith, too afraid to take their own lives, too guilt-stricken to exorcise the memory of their offences against the child, the Allmerses seem almost beyond redemption from the dark night of their earthbound souls.

In the final analysis, it is not little Eyolf as some mythical redeemer who saves them from their condition. For man is saved, in Ibsen, not by teleological means but by ethical actions: by his ability to reconcile idealism with workable human realities, and by enacting the idea of human responsibility in its most ordinary sense. Once the Allmerses are able to *see the child* they have neglected, they are then able to see the suffering of a whole world of cruelly deprived children; and, by pledging themselves to the care of the outcast waifs of the quayside settlements, they move towards incarnating the abstract thesis of Allmers's unwritten manuscript. If they can make it viable, they can also change the meaning of 'Eyolf' from an evasion of responsible commitment to others to a principle of ethical involvement. It is the pressure of human experience that ultimately gives life to teleological abstractions; and, however poorly qualified the Allmerses may seem for the life of personal dedication and self-education, however slight the probability of success, a pathetic dignity still attaches to their assertion of human value beneath 'den store stillhet' (518) – the great stillness – which is also the silence of God.

Notes

1. Muriel Bradbrook, *Ibsen the Norwegian,* new ed (Hamden, Conn., 1966) p. 10.
2. James Kerans, '*Kindermord* and Will in *Little Eyolf* ', Travis Bogard and William Oliver (eds), *Modern Drama: Essays in Criticism* (New York, 1965).
3. James Hurt, *Catiline's Dream: An Essay on Ibsen's Plays* (Urbana, Ill., 1972).
4. See Lyons, *Ibsen: The Divided Consciousness,* and 'Some Variations of *Kindermord* as Dramatic Archetype', *Comparative Drama,* I (Spring, 1967); and Orley Holtan, *Mythic Patterns in Ibsen's Last Plays* (Minneapolis, 1970).
5. Cf. Henry James, 'The Pupil'; D. H. Lawrence, 'The Rocking Horse Winner'; John Whiting, *No Why.*
6. Downs, *Ibsen: The Intellectual Background,* p. 91.

7. William Wordsworth, 'Ode: Intimations of Immortality from Recollections of Early Childhood'.
8. Peter Coveney, *Poor Monkey* (1957); repr. as *The Image of Childhood: The Individual and Society: A Study of the Theme in English Literature* (Harmondsworth, 1967).
9. Quoted ibid., p. 83.
10. Ibid., pp. 339–40.
11. Gerard Manley Hopkins, 'Spring'. Cf. Abrams, 'Freshness of Sensation', *Natural Supernaturalism*, pp. 377–84.
12. Quoted ibid., p. 414.
13. Robert Raphael, 'Illusion and the Self in *The Wild Duck, Rosmersholm,* and *The Lady from the Sea*', *Scandinavian Studies,* xxxv (1963) 38.
14. *Shaw and Ibsen,* p. 217.
15. W. B. Yeats, 'Among School Children', in *Collected Poems* (London, 1958) p. 244.
16. *The Father,* in *Six Plays by Strindberg,* trs. Elizabeth Sprigge (Garden City, NY, 1955) p. 39.
17. McFarlane, Introduction to *the Oxford Ibsen,* iii, 19.
18. Søren Kierkegaard, *Fear and Trembling,* trs. Robert Payne (London, 1939) p. 23. All subsequent quotations are from this edition.
19. 'A Discussion with Edward Bond', *Gambit,* v (1970) 19.
20. Albert Camus, *'The Myth of Sisyphus' and Other Essays,* trs. Justin O'Brien (New York, 1955) p. 5.
21. J. B. Halstead, *Romanticism* (New York, 1969) p. 23.
22. William Wordsworth, *The Prelude,* xiii. 441–5 (1850 text).
23. Mary McCarthy, 'The Will and Testament of Ibsen', *Partisan Review,* 1956; repr. in McFarlane, *Ibsen: A Critical Anthology,* p. 278.
24. Pinter, quoted in Martin Esslin, *The Theatre of the Absurd* (New York, 1961) p. 206.
25. McCarthy, in McFarlane, *Ibsen: A Critical Anthology,* pp. 273, 274.
26. Peckham, *Romanticism,* p. 27.
27. Ibid., pp. 27–8.
28. Ibid., p. 28.
29. See James McFarlane's structural analysis of *Little Eyolf* in Durbach, *Ibsen and the Theatre,* pp. 131–9.
30. Ibid., p. 136.
31. Northam, *Ibsen: A Critical Study,* p. 187.
32. Holtan, *Mythic Patterns,* p. 120.

5 'Cosmologies of Two': Romantic Eroticism in *Little Eyolf, The Master Builder,* and *When We Dead Awaken*

I

'Incest', wrote Shelley, 'is, like many other incorrect things, a very poetical circumstance.'[1] And, if *Little Eyolf* is any indication of Ibsen's treatment of 'incorrect things' in general and incest in particular, then it clearly has its place in a tradition fired by the erotic imagination of nineteenth-century Romanticism and the varieties of illicit love which constitute its peculiar poetry. One year before the publication of *Little Eyolf* there appeared that monumental study of sexual disorders, the *Psychopathia Sexualis* – but it is unlikely, as Brian Downs laconically remarks, that Krafft-Ebing had much to teach Ibsen.[2] As Freud must surely have observed in his analysis of Rebekka West,[3] Ibsen's plays exist as corroborative evidence in contemporary literature of the forms of sexual behaviour that medical science was struggling to understand – from Torvald's fantasies of defloration to the incest fantasies that govern Alfred Allmers's conduct. But Freud and Otto Rank notwithstanding, modern psychiatry has very little to add to Krafft-Ebing's bafflement in the face of incest behaviour[4] and even less to Ibsen's 'poetical' understanding of a syndrome which, of course, finds no analogies in the standard textbooks on the subject. Nor would one expect it to. His concerns lie not with the pathology of incest – unless one gives 'pathology' the widest possible meaning – but in the sexual

104

attitudes of Romanticism, where pathological diagnosis is ultimately irrelevant to 'poetical cricumstance'. *Little Eyolf,* which I
want to discuss as a paradigm of Romantic eroticism in Ibsen, is
pre-eminent among those of his plays which deal with aspects of
sexual perversity – the denial of the body as an aspect of process, the
evasion of sexual commitment through taboo or asceticism –
from Solness's fantasies of nursery sexuality with Hilde to Rubek's
sublimation of his sexual attraction to Irene. The play has an
obviously significant place among those which deal with very
different aspects of incest: most notably, *Ghosts, Rosmersholm,*
or those in which the protagonist is more fiercely drawn to his
wife's sister than to his wife. But the proper context of *Little
Eyolf,* it seems to me, is the whole range of erotic Romantic
literature fascinated, if not obsessed, with the incest theme: from
Chateaubriand's *René* and *Atala,* through the literature of the
Sturm und Drang, Wagner's *Die Walküre,* the Gothic novels of
Walpole and Lewis, the poetry of Shelley, Byron's *Cain* and other
of his plays and poems, to the post-Romantic novels of Emily
Brontë and Dickens.[5] The list is extensive, stretching beyond the
confines of the nineteenth century to Iris Murdoch's *A Severed
Head* and beyond. The centrality of *Little Eyolf* to this genre is
not merely its participation in the tradition, its dramatisation of
yet another 'poetical circumstance', but its peculiar analysis of
the theme, its explicit criticism of unstated Romantic sexual
assumptions and attitudes, and its exposé of that perverse poetry
which might have prompted Goethe to his pejorative definition of
Romanticism as sickness.

Goethe may, indeed, have had in mind Shelley's rather coy
description of incest as the poetry of the incorrect; but this has
very little to say about erotic Romanticism and much more about
erotic decadence. The distinction between these two sensibilities
may be perilously fine at times, but it is very important to
maintain it, as Goethe in his cynicism did not. Nor does George
Steiner, writing of 'Romantic' exoticism. His point of view seems
to share in the sensationalism of Shelley:

Romantic ideals of love, notably the stress on incest, dramatize
the belief that sexual extremism, the cultivation of the pathological, can restore personal existence to a full pitch of reality
and somehow negate the gray world of middle-class fact. It is

permissible to see in the Byronic theme of damnation through
forbidden love and in the Wagnerian *Liebestod* surrogates for
the lost dangers of revolutionary action.[6]

Mario Praz, in *The Romantic Agony,* has dealt at length with this
decadent aspect of the erotic sensibility. His view of Byron, for
instance, is that of a man who uses incest as a condiment, a spice
for love, in order to intensify the thrill of guilt and fatality which,
in turn, enhances the flow of life.[7] But nothing could be further
from the strange purity that defines the incestuous lovers in *Cain.*
They are not damned through their forbidden love, but saved
– paradoxically freed by it from fatality, guilt and finally even
from the flow of life itself, from what Ibsen, in *Little Eyolf,* calls
forvandlingens lov, the law of change. Decadent love may indeed
cultivate the pathological. But Romantic love, whatever its final
consequences, consciously cultivates the paradisal, discovering in
incestuous sibling relationships that ideal counterpart in whom
one sees one's self, one's soul, reflected in a union of rediscovered
Edenic wholeness. The 'poetical circumstance' of *Cain* is nothing
less than a form of Romantic religion in which the lover leads the
beloved from the Land without Paradise, from the mortality of
the body and the impermanence of desire, to an immortal realm
of imperishable bliss. This is Adah's most significant discovery in
her relationship with Cain:

ADAH: Why wilt thou always mourn for Paradise?
   Can we not make another?
CAIN: Where?
ADAH: Here or
   Where'er thou wilt. Where'er thou art, I feel not
   The want of this so much regretted Eden. (*Cain,* III.
   37–40)[8]

The imagery in which Allmers declares his love for Asta may be
less explicitly paradisal, but it shares in Adah's sense of a mystical
affinity of souls which transposes the sexually incestuous into a
religious impulse. Paradoxically, the atheist who would deny all
divinity thinks, like Keats's modern lover, 'to make itself / Divine
by loving'; and, as Allmers had once transformed little Eyolf into
a conception of immortality, so he now locates in big Eyolf a
transcendental principle of holiness – a form of love miraculously

exempt from process and mutability, from the sublunary and fallen sexuality of *eros*. His return to Asta after the trauma of his marriage will be a 'homecoming', a recovery of that lost golden world of shared adolescent affection: 'Det ble dog en deilig tid for oss i grunnen, Alfred. Vi to alene' (III. 501) – 'It still remains such an utterly lovely time for us, Alfred. The two of us, alone.' And he envisions this recovery of a vanished loveliness in images of exaltation, new baptism, and spiritual redemption:

> Og det er deg, Asta, som jeg nu tyr hjem til igjen. . . . Så kommer jeg til deg, – du kjære, kjære søster. Jeg *må* til deg igjen. Hjem til deg for å renses og foredles fra samlivet med –. . . .
>
> Å, tenk deg dog om, Asta! Hvorledes var ikke samlivet mellem deg or meg? Var det ikke som en eneste høy helligdag fra først til sist? . . .
>
> Jå, så vil vi to leve vårt fordums liv om igjen. . . . For en bror og en søsters kjærlighet –. . . . Det forhold er det eneste som ikke står under forvandlingens lov. (508–9)

> And it is you, Asta, I want now to come back home to again. . . . Then I'll come to you–you, my dear, dear sister. I *must* come back to you again. Home to you, so that I may be cleansed and made new again [literally, 'perfected'] after living together with –. . . .
>
> Ah, just think of it Asta! Wasn't our living together wonderful, just you and me? Wasn't it like an endless day of sacred exaltation from beginning to end? . . .
>
> Then let the two of us live our past life over again. . . . For a brother and a sister's love –. . . . That relationship is the only one that is not subject to the law of change.

'Where'er thou art, I feel not / The want of this so much regretted Eden.' Paradise, as Adah's words to Cain imply, may be regained through an ideal sexual counterpart in whose nature one is completed and fulfilled, who assuages one's homesickness for the land of one's expulsion, and who embodies the imperishable qualities of an Edenic relationship. To locate such absolute value in the ideal lover is to recover a divinity which opposes meaninglessness, change and death. And, like the high Romantic lovers of

Byron and Emily Brontë, Allmers's discovery of an immortal
symbolism in the sexually desirable sister satisfies an intense need
in the secular world for a reintegration of the self through soul-
kinship with one's female counterpart. In this way, the immortal
dimension of spirit, once affirmed through communion with
God, is now recovered cosmically through self-completion in the
lover – an idea definitively expressed in Catherine's declaration of
love for Heathcliff. It is not in Allmers's nature (or Ibsen's style) to
articulate ideas, but the sense of sacred alliance which underlies
his need for Asta is surely analogous to this most Romantic of all
avowals:

> I cannot express it; but surely you and everybody have a notion
> that there is, or should be, an existence of yours beyond you.
> What were the use of my creation if I were entirely contained
> here? My great miseries in this world have been Heathcliff's
> miseries, and I watched and felt each from the beginning; my
> great thought in living is himself. If all else perished, and *he*
> remained, I should still continue to be; and if all else remained,
> and he were annihilated, the universe would turn to a mighty
> stranger. I should not seem a part of it.[9]

'Her hyperbole,' writes Hillis Miller, 'is the climax and endpoint
of the long tradition making love a private religion in which the
loved one is God and there is a single worshipper and devotee.'[10]
But it is *Little Eyolf* rather than *Wuthering Heights* which is the
endpoint of the tradition – not in the sense that Ibsen is its last
exponent, but in the sense that he discredits so thoroughly the
assumptions that underlie this Romantic solution to death and
the disappearance of God.

'If you don't have a God in heaven, an invisible dimension that
justifies the visible one, then you take whatever is nearest at hand
and work out your problems on that.'[11] That process of working
out one's existential problems – what psychology terms 'projection'
or 'transference' – has been extensively dealt with by Ernest Becker
in *The Denial of Death*; and the various ways of creating sources
from which man may derive some assurance of personal significance and power over process has obvious relevance to Hedda's
relationship with Løvborg, for instance, or Allmers's with both his
Eyolfs. Projection, as Becker defines it, is that impulse to see in
the other person 'the self-transcending life process that gives to

one's self the larger nourishment it needs. . . . It represents the natural attempt to be healed and to be whole through heroic self-expansion in the "other".'[12] As such, it may be a highly creative mode of coping with the fear of death and the sense of personal insignificance. But in its obvious denial of human limitations, its insistence on man as God, projection may also constitute another form of the life-lie – an illusion which exists perilously on the line that divides life-enhancing fantasies from regressive and life-denying distortions of reality. And it is precisely on this line, at this verge, that the Ibsen protagonist tries to find his impossible point of balance. On the one hand, what Otto Rank has called the 'Romantic solution' may restore to man his spiritual powers and, by a leap of the imagination, enable him to transcend the processes that frustrate his immortal desires. It enables him to inhabit a 'cosmology of two' in which 'the guilt of the body, the drag of his animality that haunts his victory over decay and death' are all purged in 'a perfect consummation with perfection itself'.[13] But perfect consummations are obviously not of this world; and the perfect woman – Solveig, or Goethe's *Ewig-Weibliche* – can exist only in infinitude as an ideal to be reached for but never attained. The Romantic triumph, as M. H. Abrams puts it, 'consists simply in the experience of sustaining a desire which never relaxes into the stasis of finite satisfaction'[14] or, in other words, in the experience of sexual desire eternally exempted from sexual gratification.

There are many forms of sexual perversity in Ibsen, but they all seem to derive from this tendency towards an indefinite postponement of passion: the denial of love, the evasion of sexuality, the sublimation of erotic desire beneath an idealised conception of the perfect cosmology of two. Paradise regained at the cost of human joy, however, is a Paradise populated by grotesquely static forms – by the metamorphosis of women into dolls or statuary, or into Platonic forms of deathless (and therefore dead) perfection, like the figures on Keats's Grecian Urn. Sex, at all costs, must be resisted, because – in Ernest Becker's axiom – 'Sex is of the body, and the body is of death. . . . Resistance to sex is a resistance to fatality.'[15] And this is where the cosmology of two must ultimately fail, despite the magnificence of its conception. For, if one is seeking forms of immortality against the law of change, then the projection of absolute value in the lover-as-god can only redirect one to the heart of the romantic dilemma: the twinship of *eros* and *thanatos,* love and death. There is no having one without the other; and those who seek in Ibsen's world to find imperishable bliss by denying mortality and change inevitably end by denying life itself.

Allmers's sexual anxiety in *Little Eyolf* is clearly of this nature – existential, rather than symptomatic of any particular trauma, such as the maiming of Eyolf during their love-making. The child's presence merely confirms his father's deep erotic fear and intensifies his guilt without actually explaining its origins. It would be closer to the truth to say that sex, for Allmers, is the ultimate revelation of man's absurd condition: that which impels him towards self-completion and immortality, and that which, at the same time, confronts him with the imperfections of the body, the human limitations of the lover, and the failure of cosmic heroism. Sex is that which fascinates and horrifies, which attracts and repels, which confirms death in the quest for immortality. When Rita asks Allmers what he felt for her at the beginning of their relationship, he replies in a strangled monosyllable: 'Skrekk' (III. 507) – 'Terror.' And yet in the very next breath he acknowledges the ineluctable and dangerous desire: 'Du var så førtærende deilig, Rita' – 'You were so overwhelmingly [literally, 'consumingly'] lovely, Rita.' 'Dread', writes Kierkegaard, 'is a desire for what one fears, a sympathetic antipathy ... an alien power which takes hold of the individual, and yet one cannot extricate oneself from it, does not wish to, because one is afraid, but what one fears attracts one.'[16] And this is precisely how Allmers is bound in his mortal sexuality to Rita – trapped, like Ellida Wangel, in a relationship that appals in the very process of sexual allurement.

This alliance of contradictory impulses informs the very rhythm of the play with its fearful and irresistible forces, its undertows and lures; and the protagonists' rersponses to love are as horrible and compelling as their responses to death. Whatever else she might incarnate in her macabre appearance, the old Rat Wife manifests more powerfully than any other of Ibsen's strange visitors the nature of death-infected sexuality – its seductive charm, and its dangers. Ibsen calls her *Rottejomfruen* – the Rat Virgin – an almost impressionistic, Munch-like amalgam of woman as goddess and crone, a young–old emblem of love and death in part defined by the red and the black of her clothing. She charms and attracts, like the horrible–beautiful dog in her bag, compelling her beloved victims to yield to what they most resist: 'They can't help themselves! . . . Because really they don't want to do it. Because really they are horribly afraid of the water – and that's just the reason that compels them to go' (VIII, 48). And the attractive powers that seduce and drown rats are identical with the sexual forces that operate in human affairs:

RAT WIFE: . . . Ah, in my earlier days I had no need of any Mopseman. I was sufficient attraction myself. On my own.
EYOLF: And you attracted – what?
RAT WIFE: People. One in particular.
EYOLF [*tense*]: Tell me who that was.
RAT WIFE [*laughs*]: It was my own dearest love, you little heart-breaker!
EYOLF: Where's he now?
RAT WIFE [*brutally*]: Down among all the rats.   (49)

La Belle Dame sans Merci – enthralling, compelling, and terrifying. *Rottejomfruen*'s mythic identity finally subsumes all of those qualities of woman's sexuality which, for years, have frightened Allmers out of Rita's bed.

But Allmers merely demonstrates the more extreme symptoms of a condition shared by most of the other persons in the play – that Keatsian awareness of beauty that must fade, of fleeting joys, and pleasure turning instantly to poison. They all live under the shadow of the law of change, longing for infinitude and eternity, for a loveliness exempt from process. To discover the immutable in human affairs is to love forever – as Borghejm dreams of doing, and as Rita with desperate insistence demands of her relationship with Allmers. In her need, she clings to him with a determination not to admit the extreme and destructive change in their sexual lives:

ALLMERS: But my dearest Rita! People change with the years. And some time or other that's bound to happen to us, too, in our life together. As it does to everybody else.
RITA: Not to me! Ever! And I don't want to hear of any change in you either. I couldn't bear that, Alfred. I want to keep you all to myself.   (62)

But her possessive sexuality only intensifies Allmers's abhorrence;

and his need for cleansing and purification from the impulse which first brought death into the world drives him to fashion in fact what the others all dream of: *'noe* her i verden som ingen ende tar' (III, 493) – *'something* in this world which has no end'. He fashions *eros* without *thanatos*: love which defies the mortality of the body while affirming its passion, which incarnates the irresistible need while eliminating the dread of imperfection and death. And it is in his love for Asta that Allmers locates this absolute guarantee of immortal desire. The 'incorrect thing' has become transformed into the 'poetical circumstance', although not quite in the sense that Shelley might have intended: a transformation of the incestuous impulse into a perverse form of idealism where physical desire is eternally protected against sexual consummation by the operation of taboo. It is this aspect of Romantic eroticism that Ibsen might well have contributed to the *Psychopathia Sexualis* and which Ernest Becker comes closest to defining:

> Sexual taboos have been at the heart of human society since the very beginning. They affirm the triumph of human personality over animal sameness. With the complex codes for sexual self-denial, man was able to impose the cultural map for personal immortality over the animal body. He brought sexual taboos into being because he needed to triumph over the body, and he sacrificed the pleasures of the body to the highest pleasure of all: self-perpetuation as a spiritual being through all eternity.[17]

'Complex codes for sexual self-denial': these are precisely what the Ibsen protagonist seeks out as a refuge from sexual desire; and incest, as I have suggested, while not an exclusive 'code' for sacrificing bodily pleasure to immortal longings, is surely an extreme form of the various other techniques for sexual evasion. Critics who have dealt with the psychology of *Little Eyolf* – most notably Otto Rank and James Kerans[18] – have argued that brother-sister incest (what Rank calls the *Geschwister-komplex*) is essentially a recapitulation of the Oedipus Complex: the desire for sexual union with the mother displaced upon the sister. But *Little Eyolf,* it seems to me, implicitly denies the fundamental assumptions of Freud. It is not the death-wish but the fear of death, not the desire for taboo'd sexuality but the evasion of sex in the name of taboo that underlies the erotic anxieties of Ibsen's protagonists.

And their attempt to place human sexuality beyond the processes of change and death, to spiritualise the physical, is apparent throughout the literature of Romantic incest – even when, as we may assume in the case of Byron and Augusta Leigh, the taboo is actually broken. In his letters to his half-sister, Byron still appeals to the magical infinitude inherent in incestuous love which distinguishes the sublime from the merely human, the ideal from the real: 'I have never ceased', he writes, 'nor can cease to feel that perfect and boundless attachment which bound and binds me to you – which renders me utterly incapable of *real* love for any other human being – for what could they be to me after you?'[19]

Ibsen's greatest contribution to the history of Romantic eroticism is to expose, with conscious counter-Romantic irony, the failure of an erotic ideal which so insulates the lover against love in all its humanly accessible forms, and which has the effect of rendering him so 'utterly incapable of *real* love for any other human being'.

I want, briefly, to compare the iterative metaphors, the typical patterns and symbols of Romantic incest which link Ibsen to the tradition and which elucidate his themes while revealing the ironies which set him apart from high Romanticism. The Romantic source for all brother-sister incest is surely Byron's *Cain*, a storehouse of all those Romantic impulses which characterise the erotic sensibility from the 1820s to Emily Brontë and Ibsen: the grievous loss of Paradise, the absurdity of existence under the sentence of death, a yearning for the condition of immortality, and a sense of estrangement from an apathetic God whose morality is merely circumstantial and who can make sin of virtue within a single generation. Incest, for the aboriginal sibling couple, must obviously be exempt from sin – how else could the race endure? – an ingenious dramatic situation in which the magical properties of incestuous love survive the violation of taboo. But such love must be denied to the children of Cain and Adah, and to all who will replace them in mortality. This is Adah's cry of protest when Lucifer declares the incestuous passions of subsequent generations forbidden:

> Oh my God!
> Shall they not love and bring forth things that love
> Out of their love? Have they not drawn milk
> Out of this bosom? Was not he, their father,

Born of the same sole womb in the same hour
With me? Did we not love each other? And
In multiplying our being multiply
Things which will love each other as we love
Them, and as I love thee, my Cain?   (*Cain*, i. 367–75)

Sense and syntax are brilliantly fused – those phrases that wind in
on each other, statement enveloped in statement in endless circularity, and that speak so poignantly of a closed genetic circuit,
of a mathematics of endlessly reduplicated products. For incestuous love is the means not so much to sexual reproduction as to a
form of curious genetic cloning – the eternal perpetuation not of
the *species*, but of the *self*. Implicit in the passage is the idea of
self-completion through the other – the idea of 'projection'; but an
even more intriguing image is that of the incestuous family, and
both have direct bearing on the major structures of *Little Eyolf*.

What we find in Cain and Adah is Plato's parable unaltered:
male and female aspects of a single psychosome, a single self,
each discovering in the other a complement to his/her integrity –
'Born of the same sole womb in the same hour' – twins, like
Siegmund and Sieglinde, identical in all but sex. The Romantic
ego must seek out its own self image in the other until it finds the
sort of affinity that Manfred discerns in his soul-mate, Astarte:

She was like me in lineaments; her eyes,
Her hair, her features, all, to the very tone
Even of her voice. . . .[20]

The same tendency persists strongly in the Allmers–Asta relationship: that sense of a radical identity that sets them apart from all
others, their reliance upon some special or magical status conferred upon them by sharing initials:

Rita er jeg ikke i slekt med. Det er ikke som å ha en søster. . .

Rita and I don't belong together in the same family. It's not
like having a sister. . . .

Ja, *vår* slekt er noe for seg selv. Alltid så har vi hatt lyse

forbokstaver i navnene. Kan du huske hvor titt vi snakket om
det før?

Yes, *our* family is something quite special to ourselves. For

example, our names have always begun with vowels. Do you remember how often we used to talk about *that?* . . .

Og alle har vi samme slags øyne.   (III, 502)
And we all have the same kind of eyes.

They *don't,* of course – Asta's eyes are quite different as they both
admit. For an instant, Ibsen exposes the silliness of it all, and the
whole system of correspondences and likenesses begins to break
down; but Allmers saves the situation by moving from a merely
physical to a spiritual projection of shared qualities: 'Ja, jeg tror
at samlivet allikevel har preget oss begge to efter hinannens bilde.
I sinnet, mener jeg' (ibid.) – 'Yes, I believe, all the same, that living
together has imprinted upon both of us each other's likeness. In
the mind, I mean.' To which Asta replies, deeply moved, 'Å, det
må du aldri si, Alfred. Det er meg alene som har tatt mitt preg
efter deg. Og det er deg som jeg skylder *alt,* – alt *godt* i verden' –
'Ah, you must never say that, Alfred. It is I alone who have taken
my impression from you. And it's you to whom I owe *everything,* –
all that's *good* in the world.'

Each is to the other as the steel plate is to the engraving, a
mirror-image in which soul-likeness reflects soul-likeness. And the
child of such a union – Byron's Enoch, or Ibsen's Eyolf – becomes
a Paradisal image of the reintegrated self reduplicated, as images
are endlessly reduplicated on reflecting surfaces:

Oh Cain, look on him, see how full of life,
Of strength, of bloom, of beauty, and of joy,
How like to me, how like to thee, when gentle,
For then we are all alike, is't not so Cain?
Mother and sire and son, our features are
Reflected in each other, as they are
In the clear waters when they are gentle, and
When thou art gentle. Love us then my Cain!
And love thyself for our sakes, for we love thee.   (*Cain,* III.
140–8)

One has the sense, again, of a closed, perfectly contained, and
almost solipsistic system: the family as an image of eternal
circularity, rather than a linear chain of finite beings in whom
nature answers death, 'not by creating eternal organisms,' as
Becker puts it, 'but by making it possible for ephemeral ones to
procreate'.[21]

This double-family configuration, as I have suggested in the previous chapter, is one of the central structural features of *Little Eyolf*: the real family and the mythical, the sexual and the spiritual, the mortal and the miraculous. As the child of Rita's body, Eyolf is the emblem of the living family – a maimed and pathetic reminder of man's earthbound imperfections which subject him to the vicissitudes of change and the inevitability of death. But, as the child of Asta's soul, he is the consummation of the ideal family – the child whose special status as *vidunderbarnet* ranks him among those other wonderful children of incestuous love (Wagner's Siegfried, for example, culture-hero and superman). Rita is well aware of this two-family pattern and of Asta's peculiar surrogate motherhood. It diminishes her own claim to a child who is, at best, only half hers – a stranger never really part of *her* cosmology of two; and the more she rejects Eyolf as an intrusion upon her relationship with Allmers, the more conscious she becomes of Asta's claim upon the child: 'Eyolf would never wholeheartedly give himself to me. . . . Somebody stood between us. Right from the beginning. . . . Asta stood barring my way. . . . Yes. Asta – she possessed him' (VIII, 78). Ibsen's conscious intentions in exploring the Romantic symbolism of the incestuous family remain obscure, exist largely by inference or through comparison. The mystical bonding of names, for example, resembles the Siegmund–Sieglinde–Siegfried connections in the Ring cycle – the soul-likeness of the incestuous family re-echoing, as it were, with its own *Leitmotiv*. But it is not merely the initial vowels of their names that draw Eyolf and Asta into the circle of the paradisal family. They share the *same* name, big and little aspects of a single conflated identity in the mind of Allmers, which for him seems to have a magical significance abstracted from its living forms. Critics, acknowledging the esoteric symbolism of the name, have interpreted it in various ways: 'Eyolf is the name or sign of non-sexual relationships';[22] 'Eyolf remains the name for the self, the sense of security of being for which Allmers is searching';[23] and so on. I would formulate the idea in somewhat different terms. 'Eyolf' is Allmers's answer to death, a Romantic symbol of personal immortality.

It is impossible, of course, to abstract these double-family triangles from the 'eternal' triangle in the complex geometrical structure of the play. The typical situation in which the protagonist is torn between two women (or, conversely, between two men) is so recurrent in Ibsen as to assume the features of a private mythology, from the Furia–Catiline–Aurelia grouping of his first play to the Maja–Rubek–Irene grouping of his last. Orley Holtan discusses this mythic configuration as the opposition between the 'dark' and the 'light' woman, contrary forces working on the soul of the hero;[24] and James Hurt has expanded this 'fascinating'/ 'gentle' dialectic in Ibsen into an *Ur*-myth of the divided self, a paradigm of what existential psychology calls the 'schizoid position'.[25] But, again, I have the sense that comprehensive mythologies are either too vague to account precisely for the nature of this erotic opposition, or too monolithic to describe the variety of meanings in Ibsen's treatment of the theme. Which woman in *When We Dead Awaken,* for instance, is 'gentle' and which 'fascinating'? And what does the opposition of 'light' and 'dark' ultimately say about the nature of the alternatives between which the protagonist must choose? I am not entirely satisfied, moreover, that these two loves of comfort and despair, domestic and erotic, *are* in any sense choices or alternatives for Ibsen's men – since their most habitual tendency is to *evade* all sexual commitment to either. Rather, I would argue, the typical Ibsen structure relates to a binary pattern in Romantic and post-Romantic literature where the alternatives between which the hero is trapped are similar to those I have tried to define in Asta and Rita: imperishable bliss or mortal passion, the absolute necessity for a symbol of immortality (in whose name sexuality is sublimated) or the compelling lure of the flesh (which, in Ibsen, one avoids in terror). These distinctions are most clearly expressed in Catherine's definition of her two loves in *Wuthering Heights*:

> My love for Linton is like the foliage in the woods. Time will change it, I'm well aware, as winter changes the trees. My love for Heathcliff resembles the eternal rocks beneath – a source of little visible delight, but necessary. Nelly, I *am* Heathcliff – he's always, always in my mind – not as a pleasure, any more than I am always a pleasure to myself – but as my own being – [26]

That love which is visible and delightful and pleasurable is also, as the imagery suggests, organic and mutable and subject to the law of change – what Wordsworth calls 'the touch of earthly years'.[27] For sexual love is instinct with 'human fears', and as an anodyne the Romantic lover must seek out love which is necessary rather than delightful, eternal rather than temporal, and rocklike rather than organic. Heathcliff, like Wordsworth's Lucy, is placed beyond change and reduced to a 'thingness' without motion and without force – the very quest for deathlessness ironically creating merely petrified and lifeless forms as its solution to decay. It is not clear to me whether Emily Brontë actually intends this fallacy of Romantic logic (as Wordsworth surely does in the Lucy poem). The reader is usually impressed by the extraordinary intensity of Cathy's need for soul-kinship with Heathcliff. But what her definition of love ultimately amounts to is a form of sterile self-worship in which the possibility of a genuine human connection is eliminated; for one cannot mate with mere abstract necessity – especially when the relationship between soul and self is inhibited, on the human level, by strong suggestions of incest. I do not subscribe to the familiar argument that Heathcliff is in reality old Earnshaw's 'by-blow' and that Emily Brontë stopped short of making their love explicitly incestuous in deference to 'traditional canons of taste'.[28] There is no need to insist on a literal reading of, say, Werther's love for Lotte when he calls it 'die heiligste, reinste, brüderlichste Liebe'[29] – holiness, cleanliness and brotherliness being inter-changeable metaphors of incestuous (and therefore sacred) love in Romantic erotic literature. Emily Brontë merely facilitates the operation of such metaphors by naming Heathcliff after Cathe-rine's dead brother and by allowing them to share the bed and the joys of childhood. It is the strong suggestion of consanguinity, rather than any literal blood-tie, that defines the Romantic attitude towards ideal love and impels the hero to search for symbols of eternity. It is in this sense that I see the incestuous love in *Little Eyolf* as a model for all the other forms of erotic evasion–those solipsistic unions, incapable of coping with reality, perversely fearful of death and therefore needlessly destructive of life. Moreover, if prohibited love is their sole guarantee of permanence, then they must cling to each other as symbols rather than human beings, envisioning love not as process but as a static infinitude – as Heathcliff dreams of 'sleeping the last sleep, by that sleeper, with my heart stopped, and my cheek frozen against hers'.[30] This is the only sense in which any of these Romantic lovers *can* sleep together – in frozen immobility, the seat of passion stopped, and bodies mingling only in the grotesque embrace of death.

Emily Brontë, I have been suggesting, in order to create a paradigm of the new Heaven (and her novel is full of paradisal imagery) imposes upon the fallible mortality of human desire the ideal-generating metaphors of incest. What I cannot claim with any certainty is her conscious exposure of the perversity of this ideal, the failure of which (despite my emphasis) remains relatively understated. In *Little Eyolf*, however, the counter-Romantic vision dominates the tone of the play, its multiple ironies directed towards demolishing a myth which the Romantic energy of *Wuthering Heights* so powerfully sustains. From the beginning, Ibsen makes us fully aware of Allmers's betrayal of life in dealings with wife, child and sister – with everyone, in short, through whom man extends himself in relationships which enlarge and fortify the self. Terrified of sex, he interposes between Rita and his own inadequacies a series of bogus ideals deeply rooted in his guilt: in his sense of failed responsibility towards 'Eyolf' the child, and his barely repressed desire for 'Eyolf' the sister. He dehumanises both by transforming them into symbols which are a typically inept mismatching of transcendental abstraction with the human reality which must provide its substance. He ignores, with appalling insensitivity, the maiming of Eyolf, which disqualifies him from the redemptive mission he devises for the child, just as he refuses to recognise Asta's sexual love as a hopelessly unsuitable vehicle for his asexual Eden. The great pathos of the play, apart from the cruelty to Eyolf, lies in the sexual expectation and the final disappointment of Asta, who waits, with dignity and tenderness, for some response to a love no longer caught up in the trammels of incest. She waits to be freed, at last, from a long family history of sexual maladjustment. But Allmers is not the man to free her. She is not, it transpires, his half-sister at all, but an illegitimate child disgracefully treated by her mother and Allmers's father. As if to repress any incipient adolescent sexuality between the children, they oblige Asta to wear boys' clothes and call her 'Eyolf', carefully concealing the true nature of their relationship, so that any legitimate passion is constantly inhibited by taboo. For the duration of their maturity sexual commitment is held at bay until the defensively asexual nature of their relationship begins to assume the perfection of an ideal, achieved through the renunciation of all sexual desire of 'brother' for 'sister'. He marries Rita, motivated partly by the need to secure Asta's future with Rita's money, and probably to protect himself against his own incestuous impulses – but still clinging to Asta as the idealised antithesis to the frightening sexuality of his wife. Occasionally, however, he betrays his sexual attraction to Asta – as on the fateful afternoon when, making love to Rita, he reveals something unstated about his relationship with his 'sister':

> RITA: You used to call her Eyolf, didn't you? I think you once told me that . . . in an intimate moment. [*Comes nearer.*] You remember that 'devastatingly lovely' moment, Alfred?
> ALLMERS [*shrinks back in terror*]: I remember nothing! I don't want to remember!
> RITA: [*follows him*]: It was the moment . . . your second little Eyolf became a cripple. (VIII, 84–5)

Exactly what he refuses to remember of that consumingly wonderful moment (perhaps the very last in Rita's bed) remains unclear. (James Kerans suggests that at the moment of sexual climax he called out 'Eyolf' – fantasising the sister in the arms of the wife?)[31] But, whatever the trauma, he *dare* not allow his sexual desire for his sister to manifest itself as terror-inducing carnality; and he deliberately fashions the incest-ideal as a protection against this fear.

Allmers's failure of Romantic logic, which he shares with all the other Ibsenian transcendentalists, derives from the habitual confusion of finite existence and the infinite possibilities of metaphor. He fails to understand that personal relationships, as in Becker's diagnosis of Romantic fallibility, are put at terrible risk when the facts of the physical world are mistaken for spiritual ideals:

> How can a human being be a god-like 'everything' to another? . . . No human partner can offer this assurance because the partner is real. However much we may idealize and idolize him, he inevitably reflects earthly decay and imperfection. And as he is our ideal measure of value, this imperfection falls back upon us.[32]

Allmers's self-protecting response to imperfection is, like Heathcliff's, to deny that death need be a fact of existence. But Asta, however intense her own spiritual needs, is able to confront the law of change without hysterical denial or evasion and see in it not merely deterioration and decay but potential and possibility. All, in *Little Eyolf,* is subject to powerfully dynamic forces – organic life, personal relationships, family structures and even human identity, which changes with changing perspectives on the past. Asta, as she enters the play, has been utterly transformed from the 'sister' Allmers knows; and her unwillingness to go with Borghejm derives from this very alteration in circumstance and selfhood. She has become sexually eligible, now, for the man she most desires. Her love is finally freed from taboo by her new-born identity as an illegitimate child, and she waits for an appropriate moment to declare herself.

Ibsen's genius in the play is to establish a complex system of Romantic assurances of imperishable value, exposing the perverse consequences of pressing life into the service of metaphor and the devious negations and evasions of human, moral and sexual responsibility that this entails – and then, one by one, eliminating the Romantic's defences against reality until reality can no longer be denied. Each of the 'Eyolfs', Allmers's analogues of Eden, perishes in its different way. Allmers's great tome on 'Man's Responsibility' – his symbolic soul-child, inspired and nurtured by his 'sister' as Thea helps to conceive her 'child' with Løvborg – miserably fails to assert any existential meaning in the void. The scholar's answer to death is only a ream of blank pages – nothing, *nichts, ingenting.* His child saviour, fatally crippled, drowns in the sea. And his sister-as-God, Allmers's last remaining symbol, exposes the vanity of a paradise regained at the cost of all human happiness. We wait to see how Allmers will respond to the promise of a passion no longer forbidden in the drama's central revelation:

ASTA: You are not my brother, Alfred.
ALLMERS [*quickly, half-defiantly, looks at her*]: But what change does that make to our relationship? None at all.
ASTA [*shakes her head*]: It changes everything, Alfred. Our relationship is not that of brother and sister.
ALLMERS: Maybe not. But is equally sacred. Will always be

sacred.
ASTA: Remember . . . it is subject to the law of change . . . as
you said a moment ago.   (VIII. 87)

His response is typically perverse: he refuses to relinquish 'Eyolf',
insists on the sacred aspects of their relationship, and resists all
change. Asta discovers in the redefinition of her role in the family
the hope of a passion no longer incestuous – but Allmers insists on
perpetuating the sexlessness. She submits herself to the law of
change, which has miraculously given her a lover by changing her
identity – but he desperately denies any radical change in the
family structure. And Asta, in a gesture of infinite compassion,
offers Allmers a gift of waterlilies from the realm of love and
death, emblems of beautiful but perishable nature, and her final
plea for him to renounce both Eyolfs, who are dead beyond
recovery:

ASTA [*with tears in her eyes*]: They are like a final greeting to
you . . . from little Eyolf.
ALLMERS [*looks at her*]: From Eyolf out there? Or from you?
ASTA [*quietly*]: From us both.   (88)

Allmers, she seems to realise, is hopelessly lost to her. And in her
farewell gift as Eyolf she commits herself to life. Unlike the other
sisters of Romantic incest – Adah or Catherine – Asta will not
collaborate in the 'poetical circumstance' which negates her
humanity. Despite her deep and affectionate love for Allmers, she
resists the temptation of a *ménage à trois* in which she will be cast
yet again in the roles of Eyolf – both as child and sister – to assuage
the Allmerses' sense of meaninglessness and loss:

RITA: . . . Oh, Asta, I do beg and implore you! Stay here and
help us! Be what Eyolf was to us. . . . [*Seizes her hand.*] From
now on you shall be our Eyolf, Asta! Eyolf, as you were
before.
ALLMERS [*concealing his emotion*]: Stay. And share your life with
us, Asta. With Rita. With me. With me – your brother!
ASTA [*firmly, withdraws her hand*]: No. I cannot.   (96)

Her human reality no longer matches their psychic needs; and, in
the face of the incorrigible reliance of Allmers upon the brother–

sister bond, Asta has no choice but to save herself by leaving. Borghejm may be a poor second choice for her, but at least he does not constantly pretend to be her brother.

All that finally remains to the Allmerses after the destruction of 'Eyolf' is the crutch that floats to the surface of the sea – an emblem of their defective lives, a judgement on their guilt, and a reminder of what 'Eyolf' had been to them. The challenge, now, is to discard the thing by healing the life, finding some respite to the gnawing of conscience, and some meaning to an existence stripped of all consoling illusions. Asta's action is one possible response to the failure of Romantic solutions to death and the quest for immortal value in human affairs: she commits herself not to perfection or ideal marriage, but to the best she can make of her life with a pleasant-enough but rather ordinary and fallible man. Her departure leaves Rita and Allmers deprived of their last defence against cosmic emptiness, and against each other. Cut off by their atheism from the comforting reassurances of faith, incapable of leaving each other, and yet equally incapable of helping each other, they seem almost beyond redemption from the nothingness of their lives. Their dilemma anticipates, more articulately than almost any other play of the period, the existential predicament that we tend to regard as peculiarly modern, if only because D. H. Lawrence has defined it as the malaise of contemporary culture:

> We lack peace because we are not whole. And we are not whole because we have known only a tithe of the vital relationships we might have had. We live in an age which believes in stripping away the relationships. Strip them away, like an onion, till you come to pure, or blank nothingness. Emptiness. That is where most men have come now: to a knowledge of their complete emptiness. They wanted so badly to be 'themselves' that they became nothing at all: or next to nothing.[33]

Consciously or unconsciously, Lawrence's image of the romantic paradox is quintessentially Ibsenian: the onion image from *Peer Gynt*, which projects Peer's dilemma into the twentieth century and makes the Gyntian protagonists of the last plays peculiarly representative and peculiarly relevant. What we also see in *Little Eyolf*, moreover, is a prefiguration of Lawrence's solution to isolated individualism, a creatively Romantic acceptance of value in the law of change itself, and a recovery of wholeness in relationships which reject the perfection of stasis for the imperfections of process:

> The long course of marriage is a long event of perpetual change, in which a man and a woman mutually build up their souls and make themselves whole. . . . With every change, a new being emerges, a new rhythm establishes itself; we renew our life as we grow older, and there is real peace. Why, oh, why do we want one another to be always the same, fixed, like a menu-card that is never changed.[34]

But this is to state too enthusiastically, perhaps too glibly, the understanding that the Allmerses attain with hesitation and diffidence – and only sporadically. 'We Need One Another' is the title of Lawrence's essay from which these passages derive. But Ibsen, like Strindberg, sees this mutual need as both ineluctable and potentially destructive – the *nec tecum nec sine te* nexus of contrary sexual impulses which fascinate and repel, bind and break. Allmers, after all, is subject to these forces and *cannot* follow Asta. With an effort of will, he breaks through the fixed and static patterns of incest to confront the earthbound sexuality against which they had insulated him: his sense of binding attachment to Rita, that *samliv* – their living together – which has changed them, and in which they may possibly find their salvation. Both commit themselves to *forvandlingens lov,* to process, which must of necessity include birth as well as death in its rhythms, improvement as well as decay among its possible operations.

> ALLMERS: Perhaps the law of change might nevertheless hold us together.
> RITA [*nods slowly*]: A change is taking place in me. I can feel the pain of it.
> ALLMERS: Pain?
> RITA: Yes. Almost like giving birth.   (VIII, 99)

Rita's change is less equivocal, achieved through greater pain than that of Allmers. She is able to relinquish her frightening possessiveness, as exclusive in its way of other meaningful relationships as Allmers's self-insulating incest; and, as she brings

herself to admit Asta into her relationship with her husband, so
she also finds a place in their *samliv* for the new '*Eyolf*' – the child
reborn, as it were, in the socially committed conscience and the
psychic need to make good her offence against her son. She will fill
her emptiness with responsibility to a world of 'Eyolfs' – not as a
pretentious abstraction, but with a humanity that approaches
love and satisfies the quest for spiritual value in the things of the
earth. It is not a project casually adopted. She arrives at it
through the pangs of birth, and by asserting her determination
against a thorough awareness of personal failing and incapacity.
Above all, she extends herself towards her husband in compassion, offering him help in the difficult business of living, and
discovering in life itself the reason to live: 'Å, la oss bare leve livet
sammen så lenge som mulig' (III. 516) – 'Oh, let us simply live our
life together as long as we can.' There is a simple clarity in which
Ibsen's women cut across all existential pondering upon life's
abstract purposes and the constant gnawing of their men on the
bones of desiccated philosophies – as in Rita's offer to Allmers, or
Rebekka West's response to Rosmer's morbidity: 'Å livet – det har
fornyelse i seg. La oss holde fast ved det, du. – Vi kommer tidsnok
ut av det' (323) – 'Ah, life – it keeps renewing itself. Let us hold fast
to it, my dear. – We come to the end of it only too soon.' A life-
affirming common-sense, in the final analysis, is Ibsen's answer to
the Romantic's fear of change and death and his *Angst*-ridden
search for meaning in the emptiness and the silence.

An entire spectrum of such 'negative' romantic attitudes vies,
in Allmers, with the extraordinary intellectual and psychological
adjustments he is able to make to his deepest fears and anxieties.
On the one hand: echoes of Keats's flirtation with easeful death
and Rimbaud's baleful sense of dying young, contradicted almost
in the same breath by the fear of death and a perverse loathing of
a life doomed to extinction. On the other hand: a willingness to
trust to change, a recognition that the lure of the heights is as
deadly and destructive as the sea's undertow and that man's
promises are made to earthly things. His moral nature reveals the
same extremes: a punitive desire to avenge himself indiscrimin-
ately on the men and the children who let Eyolf drown, held in
check by an acknowledgment of man's social, ethical and economic responsibilities to a poor and suffering community. How,
then, are we to understand him and his motives for wanting to
share Rita's 'working day' commitment to action? As a preten-

tious existentialist? A sentimental self-deceiver? A Negative Romantic? Irony, James McFarlane suggests, undermines his every attitude and discredits all he says:

> Alfred is caught out striking attitudes, mouthing phrases, self-consciously acting a part even at moments of the greatest pathos. In its final form, the play is a technically audacious attempt to construct an action on the tensions between a suspect articulation and enactment of motives and causes and the reality of things inherent in the total situation.[35]

The tone of those final, pathetic moments is, admittedly, very difficult to account for; but irony, sentimentality, or suspect articulation seem as inappropriate to its mood as to the quiet, compassionate ending of that most Ibsenian of modern plays, Albee's *Who's Afraid of Virginia Woolf?* Confronted with the fear of living life without illusions, reaching out to each other for comfort, both couples speak a language of simple eloquence purged of the venom and the self-exposing ironies of earlier scenes. 'Kanskje jeg kunne få være med? Og hjelpe deg, Rita? . . . La oss forsøke om ikke det kunne gå' (518) – 'Could I not perhaps join you? And help you, Rita? . . . Let us try and see if it can't be done.' What they hope for is – in Shaw's phrase – 'Life with a blessing':[36] a world of mundane and workaday responsibilities, illuminated by flashes of spiritual value and a sense of life's larger purposes. Somewhere between the cold, static region of the stars and the destructive pull of the sea, Ibsen's pair see the human dimensions of the Land without Paradise:

> RITA: Where shall we look, Alfred?
> ALLMERS [*gazes at her*]: Upwards.
> RITA [*nods in agreement*]: Yes. Upwards.
> ALLMERS: Up . . . towards the mountains. Towards the stars. Towards the vast silence.
> RITA [*holds out her hand to him*]: Thank you.   (106)

Like the gesture at the end of *John Gabriel Borkman,* the holding out of hands re-establishes human connection, breaks down isolation, and reaffirms a frail mankind's need – at sporadic moments – to hold to ties that save them from utter meaninglessness. Allmers's ability to *see the child* is complemented, here, by his willingness to *see the woman*; and, although there is the danger of claiming too much for his recovery (as there is in denying it altogether),[37] he seems at least to have made an important preliminary accommodation to life. In the closing moments of the play he may speak of infinitude – but he looks at his wife. And Ibsen leaves us with the sense that ideals and realities, Romantic metaphors and the actual business of life, have at last been creatively realigned. 'The peaks are there, the stars are there', as John Northam puts it, 'not for him to dwell among but to strive towards, strenuously, intermittently.'[38]

II

Master Builder Solness makes no concessions whatever to this fine distinction between human aspiration and inhuman achievement. He commits himself, in soul-comradeship with Hilde Wangel, to that most Romantic of impulses: the lure of the impossible, the temptation to transcend not only his own physical infirmity in high places but the mortal and temporal limitations of mankind. *Det umulige* – the impossible – has the same seductive fascination in *The Master Builder* as the ineluctable tides of sexuality in *Little Eyolf* or the siren-song of the mines in *John Gabriel Borkman*. 'Har De aldri merket det, Hilde, at det umulige – det liksom lokker og roper på en?, (III. 462) – 'Have you never noticed, Hilde, that the impossible – it's just like something enticing you, and crying out to you?' But not all the protagonists are so attracted to *det umulige,* each understanding the phrase and using it in different ways. For Aline Solness and Ragnar the impossible is synonymous, as it is in casual speech, with the difficult or the dangerous – like the 'impossibility' of Solness's actual ascent of the spire. 'Dette her er som å stå og se på noe rent umulig' (482) – 'This is like standing and looking at something utterly impossible', says Ragnar. What is merely a figure of colloquial speech for him, however, becomes a near-mystical experience for Hilde, who sees the 'impossible' through the haze of a self-induced trance: 'Ja, det *er* jo det *umulige,* det som han nu gjør! [*med det ubestemmelige uttryk i øynene*]. Kan De se noen annen der oppe hos ham?' (ibid) – 'Yes, it *is* surely *impossible* what he's doing right now! [*with that nebulous expression in her eyes*]. Can you see anyone else up there with him?' With the pre-

ternatural sensibilities of one drunk on the milk of Paradise, she
has visions of her master builder locked in a struggle with divinity,
while a heavenly ethereal music celebrates his apotheosis. 'For nu,
nu er det fullbrakt! (ibid.) – 'Now, now it has been fulfilled!'
Consummatum est. It is a consummation, devoutly wished and
miraculously achieved in her mind, both spiritually and erotically, by a man's 'impossible' realisation of the impossible.

Sexual sublimity? Cosmic orgasm? It is difficult to define
precisely the nature of the erotic ideal that Hilde demands of
Solness or the divine component of her Romantic yearning for a
kingdom not of this world. Both are clearly located in her
memories of the spire; and the account of her response to
Solness's superhuman ascent at Lysanger when she was thirteen
combines the physical thrill of a nubile adolescent's first sexual
experience with angelic intimations of transcendence. The *'real
thing'* that follows – wish-dream or fantasticated memory or
fact? – is an act of passion, the most erotically explicit in Ibsen,
which verges upon the seduction of an enthusiastically acquies-
cent child. 'You went and kissed me, Mr. Solness. . . . You took
me in your arms and bent me backwards and kissed me. Many
times' (VII, 383–4). But nothing more, she cries out in annoyance
and disappointment. Now, ten years later and sexually eligible,
she comes to claim a kingdom freed from nice restrictions and the
conventions that govern the actual and the ordinary. She has
been dreaming of sensational sexual experience, finding in the
Norse sagas Romantic tales of rape and seduction by splendid
troll-like Vikings. But, at the same time, her kingdom is to exist
beyond the flesh, beyond the possible – a castle in the air, a
projection of the visionary imagination described with her habitual 'ubestemmelige uttryk' (III, 476) – the nebulous gaze in the
eyes, which is Ibsen's dramatic notation for her regression from
reality into dream, from actuality into impossibility. (The
demands made by the stage-directions upon the actress are con-
siderable – glances that grow increasingly more opaque as the gaze
shifts from an outer to an inner reality, lapses from vitality into
somnolence, which seem to require television close-ups to register
these and other withdrawals into Romanticism.) In the language
of the 1960s – not too far removed from Hilde's own clichés of
enthusiasm – she is on the sort of 'trip' which later generations of
Romantics will induce artificially, rather than envision Paradise
as an act of the imagination. Hilde, the mythopoeic critics

suggest,[39] has affinities with the Norns, who tempt men to
heroism and death, with the Valkyries, and with the spirit-guides
who lead the hero through dark regions to magnificence. But the
mythic must be seen within the ironic context of Ibsen's dramatic
image: the hiker with the back-pack, with no clothes or money,
and a single change of underwear – a Romantic flowerchild who
needs Solness to realise her own quest for the impossible just as he
needs her, a sensationalist who craves superhuman satisfaction,
and a dreamer who demands Paradise *now*. The call of the
impossible comes, as she puts it, from the 'troll within' – 'Well,
what would *you* call a thing like that?' (vii, 406). Freud had
similar difficulty in defining that impulse which defies
rationality, conscience and the trammels of middle-class
Christian guilt, and which impels man – with all the power of the
erotic – towards an absolute assertion of freedom.

> HILDE [*utterly serious*]: Something inside me forced me, drove
> me here. Drew me, tempted me, too.
> SOLNESS [*eagerly*]: There you are! There you are, Hilde! There's
> a troll in you, too. Just as in me. And it's the troll in us, you
> see, that calls on the powers outside. Then we *have* to give
> in – whether we like it or not.   (413)

What each becomes, it seems to me, is the complementary
response to the troll-call in the other: minister and server to the
most insistent demands of the Romantic temperament for an
absolute satisfaction of man's drive to freedom, ecstasy, timeless-
ness and godhead. To yield to the implications of the troll within
is to yield, finally, to death – the only guarantee of absolute freedom from entanglement in time and the limitations of human
possibility.

Solness's response to Hilde, her fantastic memories and her
demands for kingdoms and castles is ambiguous to the point of
bafflement. Does he or does he not remember the erotic events of
19 September ten years ago? And do his memories coincide with
the facts as Hilde relates them? Speculation ultimately leads
nowhere, resolves no difficulties; and what the text finally persuades one to acknowledge in Solness's equivocation is a grabbing
at the straws of salvation as they suit his particular purposes.
Unlike Allmers, he has no carefully structured mythic solution to
his anxieties and fears: and so he accepts at face value the

mysterious and impossible elements of an *ad hoc* Romanticism as
he goes along, participating in Hilde's creative fantasies without
undue concern for their veracity. Hilde offers him a life-lie, and
he accepts it as a truth – a way of coping with failure and guilt,
anxiety bordering on madness, tormenting fears of retribution,
process and death. The language of his anxiety is, in many ways,
similar to Allmers's – a sense of being determined by a law no less
tenacious in its operation than the law of change. But Solness's
term for 'change' and his understanding of process is not entirely
synonymous with *forvandling* and its suggestions of organic deterioration and decay. With an almost obsessive reiteration of the
phrase, he cries out against change – *omslag* – as the source of his
greatest fear: 'Både sent og tidlig gjør da meg så redd, – så redd.
For en gang må da vel omslaget komme . . .' (III, 446) – 'Night
and day it makes me so terrified, – so terrified. For some day the
change must come.' *Omslaget kommer.* The thought haunts him
both existentially and professionally: the sense of age having to
yield to youth, of the less potent to the more, of one generation to
the next as part of the process of surrender and retirement
endemic to life. *Omslag*, as distinct from *forvandling*, envisions
change as revolution, or the circular motion of Fortune's wheel,
rather than the linear processes of gradual evolution and loss. Its
span is generational, and its operation may be accelerated – as in
Solness's take-over from old Brovik – by usurpation or deposition.
Its typical pattern is recurrence; and with almost irrational
anxiety he sees his fate forecast in the career and the debility of
the old builder he has dispossessed. It is, admittedly, a discon-
certing image of age that old Brovik presents: a shrunken and
poverty-stricken failure, seized as soon as the curtain rises by a
spasm which will finally lead to the fatality of a stroke. His dying
hangs like a pall over the action of the play. But what is most
pitiful in the old man's condition is that *omslag* in its most
creative aspect – the natural passing of a living heritage from the
father to his son, that assurance against absolute finality – is
denied him by Solness's devious subordination and frustration of
Ragnar. And it is precisely here that the two men share a common sorrow. Neither is permitted redemption through his child:
Brovik because his son is fettered to the whim of a man who deliberately negates his potential, and Solness because his sons are
dead. With pathetic insistence he maintains their nurseries and
even builds them into his new house, hoping (as he explains his

'madness' to Hilde) for the impossible, for the redemption of age by youth. Lacking this assurance, he develops an inordinate and consuming fear of *omslag* – a sense, like Macbeth's, of his own barren sceptre wrenched from his grip by other men's sons as he had wrenched it from Brovik: 'Ungdommen, – det er gjengjeldelsen, det, ser De. Den kommer i spissen for omslaget' (453) – 'Youth, – it means retribution, you see. It comes as the spearhead of change.' Only the impossible can save him – the impossibility of childbirth in his burned-out marriage, or the impossibility of reversing process by becoming young again. This is what Hilde offers him: a means of eluding *omslag* through the agency of youth, a perfect cosmology of two in which each reciprocates the other's need for transcendence by embracing the impossible. In the intensely private architecture of their relationship, man can burst out of time by recovering youthfulness, defy God in his assumption of immortal powers, and eliminate the consequences of the past by recreating Paradise before the Fall. 'To be free from guilt is to be young again', writes Charles Lyons of *The Master Builder*, 'and the return to youth is an inversion of life: that is the inescapable fact of Ibsen's drama.'[40] And, like the other impulses towards impossibility in Ibsen, it is both magnificent and utterly mad.

What is most surprising about the erotic sensibility of *The Master Builder*, however, is that, like Antony and Cleopatra's, it is almost entirely retrospective: *memories* of heaven in the lips and eyes, held in check by a careful avoidance of physical contact and characterised by an extraordinary formality of address. Never, as Muriel Bradbrook points out, do they use the intimate *du* to each other; there are no words of endearment; and Solness's similes of love are curiously dispassionate in tone.[41] But the strategies of sublimation are, by now, all too familiar; and the indictment that Dorothy Van Ghent levels against Emily Brontë's Romantic lovers is equally applicable to Ibsen's asexual erotic couples. 'The relationship and the destiny suggested are not those of adult human lovers,' she writes, 'because the complex attendant motivations of adult life are lacking.'[42] If Allmers is not fully 'adult' in his perverse reliance on the safeguards of the incest myth, then the defective maturity of Hilde and Solness must derive – almost literally – from a regressive movement towards childhood as a condition of innocence, protected by social mores from violation. Kissing a thirteen-year-old 'dævelunge' (III.

449) – a child devil – is sexually quite safe, in a way that kissing a
sexually eligible adult devil is not; and, although the terrors of
sexuality are far less insistent in this play, the techniques of erotic
evasion are as complex and elaborate as those in *Little Eyolf*.
Solness, it appears, habitually seeks out the sexually safe relationship, which, by definition, eliminates the possibility of commitment or fulfilment – as in his manipulation of Kaja's youth against
Ragnar's youthful threat. Binding her sexually to him without
any genuine reciprocation, he enslaves her fiancé as well. Moreover, as he tells the doctor, his simulated 'affair' enables him to
luxuriate in the self-torture of allowing his wife to do him an
injustice. Sex enmeshed in guilt, and sex perverted into power.
Sterility, neurosis and incipient madness are the afflictions
which Solness heaps upon himself in the attempt to control the
flow of life, the order of nature, and the threat of youth. And
what Hilde offers him is an escape from the meshes of guilt and
the sickness of mind: relinquish youth to life, and fortify yourself
against it by becoming young again – by recapturing past conviction and strength and the qualities of a Viking conscience. To
enter their Kingdom of Orangia is to recover the lost world of
innocent childhood – or, as Brian Johnston puts it, 'the heaven
that Solness and Hilde envisage clearly requires that they become
as little children'.[43] But I am not entirely convinced, as Johnston
is, that 'childishness' sheds all pejorative implications in their
strangely chaste eroticism. Ibsen's lovers are committed to an
impossible recreation of the circumstances of their original sexual
encounter which, at its most Romantically magnificent, promises
a Nietzschean redemption through reconstituted time:

> I taught them to work on the future and to redeem with their
> creation all that has been. To redeem what is past in man and
> to re-create all 'it was' until the will says, 'Thus I willed it: Thus
> I shall will it!' – this I call redemption and this alone I taught
> them to call redemption.'[44]

Johnston's quotation from *Zarathustra* may indeed clarify the
ideal intentions of Solness and Hilde. But their actual achievement is inseparable from the irony which emphasises the fallibility, without actually discrediting the splendour, of their impulse.
To put it crudely: time, turned ten years back, has the effect of
relocating Paradise in the nursery. For ideal, prelapsarian sexua-

lity, in the final analysis, makes Romantic nonsense of hun
consummations.

In few other plays are the tensions between Romantic and
counter-Romantic impulses more difficult to resolve – as if the
essential tone of The Master Builder were located in pulsation
itself, in the systole and diastole of magnificence and madness,
creation and destruction. It is a question, as always in Ibsen, of
striking a delicate balance between life-enhancing illusion and
regressive fantasy or, in the imagistic terms of the play, between a
Wordsworthian recreation of the child in the consciousness of the
adult and childishness as an evasion of responsible engagement in
life. Aline Solness is a gloss upon this central difficulty – a woman
for whom 'playing with dolls' is symptomatic of a frightening
withdrawal from reality. 'I carried them under my heart', she
cries of her nine burned homunculi. 'Like little unborn children'
(vii, 425). And she mourns the loss of the unborn – the eternally
potential – with an intensity quite absent from the memory of her
real children. She has never quite grown up, never quite come to
terms with experience; and her regressive childishness exists in
thematic tension with positive Romantic suggestions of youthful
self-renewal. Hilde's role is subject to the same Romantic/
counter-Romantic pulsation. Her sailor-suit and hat, her insouci-
ance, and the 'excited and slangy gallop'[45] of her speech all hint at
a coy girlishness in this woman of twenty-three. And Solness's
condescending manner, his teasing references to 'Princess Hilde
of Orangia' and his strange suggestion that she be accommodated
in one of the nurseries conspire with her to impose another aspect
of the incest-taboo upon a sexually threatening liaison. 'No, we
have no children', he tells her. 'But now you can be the child
while you're here' (378). She playfully accepts the part. 'Slept
well?' he inquires next day of the nursery inhabitant; and she
replies, 'Like a child in a cradle. Oh, I lay there and stretched
myself like . . . like a princess!' (396). Perhaps, as their relationship deepens, the return to childhood gradually sheds the cute
and the facetious. But even in Act iii the tonal pulsations between
high seriousness and baby-talk, animated conviction and dreamy
withdrawal persist as the basic rhythm of the play:

HILDE [animatedly]: . . . We two will do it together. And we'll
build the loveliest . . . quite the loveliest thing in all the
world.

133
·n

'de! Tell me what that is!
  *vith a smile, shakes her head a little, pouts,
  as though to a child*]: These master build-
  .y, very stupid people they are.
  ., of course they're stupid. But tell me what it is!
  .t is it that's quite the loveliest thing in all the world.
Which we two are to build together?
HILDE [*is silent for a moment and then says with an enigmatic
expression in her eyes*]: Castles in the air. (431)

The tone, it seems to me, is quite deliberately located midway
between creative illusion and embarrassment, rather like the 'silly
symphony for two' that brings the curtain down on Osborne's
Look Back in Anger.
 Of course, what has happened to the Romantic archetypes and
images associated with the 'cosmology of two' since Ibsen is their
passing – intact but sentimentalised – into the conventions of the
popular love-song; and there is obviously the danger of filtering
Hilde's 'castles in the air' through a sensibility already permeated
with lyrical celebrations of rooms with a view, high above mountain and sea – a Paradise for two, far removed from the ordinary
world, which blends the heavenly and the domestic in varying
proportions. It is all too easy to miss the intensity of Hilde's vision.
But the fanciful and the sentimental have always been one
hair's-breadth removed from *lengslens vei, Sehnsucht,* and the
high Romantic quest for infinitude; and the interpenetration of
the sublime and the ridiculous seems to me Ibsen's most
audacious and carefully calculated achievement in *The Master
Builder.* A delicate irony – touching, perhaps, on parody every
now and then – envelops the Romantic structures of the play, so
that what finally happens to Solness, totally absorbed in a world
of private mythic symbols, becomes inextricable from the double-
vision and the crucial tonal ambiguities. 'Solness's climbing the
tower is an action which makes him great,' writes a modern
critic, 'and that greatness is worth more than life itself.'[46] The
first half of the statement is incontrovertible – Solness's purely
human achievement, conquering fear and vertigo, is an exhilarating dramatic experience; but what the rest of the sentence
claims so confidently is precisely what Ibsen's irony calls in
doubt – the denial of life in what is also a quest for immortality,
impossibility and transcendence. The Kingdom of Orangia, the

castles in the air, the cosmology of two – all these analogues of
Paradise are *symbols* of reality but not reality itself, just as Hilde's
thrilling demand that Solness climb the spire is an *objective
correlative* for the sexual experience but not sex itself. What
neither of them acknowledges in their Romantic questing is that
these myths are so structured as to suspend life – and especially the
demands of sexuality – in an ethereal limbo. And the consequence
of climbing as loftily as one's Romantic architecture towers above
the 'alminnelig, riktig kongerike' (III, 452) – 'the realm of the mundane and the ordinary' – is an ascent into the no man's land of
stasis, from which all human vitality has been purged and
drained away. There is ultimately no distinction between experience at the one and experience at the other extreme of the
Romantic spectrum – Paradise at the summit of the spire, and the
abyss at the bottom of the quarry. Both are deadly, although in
different ways. And Solness, striving for an impossibility beyond
existence, ironically confirms the morbidity that is inseparable
from his 'greatness'.

The image of Solness finally restored to heroic Viking splendour depends very largely on one's view of Hilde. Is she the
archaic Valkyrie spirit redeeming the sickly Christian conscience,
or a post-adolescent Romantic for whom the Viking saga is
merely sensational and who demands the impossible to satisfy her
need for the impossible lover? Does Solness's fate confirm the
apotheosis she envisions in those final cries of rapture, or does it
merely recapitulate her erotically terrifying and thrilling dream
of falling? In administering to the *man*, she clearly achieves the
sort of human transformation that the cosmology of two provides
– not as an impossibility, but as the creative influence of one personality upon another: she opens the door behind which he had
locked and bolted himself against life, assuages the guilt of a
flayed and lacerated conscience, and frees him from perverting
his sexuality for expedient ends. But, in urging her liberated man
towards godhead, she etherealises the most vital aspect of their
relationship – its affirmation of life, sexuality, and spiritual
vigour – into illusions that deny its human reality: *eros* without
thanatos, a timeless existence beyond death, and youth forever
freed from change and therefore from the maturity of adult
experience. She clings to this mythology to the end, but her
dream can survive only by ignoring reality; and there is something
deeply pathetic in her denial of Solness's death at the end of the

play, in her strenuous effort to keep the triumphant vision alive.
She refuses to *look* at what happens, rivets her gaze upwards, and
'forstenet' (482) – like one petrified – insists on the impossible in
full sight of its impossibility. 'I can't see him up there now', she
whispers to Ragnar, in what is probably the most poignant line in
the play. And the only way she can protect herself against the
horror is to recede into the world of her imagination, roused once
again to 'fortvilet triumf' (ibid.) – confused triumph – where life
remains terribly exciting and death has no dominion. For all
Hilde's cries of intensity and exhilaration, there remains an
undertone of deep and compassionate sadness for the self-de-
luded dreamers whose spendid visions fail, in the last analysis, to
console mankind against the death of children, the apathy of
God, the loss of happiness, the fear of age and death, and the
limitations of human capacities. If castles in the air had solid
foundations, and if Paradise were inherent in an earthly humanism, then, perhaps, in Brand's imagistic vision, man could build
bridges between the worlds of flesh and spirit, the mundane and
the divine. But in *The Master Builder*, with its empty nurseries
and uninhabitable houses and illusory castles, the impossibility of
constructing such an innovative architecture underscores the
tragedy of Solness's and Hilde's romaticism.

III

When We Dead Awaken, too, has its architectual structures – its
castles and towers, and houses which are decidedly *not* homes for
people to be happy in. There is the opulent Rubek mansion in the
city, where Maja feels stifled as in a dank cage, and the villa on
the Taunitzer See, where she feels herself to be a mere adjunct to
the general affluence to which her husband has sold his soul. The
villa stands on the site of the little farmhouse, now razed to the
ground to make way for parklands but remembered by Irene as a
place of beauty where she and Rubek might have lived in joy. At
the end of the play, in typical fashion, the two of them try to
redeem their erotic failure in a dimension of existence beyond all
human possibility: they ascend, if not to one of Hilde Wangel's
castles in the air, then to a very similar analogue of Eden, to glory
and splendour and light, up the Peak of Promise (with its echo of
some 'promised land') to the very pinnacle of the mountain-

tower – 'Opp til forjettelsens tinde! . . . opp til tårnets tinde' (III. 600). The Paradisal architecture is all too familiar, counterpointed not only by desolate or forfeited human habitations, but by the anti-Romantic architecture of the bestial: the ramshackle 'castle' among the rocks, where kings' daughters once copulated with mythical bear-men and where Ulfheim promises Maja a whole summer of sexual gratification. And when she responds to his 'castle' as 'den gamle svinestien' (596) – 'that old pigsty' – he offers her romance less brutally carnal, but no less physical, in the fallen world of human sexuality. It is an invitation framed in the echoing phrases of The Master Builder's romanticism:

> ULFHEIM: I can offer you a castle. . . .
> MAJA [points to the hut]: On the style of that?
> ULFHEIM: It hasn't collapsed yet.
> MAJA: And all the glory of the world perhaps?
> ULFHEIM: A castle, I said. . . . (VIII, 292)

Romanticism, perhaps – but a carefully qualified romanticism. Ulfheim's castle stands midway between the impossible glory of 'forjettelsens tinde' and the animal squalor of 'den gamle svinestien', while also lacking the material vulgarity – the gilded walls – of the mansions she hates. What he offers seems very human, very readily accessible. But the way down the ravine into the world of men is only minimally less dangerous than the way up to Eden. Up or down, the same mountain-track is 'en dødsens vei' (III. 598) – a path of death – whether it leads to mortal sexuality in the castles men construct in the abyss, or to seraphic sexuality in the metaphysical castles on the heights of splendour. With Maja in his arms, Ulfheim clambers down the difficult dødsens vei to patch up their tattered lives; and Rubek and Irene, hand in hand, climb up the snowfields and through the mist towards their consummation in a world beyond life. The cosmologies of two in When We Dead Awaken are neither antithetical versions of experience, nor opposed strategies of consciousness. They are mirror images of each other, obverse likenesses, Ibsen's final and most complex juxtaposition of related responses, Romantic and counter-Romantic, to the existential problems of sexuality and death, the quest for freedom and assurances of permanence, and man's desperate need for completion and wholeness in soul-kinship with his lover.

'I feel a deep . . . a tormenting need of having somebody near who is really close to me', cries Rubek; (VIII, 268); and in this and other analyses of his grief he is possibly the most articulate of Ibsen's studies in Romantic alienation – a man forced to endure the consequences of momentous choice in appalling loneliness, searching in life for the fallible guarantees of imperishable value once located in art. 'I need to live with somebody who can fulfil me . . . make me complete . . . be as one with me in everything I do', (ibid.) he tells Maja, defining the 'cosmology of two' in terms quite unlike Catherine Earnshaw's, but with an identical conception of soul-partnership in which the lover plays God by redeeming man from his sense of cosmic nothingness. As the divinely inspirational muse to the artist, so the perfect woman must enter into creative union with her lover. But Maja is no longer necessary to Rubek, and never was. Her name may have the archetypal connotations of sensual life and the erotic; and yet she is boring and trivial – life without spiritual substance, sexuality subject to change. In his unhappy marriage, Rubek realises the disastrous nature of his choice, which, at its most schematic, recalls the impossible alternatives in Yeats's poem 'The Choice':

> The intellect of man is forced to choose
> Perfection of the life, or of the work,
> And if it take the second must refuse
> A heavenly mansion, raging in the dark.[47]

The point, perhaps, is that perfection is not of this world and that neither alternative can possibly ensure the paradisal mansion. But, having once chosen perfection of the work, Rubek is forced to endure the consequences of vanity and remorse – the sacrifice of love and life's happiness in a sexual relationship with Irene to the cold idealism of art. The irony, of course, is that, in dissociating his ideal from the inspirational passions of life, he has merely desecrated his work and dehumanised his living muse, Irene. Art without life, as Wilson Knight puts it, proves sterile; and life without art – his attempt to remedy the consequences of his choice by marrying Maja – proves empty.[48] Rubek is powerless to reconcile these antinomies, powerless – in terms of his real and symbolic relationship with the two women – to restore Irene to life, or to rediscover the principle of artistic creativity in his desiccated union with Maja. His most recent art-works reflect this failure: a

series of brutish portrait-busts which mocks the 'mob' who com-
missions them, leaving Rubek with the sense of having forfeited
his integrity to gain the world. Cynicism, misanthropy and a consciousness of terrible failure are the symptoms of his disappointed
quest for perfection in life and art; and the play opens with his
awareness that to choose life above art is merely to repeat the
nature of his original mistake:

> I've come to realize that to seek for happiness in idle pleasure is
> not for me. Life isn't like that for me and my kind. I must keep
> on producing . . . creating work after work . . . until my dying
> day. [*With an effort.*] That's why I can't get on with you any
> longer, Maja. Not with you alone.   (VIII, 271)

Life sacrificed to art, or art to life: there is no way out of the
impasse, no redemption for the spiritually dead. His 'cosmology
of two' with Maja has proved disastrously ineffectual – an image of
marital incompatibility which denies every creative impulse of the
Romantic solution. Neither completes the other. Neither sustains
the physical demands for happiness, nor the metaphysical vision
of wholeness. A desperate sense of *change* hangs over their
marriage, an awareness of time passing aimlessly by, of relationships lapsing into a state of terminal boredom, of age advancing
and beauty wasting, of alteration in all the familiar things of life:
'Men herregud, – hvem kunne også ane at allting skulle ha for-
vandlet seg så forferdelig her hjemme!' (III, 568) – 'But good God,
– who could possibly have imagined that everything would
have changed so horribly here at home!" Marriage and affluence
have obviously changed Maja for the worse in a world where *forvandling* and *forandring* – 'change' and 'transformation' – govern
all. But it is in Rubek's ruined masterpiece, his cancelled vision of
Resurrection, that the Land without Paradise and man's fallen
state – mired in guilt and mortality – are most appallingly
envisioned:

> In the foreground, beside a spring – as it might be here – sits a
> man weighed down with guilt. He cannot quite break free from
> the earth's crust. I call him remorse for a forfeit life. He sits
> there dipping his fingers in the rippling water – to wash them
> clean. He is racked and tormented by the thought that he will
> never, never succeed. Never in all eternity will he win free to

e life of the resurrection. He must remain forever
in his hell.   (VIII, 279)

'The life of the resurrection' – 'oppstandelsens liv' (III, 590) – eludes
precise paraphrase. It implies the sublimation of mortal passion
into imperishable forms of art, a metamorphosis of the sexual
into the sacred, flesh into spirit, *eros* into *agape.* The idea is
expressed most articulately through the extraordinary vision
carved into the marble; and what Rubek and Irene strive to enact
through their own 'awakening' is the symbolism of art which
defies all human equivalence, which holds impossibility in the
stasis of eternal form. It takes two separate descriptions of the
'Resurrection Day' statue to encompass the multiple impossibili-
ties of Rubek's Romantic yearning:

> This waking girl was to be the world's noblest, purest, most
> perfect woman. . . . I wanted to create my vision of how the
> pure woman would wake on Resurrection Day. Not wondering
> at things new and unfamiliar and unimagined, but filled with a
> holy joy at finding herself unchanged – a mortal woman – in
> those higher, freer, happier realms, after the long and dream-
> less sleep of death. [*Speaking softly.*] That is how I created her.
> Created her in *your* image, Irene.   (VIII, 259)

Not only is the marmoreal woman–child to be the 'cunning'st
pattern of excelling Nature' – pure Platonic form – but she is to
awake, miraculously, from innocence into transcendence, as if
bypassing the whole world of human experience. She is to be
transformed, 'uforvandlet' (III, 578) – unchanged – from mortal
into immortal existence, from the world into Paradise, without
shedding her human identity and without suffering the consequences of the Fall, 'jordlivs opplevelser' (589) – 'the life of
earthly experience' – with all its filth and ugliness and impurity.

> My vision to Resurrection – the loveliest, most beautiful image
> I could think of – was of a pure young woman, untainted by the
> world, waking to light and glory, and having nothing ugly or
> unclean to rid herself of.   (VIII, 278)

It is a composite image of nearly every Romantic symbol in the
sequence: *eros* without *thanatos;* the 'child' as an emblem of

immortality and divinity; an analogue of Eden, static and imperishable in its inhuman perfection; the impossible given mythic form. It is that thing, both dead and deathless, which the Romantic visionary interposes between his anxious experience of life and his desperate search for permanence in the midst of process and death.

We should not read *When We Dead Awaken* as Ibsen's rejection of *all* art, argues James Hurt; for 'Rubek's art is a false art, not a means of "seeing" life but a defence against it.'[49] This is surely true. But what the play investigates most profoundly, it seems to me, is not 'true' art or 'false' art but that specifically Romantic attitude to art as creative solution to life's dilemma, a substitute religion in which a god-like creator locates the redemptive hopes of a now effete Christian dispensation. Not only is Rubek's masterpiece of sculptural art a transcendent religious vision, but the very process of creation becomes 'en andakt' (588) – a devotional rite – an act of worship in which the divinely inspired artist shapes human meaning out of inanimate matter:

> IRENE: . . . But that statue in wet, living clay . . . *it* I loved. As out of that raw and shapeless mass gradually there emerged a living soul, a human child. That was *our* creation, *our* child. *Mine*, and *yours*.
> RUBEK [*heavily*]: It was. In spirit and in truth.   (VIII, 276)

Images of conception, of foetal growth and parturition, coexist with echoes of the Creation, the compounding of dust and spirit into the new-made Adam. And, if the living child is a *human* answer to man's need for an existence beyond finite mortality, then the art-'child' is Rubek and Irene's *ideal* answer to that existential demand. Out of his creative impulse the artist fashions his own divinity, an act of projection in which the self finds permanent value in the artefact itself, in what Yeats calls 'the artifice of eternity'.[50] 'It is his "private religion"', writes Ernest Becker of the artist. 'Its uniqueness gives him personal immortality; it is his own "beyond" and not that of others.'[51] It also offers man godhead as in no other comparable human activity. Of all the Romantic types in Ibsen's world – the transcendentalists and Napoleons, virtuosos and Promethean rebels – Rubek is the epitome: the artist as hero, saviour, genius, creator and supreme individualist – 'a divinity', as Lilian Furst describes the figure, 'endowed like God himself with the power of creation, for all art is, according to Schelling, a direct reflection of the absolute act of creation and consequently an absolute self-affirmation'.[52] It is this aspect of the Romantic personality, with its promise of personal and cultural redemption, that Ibsen finally measures against the humanity that must be sacrificed to the ideal.

'Jeg var kunstner, Irene' (III, 578) – 'I was an artist, Irene' – says Rubek in defence and explanation of his past predicament; and the Romantic implications of this excuse become tragically clear. To be an artist, to create perfection out of the raw material of life, he felt compelled to purify and refine life itself until it approximated to that state 'out of Nature' where all gross imperfections are purged away – mortal flesh, impure human passion, man's fallen nature. The idea is a familiar one in Romantic poetry: before the artist can enter the Paradise of art – Yeats's Byzantium, the artifice of eternity, the world of the Grecian Urn – he must shed his humanity; his heart, 'sick with desire and fastened to a dying animal',[53] must be consumed in the fires of holiness and all sensual dross burned away. For he cannot be both man *and* artist. And, trapped between the contrary demands of intense passion for Irene and his search for transcendence in the world of process, Rubek chooses to renounce sexuality, children and mortal pleasure for the absolute reassurances of art. He may be driven out of his mind by desire for Irene; but, as the human correlative for a vision to be created in her image, her perfection must be protected against the realities of sex:

> For me you became a sacred being, untouchable, a thing to worship in thought alone. I was still young then, Irene. I was obsessed with the idea that if I touched you, if I desired you sensually, my mind would be profaned and I would be unable to achieve what I was striving to create.   (VIII, 259)

This is what it means to be down among the dead men: to put the imperishable images of art above humanity and life. Nor is it merely the tragic mistake of a naïve Romantic youth, as Rubek suggests. The old artist clings all the more tenaciously to his mythic structure, still believing in its truth; and with ominous insistence he looks at Irene as 'den levendegjorte oppstandelse' (III, 586) – Resurrection given human form, transfiguration incarnate. As he had once created his vision of Resurrection in Irene's image, so he will now recreate Irene in the image of his marble masterpiece. In his new 'cosmology of two' with Irene, infused with all the magical properties of art, Rubek now sees salvation from his hopeless marriage to a merely mortal woman. In Irene's physical presence realism strains against its boundaries to dramatise the living death. She is a sculptural form invested with attenuated breath, life sacrificed to art, an inversion of the Pygmalion–Galatea myth[54] in which human passion is petrified when dead clay is invested with soul. 'I gave you my young, living soul', she cries. 'Then I was left standing there, all empty within. Soul-less. . . . That's what I died of, Arnold' (VIII, 262). This indictment re-echoes from play to play, Galatea's cry against Pygmalion's essential lovelessness and his inability to reciprocate passion – Rosmer's offence against Rebekka, Borkman's murder of Ella Rentheim's ability to love, Rubek's destruction of Irene's soul. If the creative principle which turns stone into flesh in the Ovidian myth is Venus, goddess of erotic desire, then the discreative principle in the anti-myth is the denial of Venus, the flight from sexuality and the sacrifice of human need to ascetic idealism. This is what Irene rails against most bitterly: Rubek's 'I-am-an-artist' argument, which she rejects as 'slapp og sløv' (III. 590) – 'flaccid and apathetic'; for when art becomes an insulating device rather than a heightening of life, then the creative justification of the artist merely degenerates into self-exoneration and an excuse for personal fallibility. She condemns him for being an artist and not a man, and the vehemence of her frustrated sexuality and the justice of her accusation carry great conviction. But, like Ella Rentheim, Irene also protests too much. No woman of flesh and blood can possibly be petrified without her acquiescence in the process. And, just as Nora, in Ibsen's prime example of this axiom, plays a willing capitulant to the social and sexual roles imposed upon her by male sovereignty, so Irene participates in the romanticism that destroys them both. Like Nora, she acknowledges 'en dødsens brøde imot meg selv' (590) – 'a mortal sin against myself' – tantamount to suicide; and she defines that sin as her throwing away of 'human destiny' – motherhood and joy – in order to serve the artist in Rubek. But there is something devious in her rhetoric, something equally 'slapp og sløv' in its suppression of her collaboration and her dedication to the idea of 'Resurrection' no less intense than

Rubek's. Trapped, as *he* is, in the hiatus between sexual desire
and ascetic transcendence, Irene's choice determines her destiny
as an autonomous and voluntary decision:

> Yes, I served you with all the throbbing blood of my youth. . . .
> I fell at your feet and served you, Arnold! . . . I offered myself
> wholly and completely to your gaze . . . [*Quieter.*] And never
> once did you touch me. . . . And yet, if you *had* touched me, I
> think I'd have killed you on the spot. I always had a sharp
> needle by me. Hidden in my hair . . . .   (VIII, 258)

Her response seems at best erratic, at worst neurotic. But it is
perfectly consistent with her motive for participating in the
romanticism of artistic creation. 'My going with you', she admits
in an extraordinary phrase, 'was my childhood's resurrection'
(259) – 'min barnealders oppstandelse' (III. 578). And what the
phrase would seem to imply is her recovery of radical innocence in
artistic union with Rubek, the suspension of process in redeeming
the past, and the discovery of self-perfection in the stasis of art.[55]
Again, the regressive patterns of *The Master Builder* are invoked
– their escape into a golden age of childhood innocence from the
compromising demands of adult sexuality. It is not surprising
that Irene, whether literally or metaphorically, should sleep in
her various marriage beds with a fine sharp dagger beside her;
and it is fully in keeping with the contradiction at the heart of her
nature that she should have 'obliterated' herself after the completion of the statue, perpetuating their evasion of sex in the
name of sacrifice. Her subsequent career of vengeful self-humili-
ation and debasement can no more be attributable to Rubek's
erotic denials than Nora's pirouetting like a Neapolitan doll can
indict her husband as a chauvinist. The crucial distinction between the two women, however, is that one is vitally alive and the
other dead and therefore beyond creative possibility. The Nora
who takes off her doll's dress, transfigures herself from a toy into a
woman, is an heroic paradigm of the liberated spirit in Ibsen – the
self-creating being who discovers in her own capacity for change
the god within, the vivifying force which Ovid called Venus. But
Irene, like the damned in Sartre's *Huis Clos,* is dead beyond all
hope of change, and therefore incapable of creative, existential
choice. With dreadful clarity, she sees only the irremediable, the
loss of children, and her eternal exclusion – like the statue on the

stream's edge – from process, flux and generation. Even to acknowledge the perversity of past choices and awake from the dead is merely to recognise – too late – the operation of the Romantic paradox at its most cruelly ironic:

> IRENE: We only see what we have missed when . . . [*She breaks off.*]
> RUBEK [*looks questioningly at her*]: When . . . ?
> IRENE When we dead awaken.
> RUBEK [*shakes his head sadly*]: And what then do we see?
> IRENE: We see that we have never lived.   (VIII, 285–6)

The basic structure of *When We Dead Awaken* is a highly formalised grouping and regrouping of a quartet into a series of alliances and 'cosmologies', all searching, through their realignments, for some solution to the failure of relationships and their inability to assuage the human wound – the fear of death and sexuality, man's loneliness and incompletion, emptiness and despair. Marriage, the most conventional of these cosmologies, becomes a study in alienation and unhappiness, a yoking together of incompatible beings in a spiritual union where neither satisfies the other's need for wholeness. And yet the love-relationship in which a creative and fulfilling alliance might have been possible proves no less sterile and deadly in its attempt to possess an artificial paradise. A stultifying marriage and memories of an erotically frustrated 'episode': Rubek's union with Maja is intolerable, and his union with Irene a disastrous confusion of life's priorities. But under the pressure of analysis and exhumation, the patterns begin to change. The *pas de quatre* regroups into reflecting cosmologies, 'marriages' which impel the protagonists – literally and metaphorically – upwards into the dangerous regions of aspiration, or downwards into the impenetrable forests where brutality lurks. Either way, however, their search is for the promise of life's satisfaction, however one assigns meaning to that insistent demand for 'all verdens herlighet' (III, 592) – 'all the glory of the world' – with its suggestions of diabolical temptation, fantastic splendour and sexual epiphany. The phrase, loosened from its original context in Matthew 4:8–9, is clearly part of Rubek's playfully blasphemous language of sexual flirtation, the inevitable promise made (and usually broken) to all his women, who understand the temptation in varying degrees of literal and metaphorical significance.[56] 'Perhaps you have taken me up a pretty high mountain, Rubek', Maja says to him. 'But you haven't shown me all the glory of the world.' 'Never satisfied!' he retorts (VIII, 270). The interchange, however witty, is heavy with insinuation, with the sort of unspoken accusation which eventually drives Maja to seek the 'glory' with Ulfheim: the purely carnal satisfaction of life in their earthly castle in the valley. Irene's invocation of the phrase is equally impassioned, but her vision of 'glory' is all radiance – an image of flesh-become-spirit, a flash of desire sublimated into divine revelation. Sexual surrender and religious ecstasy are inseparable in her memory of yielding, like a fallen spirit, to the ultimate temptation:

> IRENE [*smiles as though lost in memory*]: I once saw a marvellously beautiful sunrise.... High, high up on a soaring mountain peak. You lured me up there, and promised me I should see all the glory of the world, if only I .... I did as you said. Followed you up to the heights. And there I fell on my knees ... and worshipped you. And served you. [*Is silent for a moment; then speaks softly.*] Then I saw the sunrise.   (283)

Like Hilde's thrilling response to harps in the air or Hedda's cry of 'befrielse' (III. 431) – that ineffable sensation of release as she envisions Løvborg's death – so Irene speaks in the metaphors of ecstasy and sexual joy, a 'lived-through' memory of radiance which invests spirit with all the 'glory' of the flesh. James Joyce, surprisingly, speaks of Irene's 'aloofness from passion'.[57] But passion is what ultimately impels them all towards self-definition in the existence of their lovers. And the 'cosmologies of two', in their final recombination of living elements, dramatise a universe of antinomies in which the contrary impulses towards passionate self-completion and wholeness remain eternally compelling, but eternally unreconciled: *eros* and *agape,* desire fulfilled and sublimated, the pleasures of the body and the necessities of soul, all the glory of the world and all the glory of Paradise.

By the time their paths cross on the *dødsens vei*, the extreme varieties of passion have been tempered and refined, and the quests for glory revealed in all their splendour and limitations. Stark antitheses have been complicated, and there are no easy choices between alternative visions of coping with life. What remains at the play's end, as Wilson Knight puts it, is a 'quartet of positive powers, but a difference in value, or level'.[58] Ulfheim's bestial associations with goatish sexuality and satyrism gradually yield to the human in his relationship with Maja. And, as he wakens her to physical life, so she tempers his carnality until, by exchanging confidences and sexual sorrows, they arrive at something approaching tenderness and compassion. In a world of infidelity and betrayal by lovers, of terrible disappointment and the failure of glory, they find solace in each other and in the hope of salvaging what remains of their lives. To accept each other 'fritt og freidig, – som de vi selv er!' (III, 597) – 'free and unashamed, – for what we really are!' – is to make a genuine commitment, even if what they really are to each other is *eros* untroubled by the metaphysics of spirit. 'You with your goat's legs, eh!' 'And you with your –.' The crude biological order may not encompass 'menneskeliv' (597) – 'human existence' – in its entirety, but it cannot be denied without loss. For all its incompleteness and deficiency, the passionate earthly life of the Maja–Ulfheim cosmology offers one possibility of survival in the Land without Paradise: an immersion in experience and the body, dignified by the illusion of freedom from existential anxiety that such sporadic glory confers. 'I am free! I am free! I am free!' Maja sings on their descent to the castle in the lowlands. But there is a fine irony in her confidence. No one on the *dødsens vei* is free. To move into the abyss of process, sexuality and change is to embrace death as surely as to transcend life in mythical constructs of the Romantic imagination. For death, as Rubek and Irene discover, is the only absolute guarantee of freedom from deadliness itself.

Man's elusive quest for wholeness is a world of eternally unreconcilable antinomies, Yeats implies in one of his most poignant poems, is the supreme theme of art and song.[59] It is the predominating vision of the final act in *When We Dead Awaken*, when all attempts to define existence – 'oppstandelsens liv', 'jordliv', 'menneskeliv' – merely reveal the tragically incomplete condition of human life. There can be no synthesis for these people, no Third Kingdom, no midpoint between passionate flesh freed from spirit and passionate spirit freed from flesh. Although each couple awakens to desire, their definitions of existence are complementary aspects of life's integrity, factors with common denominators in an equation which frustrates solutions. Like Maja and Ulfheim, Irene and Rubek awake to passion. But, for them, to embrace desire is to relinquish a lifetime of self-protective ploys and erotic evasions, to accept process and the consequences of choosing life. To be 'dead' as they have been 'dead' is, paradoxically, to have been exempt from dying – rather like Beckett's damned in their deathless kingdoms. This is why Irene has no need to kill Rubek for his offences against her and their 'child'. The dead cannot die. But to *rise* from the dead, to *awaken,* is to expose the Self to 'jordliv' (III. 599) – earthly life – with its glories and wonders, change and erotic desire. This is the central challenge that Rubek and Irene must face when, at the close of the play, the 'dead' finally awaken: how to reconcile 'det brennende begjær' (ibid.) – 'the burning passions' of earth-love which Rubek experiences as pulsation in the blood and the cosmos, earth-life lived to the full – with their equally compelling visions of resurrection and spiritual transfiguration which transcend passion even as they incorporate it. 'We are free!' cries Rubek. 'And there is still time for us to live, Irene!' (VIII, 296). And so we watch them, in pathos and irony, enacting their freedom and their sense of life's supreme meaning. The *dénouement* is inevitable, already foreshadowed by the images in which they conceive of each other: Resurrection incarnate, the restitution of childhood, the agent of a glory beyond the flesh. They confirm their visions more dramatically than any of Ibsen's other Romantics. They enter the world of metaphor, not 'poetically', as Keats enters the Urn-world or Yeats Byzantium, but by moving physically into Paradise, by enacting literally the mythical scenario shaped by the artistic vision out of the realities of experience. They *become* the art-work, 'Resurrection Day', with all the accretions of meaning that cling to it from Rubek's impossible conception of unfallen and immortal flesh, to Irene's ecstatic sublimation of erotic desire into divine epiphany. The roaring winds that chill the bone and send down the avalanche are merely sound effects for their dramatic poem, 'forspillet til oppstandelsens dag' (III, 598) – 'the prelude to Resurrection Day'. And the landscape of death becomes a stage-set for re-enacting their experience of a glory and a radiance out of time, beyond *jordliv* and *menneskeliv* towards that final consummation: the marriage of souls in a *consummatum est* of art:

IRENE: . . . Up into the glory and splendour of the light. Up to the promised peak!

RUBEK: Up there will we celebrate our wedding feast, Irene – my
    beloved!
IRENE [*proudly*]: Then the sun can look down upon us, Arnold.
RUBEK: All the power of light can look down upon us. And of the
    darkness, too. [*Takes her hand.*] Will you come with me
    now, my bride of grace?
IRENE [*as though transfigured*]: Gladly and willingly, my lord
    and master . . . right to the very top of the tower, lit by the
    rising sun. (VIII, 297)

And so they ascend. And so they are annihilated. What we finally
witness, in Wilson Knight's excellent description of the central
experience of the play, is

> an exploration in dramatic terms of the inmost enigma of art,
> at once sex-flooded and asexual; physically sex-prompted, and
> yet, at the moment of artistic living, utterly quiescent, the sex-
> ual energies no longer specifically located, and indeed seeming-
> ly absent, but in fact so richly percolating the whole physique
> that it becomes, in Nietzsche's phrase, 'light as a bird', enjoying
> intimations of etheric life.[60]

But 'etheric life' is not *jordliv* – and neither, in isolation, is a full
expression of *menneskeliv*. Nor is 'artistic living' humanly possible, inhering as it does exclusively in metaphors, in visions of
spiritual union with brides of grace or 'den kvinne jeg drømmer å
se i deg' (III. 600) – the woman one dreams of seeing in human
form. Art and life, eternal desire and mortal passion, may enhance each other. But to inhabit the artifice or eternity, to
immortalise the self in art, is merely to ensure that one never *lives*
'the glorious, marvellous, mysterious life on earth' (VIII. 295),
however imperfect, however tormented with anxiety and fear, or
limited by the restraints imposed by life on dreams of freedom, or
wracked by yearning for all the glories of the world.

Notes

1. Shelley's comment on Calderón's *Cabellos de Absalon,* in Mario Praz, *The
    Romantic Agony,* 2nd end (London, 1970) p. 118.
2. Downs, *Ibsen: The Intellectual Background,* p. 180.
3. See Freud's analysis of Rebekka West in 'Some Character-Types met with in

Psychoanalytic Work' (1916), repr. in McFarlane, *Ibsen: A Critical Anthology.*

4. Cf. R. E. L. Masters, *Patterns of Incest* (New York, 1970) p. 80.
5. For other views of incest in Romantic literature, see Eino Railo, *The Haunted Castle* (London, 1927); Praz, *the Romantic Agony;* and Russell Goldfarb, *Sexual Repression and Victorian Literature* (Lewisburg, Pa., 1970).
6. George Steiner, *In Bluebeard's Castle* (London, 1971) p. 25.
7. Praz, *The Romantic Agony,* p. 73.
8. Act and line references to *Cain* derive from Truman Steffan's edition, *Lord Byron's 'Cain': Twelve Essays and a Text with Variants and Annotations* (Austin, Tex., 1968).
9. Emily Brontë, *Wuthering Heights,* ed. David Daiches (Harmondsworth, 1965) p. 122.
10. J. Hillis Miller, *The Disappearance of God* (Cambridge, Mass., 1963) p. 175.
11. Becker, *The Denial of Death,* p. 162.
12. Ibid., p. 157.
13. Ibid., p. 162, 161. The 'cosmology of two' is Otto Rank's phrase.
14. Abrams, *Natural Supernaturalism,* p. 245.
15. Becker, *The Denial of Death,* pp. 162, 163–4.
16. From Søren Kierkegaard, *The Concept of Dread,* quoted in W. H. Auden, *The Enchafèd Flood; or The Romantic Iconography of the Sea* (New York, 1967; first published 1950) pp. 75–6.
17. Becker, *The Denial of Death,* p. 163.
18. Otto Rank, *Das Inzest-Motiv in Dichtung und Sage* (Leipzig, 1912); Kerans, in Bogard and Oliver, *Modern Drama.*
19. Lord Byron, *Selected Verse and Prose Works,* ed. Peter Quennell (London, 1959) p. 35.
20. Ibid., p. 248.
21. Becker, *The Denial of Death,* p. 163.
22. Kerans, in Bogard and Oliver, *Modern Drama,* p. 197.
23. Hurt, *Catiline's Dream,* p. 180.
24. Holtan, *Mythic Patterns,* p. 19.
25. Hurt, *Catiline's Dream,* pp. 8, 21–3.
26. Emily Brontë, *Wuthering Heights,* p. 122.
27. See Wordsworth's 'A Slumber Did My Spirit Seal'.
28. See Eric Solomon, 'The Incest Theme in *Wuthering Heights*', *Nineteenth Century Fiction,* xiv (1959) 83.
29. J. W. von Goethe, *The Sorrows of Young Werther,* Book ii, letter dated 14 December.
30. Emily Brontë, *Wuthering Heights,* p. 320.
31. Kerans, in Bogard and Oliver, *Modern Drama,* p. 194.
32. Becker, *The Denial of Death,* p. 166.
33. D. H. Lawrence, 'We Need One Another', in *Phoenix: The Posthumous Papers of D. H. Lawrence* (London, 1961) p. 193.
34. Ibid., pp. 193–4.
35. McFarlane, Introduction to *The Oxford Ibsen,* viii, 24.
36. G. B. Shaw, *Heartbreak House,* Act iii.

37. For radically diverse views of the play's *dénouement*, see Raphael's highly ironic reading in 'From *Hedda Gabler* to *When We Dead Awaken*: the Quest for Self-realization', *Scandinavian Studies*, XXXVI (1964), and Wilson Knight's reading of the play as an education in the values of spiritual righteousness in *Ibsen*, pp. 82–3.
38. Northam, *Ibsen: A Critical Study*, p. 215.
39. See Holtan, *Mythic Patterns;* Johnston, *The Ibsen Cycle;* Sandra Saari, 'Of Madness or Fame; Ibsen's *Bygmester Solness*', *Scandinavian Studies*, L (1978).
40. Lyons, *Ibsen: The Divided Consciousness*, p. 131.
41. Bradbrook, *Ibsen the Norwegian*, p. 128.
42. Dorothy Van Ghent, *The English Novel: Form and Function* (New York, 1953) p. 158.
43. Johnston, *The Ibsen Cycle*, p. 256.
44. Ibid., pp. 281–2.
45. Bradbrook, *Ibsen the Norwegian*, p. 127.
46. Saari, in *Scandinavian Studies*, L, 13.
47. W. B. Yeats, 'The Choice', in *Collected Poems*, p. 278.
48. Wilson Knight, *Ibsen*, p. 100.
49. Hurt, *Catiline's Dream*, p. 198.
50. W. B. Yeats, 'Sailing to Byzantium', in *Collected Poems*, p. 218.
51. Becker, *The Denial of Death*, p. 171. The entire section on 'The Creative Solution' is relevant.
52. Furst, *Romanticism in Perspective*, p. 67. See also J. B. Halstead, *Romanticism*, pp. 19,ff.
53. Yeats, 'Sailing to Byzantium', in *Collected Poems*, p. 218.
54. This mythic reading of *When We Dead Awaken* is suggested by Leo Lowenthal in 'Henrik Ibsen: Motifs in the Realistic Plays', *Literature and the Image of Man* (Boston, Mass., 1957).
55. There is an excellent discussion of the 'childhood' theme in Lyons, *Ibsen: The Divided Consciousness*, pp. 143–4.
56. Inga-Stina Ewbank discusses Ibsen's use of the language of Christ's temptation in great and illuminating detail in 'Ibsen's Dramatic Language as a Link between his "Realism" and his "Symbolism"', in Daniel Haakonsen (ed.) *Contemporary Approaches to Ibsen*, I (Oslo, 1965).
57. James Joyce, '*When We Dead Awaken*', *Fortnightly Review*, LXXIII (1900); repr. in McFarlane, *Ibsen: A Critical Anthology*, p. 176.
58. Wilson Knight, *Ibsen*, p. 104.
59. W. B. Yeats, 'After Long Silence', in *Collected Poems*, p. 301.
60. Wilson Knight, *Ibsen*, p. 102.

6 'High Romantic Words': Responsible Freedom and Tragic Joy in *The Lady from the Sea* and *Rosmersholm*

'Are Ibsen's principal works to be interpreted primarily as a sum of destructions aimed at scourging the lies and idolatries of an errant civilization, or do they in fact embody a positive philosophy at their core?'[1] Or, to rephrase Rolf Fjelde's crucial inquiry, is Ibsen no more than a black satirist of Romanticism, a negative visionary for whom freedom and joy – the central, life-affirming values of the Romantic – are mere delusions of a neurotic society hell-bent on evading commitment, sexual love, and the fleeting pleasures destined for the grave? The most stringent critics of Ibsen's vision, it seems to me, are not those whose dissenting views call in question his genius, but those genuine admirers for whom that genius is expressed most characteristically in destruction, ironic subversion of values, harsh judgements upon man's frailty, and an inability to place sexuality creatively in human experience. Acts performed in joy and impelled by love lead to the mill-race. The free self proclaims its autonomy in suicide. And life seeks its apotheosis in the Ice Church of the Romantic imagination, where death alone confirms the impossibility of the quest. Ibsen's last plays, writes James McFarlane,

> constitute a general declaration that great art is, and must inevitably be destructive: destructive on the one hand of all that is spurious, inauthentic, meretricious, degenerate; destructive on the other of the lives and happiness of those who are sacrificed to it. . . . What little there is in these plays of positive

asseveration is generally either naïvely superficial or ironically undermined[2]

– as in Erhart's affirmation of happiness in the *ménage à trois* with Fanny and Frida, or Maja's song of sexual freedom with Ulfheim. In Ibsen, Wilson Knight reiterates, the sexual passions are regularly slighted and one searches in vain for the values of 'life' against which to measure the manifest failures of the Ibsen protagonists. What we hope to find, he suggests, is

a full release and incorporation of the life-fire, and yet this cohabits ill with domesticity, especially when the life-fire is the romantic vision itself. The problem is not new; from Plato onwards it has forced answers in terms of art; and in so far as sex touches art or art sex there is hope.[3]

But the physical promptings of sexuality, Knight argues, remain forever unplaced; and he is driven to extrapolate from the failures of art and love the kind of positive counter-vision that resists dramatic life in Ibsen, rather like one reconstructing a temple from the ruins on a devastated site:

What is wanted is a state of being, such as that which Svanhild demanded of Falk, that corresponds to the purity and love-dreams of youth and all the delicate harmonies of art, and yet possesses, as Falk and Svanhild did not, a full, physical or in some sense super-physical, enjoyment, with, as in the biological order, a child; and after Ibsen's recent explorations there must be overtones of immortality.
It is a lot to ask.[4]

Given the habitual failure of Ibsen's protagonists to reconcile the Romantic love-dream with the realities of sex, the death of children, and the subordination of mortal life to the quest for immortality, this synthesis of positive values *does* seem much to ask for. But, unless one demands a burst of positive Ibsenism to manifest itself unequivocally in a definitive dramatic statement, it still remains possible to discover, even in the world of the last plays, a life-affirming albeit tragic resolution to the existential crises of Romanticism: the creation of value out of nothingness, the discovery of man's place in an empty universe, and an affirmation of freedom and joy redeemed by the moral temperament and saved from the chaos implicit in the search for an absolute freedom. The values of *The Lady from the Sea* and *Rosmersholm*, those plays which deal most insistently with the concepts of responsible freedom and tragic joy, may not conform to Wilson Knight's paradigm of positive Ibsenism. But, in valuing Ellida's accommodation to life's limitations in favour of the dream of Romantic freedom, Ibsen also values sanity above madness – just as Rebekka West, in accepting the moral consequences of her past actions, acknowledges the priority of cosmic order and justice above the chaos of licence masquerading as the liberal impulse. And yet those two plays have revealed more clearly than any others the determination of the modern temperament to see in Ibsen's *dénouements* nothing but failure and gloom, dismissible (because too glib) resolutions, or mock-heroic pretension meeting its just desert. As Rolf Fjelde points out, the positive ending of *The Lady from the Sea* has opened it to 'charges of artistic deficiency, of being somehow not *echt* Ibsen'[5] – defying, as it does, the stereotypical image of Ibsen as the prophet of doom, while affirming the bourgeois carp-pond of marriage and family and distressing those modern Romantics for whom the *dénouement* betrays the vigorous Romantic spirit, 'as if Catherine Earnshaw had turned from the moors and Heathcliff to the comfort of Thrushcross Grange'.[6] This, then, in the *impasse* in which Ibsen is trapped: as the dramatist of Romantic tragedy, he is merely destructive, anti-sex and anti-art; and, as the dramatist of existential resolutions to the Romantic dilemma, he is charged with imprisoning the Romantic spirit in the bourgeois parlour.[7] On the one hand: Ibsen the counter-Romantic. On the other: Ibsen the anti-Romantic. Somewhere in the evaluation, Ibsen the Romantic, the celebrant of life's realities, of freedom saved from licence, of a joy far deeper than pleasure, is obscured or lost. And it is to re-establish this image of Ibsen the Romantic that I turn, finally, to the *dénouements* of two 'middle' plays, two positive centres, variously dismissed as glib or tolerated as ironically discrediting the resolutions they posit.

I

Ordinary people, leading their bourgeois lives in a remote Norwegian backwater: *The Lady from the Sea* is the most 'Chekhovian' – which is to say, the most normative – of Ibsen's plays. There is no magnificence, no grand madness, no Faustian aspiration towards godhead. Its very romanticism is the middle-class malady of a whole chorus of nineteenth-century provincials, ladies of a highly-strung disposition with an inexpressible yearning for some Edenic condition, dimly remembered as a lost possibility, and vaguely hoped for as the ultimate release from boredom, lack of purpose, and a deeply unhappy sexual life. Chekhov's three sisters may be able to assign a specific geography to their Eden, but 'Moscow' is no less a dream-city of the Romantic fancy than the 'Paris' of Emma Bovary's fantasies. And Ellida Wangel's Bovary-ism, her desperate longing for the sea and the lover from the sea, expresses the quintessential spirit of a romanticism that has remained remarkably persistent in the literature of woman's psychology. 'Is there any way to hypostasize this spirit', asks Francis Fergusson, 'or to define it accurately? I doubt it. The late Paul Elmer pointed out that the literature of the last century is full of it, "the Demon of the Absolute" as he called it; but he did not succeed in making a very satisfactory description of it.'[8] George Steiner has defined that spirit as 'The Great "Ennui"', tracing through the cruelly trivialising small-'r' romanticism of Emma Bovary the great social and metaphysical issues of the Romantic dilemma – '*ennui,* a feeling of impotence in the face of political reaction and Philistine rule, a hunger for new colours, new shapes, new possibilities of nervous discovery, to set against the morose properties of bourgeois and Victorian modes'.[9] In varying degrees, all the women in *The Lady from the Sea* suffer the symptoms of this condition – frustration, resentment, claustro-phobia, an appetite for sensationalism – even if they cannot relate their specific unhappinesses to the larger cultural issues that make them exemplars of a European malaise. Ibsen's emphasis, moreover, is on psychic rather than social analysis – Romanticism as a potentially dangerous affliction of the soul, no less prevalent in the 1880s than in the 1980s, and as accurately diagnosed in Sainte-Beuve's review of *Madame Bovary* as in Erica Jong's por-trayal of the Romantic heroine:

> At last she is seized by a kind of disease; they call it a nervous condition, but it is like a nostalgia, a homesickness for an *unknown country.* [10]

She lives as if she were constantly on the brink of some great fulfillment. As if she were waiting for Prince Charming to take her away 'from all this'. All what? The solitude of living inside her own soul? The certainty of being herself instead of half of something else?[11]

Ellida diagnoses her own malady as 'denne dragende hjemve efter havet' (iii, 346) – 'this relentless undertow – this homesickness for the sea' (vii, 59); and the language of her Romantic yearning is permeated with the tones of a regressive nostalgia, dragging her from the delightful realities of a golden summer bathed in light and profuse with flowers, towards a private region of secret sorrows which negate present joy and present pleasures in dim forebodings of winter and death:

The joy . . . is a bit like the kind of joy we take in the long sunlit summer days. It contains a threat of the long dark days to come. And this threat casts its shadow over human joy . . . like a passing cloud that casts its shadow over the fjord. There it lay so bright and blue. Then all of a sudden . . .   (75)

Unlike the language of *Little Eyolf,* another play set in burgeoning summer and lush with growth and vegetation, there are no hysterical responses here to the law of change, no cries of fear, but a quiet awareness of death as the deepest spring of human melancholy, marring all joy with thoughts of inevitability. Seasonal change hangs over the entire action of the play: a sense of high summer already turning, of the last steamer leaving for the season, and seaways that will soon be locked. Only the sea seems to know no extremes of change or season or climate, no limits or limitations, no bonds of land-folks' responsibility to husband, children, or community. It lures Ellida, and its terrible attraction is that 'homesickness for an *unknown country*' which promises freedom from the processes of land-life, where the consequences of sexual love are sickly children that soon die, and where man is trapped in a round of marriage, copulation, birth and death. The inexhaustible dichotomies of sea and land – the boundless and the bounded, the formless and the fixed, the infinite and the finite – finally resolve, as in W. H. Auden's analysis of the Romantic iconography of the sea, into a central statement about man's ambiguous situation in the world:

Land is the place where people are born, marry, and have children, the world where the changing seasons create a round of different duties and feelings, and the ocean, by contrast, is the place where there are no ties of home or sex . . . so that to leave land and put out to sea can signify the freeing of the spirit from finite nature, its ascetic denial of the flesh, the determination to live in one-directional historical time rather than in cyclical natural time.[12]

Ellida's yearning may express itself in the language of middle-class neurosis, but it articulates – no less urgently than Hedda Gabler's – a desperate Romantic need to burst out of time into infinity, and out of nature into the supranatural. The dimension for which she yearns finds its correlative in the sea – not as some external force, but as the undertow of the mind, the deep-seated impulses of the psyche. And its significant attributes – 'det ukjente', 'det grenseløse og endeløse', 'det uoppnåelige' (III, 380) – are those same qualities of Paradise for which all Ibsen's Romantics yearn:

> ELLIDA: . . . But my mind . . . my thoughts . . . my desires and longings . . . these you cannot bind! They will go roving, ranging . . . out into the unknown . . . which I was made for . . . and which you have shut me away from!
> WANGEL [*quietly and sadly*]: I see it, Ellida! Step by step you are slipping away from me. This craving for the unattainable . . . for the limitless, for the infinite . . . will ultimately put your very mind in darkness.
> ELLIDA: Oh, yes, yes! I feel it! Like black soundless wings above me! (VII, 120)

What makes Ellida an infinitely more complex study in this aspect of Romanticism than, say, Madame Bovary is her inner division – a wonderfully lucid ability to evaluate her own Romantic impulses, and her agonising consciousness of slipping away into darkness and insanity. She speaks of having been made for the sea. But, in truth, she is an amphibian tragically 'at home' in neither element and caught, like so many of Ibsen's other protagonists, between equally terrifying and attractive impulses – contradictory needs for the human and the suprahuman, the mutable and the imperishable, the pleasurable and the necessary.

The 'halfness' of the mermaid's divided nature is located not only
in the sea-land dichotomy, but in the tension between Romanticism and reality, dramatised most brilliantly in what Rolf Fjelde
calls Ellida's psychic bigamy'[13] – her legal and binding land
marriage to a fallible and very ordinary man, and her mystic sea
marriage to a demonic and mysterious prince of darkness. There
is no question, for Ellida, of living within a single 'cosmology'. She
is committed to both: to land marriage, which satisfies her urgent
need for security but which negates her freedom, and to sea
marriage, which satisfies her Romantic yearning for an absolute
freedom but which provides no security whatever against the fears
of freedom itself. And linked to these two cosmologies is a corresponding series of sexual attitudes which relate to the central issue
raised, at the start of this chapter, by Wilson Knight: love as an
enduring value, and its place in the Ibsen world.

It is typical of Ibsen's heroine that her bigamy, unlike Anna
Karenina's for example, should be entirely psychic. Not only does
she shun all thoughts of adultery, unlike the other heroines of
high Romance, but she avoids all sex and has not slept with her
husband for three years. The anomalies proliferate. Anna Karenina abhors her husband while morally and spiritually dedicated
to the values of marriage, family and civilised decorum; Emma
Bovary, fleeing the boredom of marriage, discovers in her sexual
liaisons an equally tiresome and trivial form of pseudo-marriage;
but Ellida loves both her husband *and* the deeply satisfying
relationship she shares with him: 'Oh yes, I do . . . I have come to
love him with all my heart! That's what's so terrible . . . So inexplicable . . . So completely incomprehensible . . .!' (vii, 50). And
it is this consideration – the security that she feels in marriage, her
genuine love for her commonplace husband, and her sexual
indifference to the mystic lover – that makes *The Lady from the
Sea* so extraordinary a variation on a familiar Romantic theme.
But what is inexplicable and incomprehensible to Ellida is
nevertheless not absolutely so. The *play* is the context of her
dilemma; and it elucidates it by rational analysis, by dramatic
parallels which reveal a pervasive condition of soul with which an
entire community must come to terms, and by a thematic
juxtaposition of ideas which mirrors Ellida's fears and concerns.
Ballested, for example, that jack of a hundred different trades,
not only enacts his schizophrenic accommodation to each of his
professions, but actually defines the process of acclimatising the

self to its condition: 'I feel bound to the place', he says, 'by ties of time and custom' (31). He is, of course, the comic or parodic counterpart to Ellida's resolution; but the comedy does not necessarily discredit the positive enactment of identical concepts in other contexts. Time and custom may habituate, but it may also deaden – just as continuous change (from barber, to dancing master, to tourist-guide) may enliven but also fragment the sense of selfhood. There are no absolutes in this world; there is no possibility of legislating choices or assigning unequivocal value to existential decisions. 'Liberty', as Ibsen noted in his jottings for *The Wild Duck,* 'consists of giving the individual the right to liberate himself, each according to his personal needs' (VI, 431) – an idea so central to *The Lady from the Sea* as almost to shape its vision. A similar idea is also hinted at by that phrase of Arnholm's which both Fjelde and McFarlane have commented on:[14] 'tegn imot tegn' (III, 366) – 'sign against sign' – equally weighted alternatives in which contradictory truths are held in equilibrium. Conceptions of marriage are no less *tegn imot tegn,* images in which even the most positive values point towards a set of negative corrolaries. Just as Ballested's definition of accommodation 'cuts both ways', so marriage as defined by Lyngstrand – the play's arch-romantic – becomes, simultaneously, a composite of the marvellous and the suspect:

> LYNGSTRAND: . . . I think that marriage must be considered rather like a kind of miracle. The way a woman gradually comes to be more and more like her husband. . . .
>
> BOLETTE: And the things a man acquires by reading and study – perhaps you think they too somehow pass over to his wife?
>
> LYNGSTRAND: Yes, that too. Little by little. By a kind of miracle. Though I know this only happens in a marriage built on love and faith and genuine happiness.
>
> BOLETTE: Has it never occurred to you that a man might also be drawn closer to his wife, somehow? Grow more like her, I mean.
>
> LYNGSTRAND: A man? No, I never thought that.   (VII, 86)

On the one hand, there are intimations of a genuinely creative projection, a fulfilment of self in the love of one's counterpart; on the other, a conceited negation of Nora's dream of the miracle – a *loss* of self when mutuality is a one way process, where the woman is a merely passive factor in the union, and where her role (as Lyngstrand later suggests) is that of *das Ewig-Weibliche* 'sitting and silently dreaming of you' (117) like some disembodied Solveig. Lyngstrand's dream of marriage to Hilde, Bolette's brow-beaten acceptance of Arnholm's offer, and Ellida's final reconsti-tution of her marriage to Wangel all reflect that multifaceted nature of Ibsen's central theme: *tegn imot tegn imot tegn.*

Because Ellida's marriage to Wangel is a human and not an ideal union, it is by definition imperfect. And the imperfections are manifest. She is his second wife – too young to relate maternally to his grown daughters, too inexperienced to find a place in the well-managed domesticity of his household, and apparently frustrated in her need to be needed by the children. She believes them all nostalgically bound by memories of the dead wife and mother, just as she feels bound to her past life with the Stranger from the Sea; and she excludes the family from her secret memory as they exclude her from theirs. There is nothing in the family structure, she says, 'to support me . . . to help me. Nothing to draw me in, no sense of things in common, of shared intimacies' (108). She seems, in other words, *free* of all the ties that normally bind one to home, children and husband; and it might seem perverse for her to cry out so insistently against a *lack* of freedom. But to be rootless in a house, on the outside of everything, is not to be *free.* The stepmother–second wife is, like the mermaid, an ambiguously 'half' being; and this is what makes her predicament intolerable. Neither free nor bound, she is merely *de trop*, an alien. To exchange alienation for com-mitment, which will be Ellida's implicit choice at the end of the play, may seem like the ultimate abandonment of the free spirit to the roles of bourgeois domesticity. But – *tegn imot tegn* – it may also be the complete fulfilment of the self in the needs of the human family. The structure of her life, in other words, is an amalgam of positive and negative factors inhering simultaneously in the same set of marital circumstances. 'Så trygg! så trygg' (III, 354) – 'So secure! So secure', she says of herself a few seconds before glimpsing the English steamer bringing the Stranger to her shores; and the consequences of standing in the presence of this alternative to imperfect human marriage is to revaluate ideas of 'security' and 'safety', to see them rather as claustrophobic limitations upon her freedoms. Again, it 'cuts both ways': Ellida, in retrospect, now envisions her whole life from an altered angle. Like John Gabriel Borkman's, her eye, born anew, transforms the structures of the past so that present unhappiness is seen as the unpitying consequence of disastrous initial decisions. The Stranger drops the phrase 'free will', and like a pebble in a stream it ripples through Ellida's consciousness in ever-widening circles until it engulfs the whole being. 'Everything lies in that phrase', she cries. 'It has opened my eyes. And now I see' (VII, 99). And what she sees, now, is that her marriage to Wangel has been a mere contract of buying and selling, an abnegation of choice and free will. The poor man looks on helplessly as she annuls the six years of their relationship as no 'real' marriage, in favour of her ideal spiritual sea marriage to the Stranger. What she *will not* see, although Wangel comments bitterly on the paradox, is that their life together is no 'real' marriage not because of the lack of existential choice and freedom six years previously, but because Ellida, of her own will and volition, has refused to sleep with her husband for the past three years.

The syndrome is all too familiar already: the consequences of sex are death, maiming, guilt. Allmers will not sleep with Rita after their child is crippled during their love-making. Ellida will not make love to Wangel after her baby dies. For how is one to explain the death of children if not as retribution for some undisclosed offence? And how is one to rationalise one's fear of the erotic if not by devising forms of moral censure against sexual contact? The denial of death and the denial of sex, as I have already suggested, are subliminal if not articulated or conscious strategies in *The Lady from the Sea* – defences against the most appalling implications of land marriage, of which sex is the primal and predominating imperfection. Like Ranevskaia's response to the drowning of her little son in *The Cherry Orchard*, so Ellida envisions the death of her baby as some obscure judgement, investing what in ordinary terms must be a sufficiently traumatic and distressing event with extraordinary Romantic meanings. It becomes a form of punishment, like that inflicted on Ranevskaia, for a curious kind of sexual promiscuity – for what, in Ellida's case, approximates to a form of 'psychic' adultery. What she persuades herself to believe (infected, no doubt, by Lyngstrand's lurid Gothic imagination) is that her baby has been fathered by two men: by the carnal land husband, and by the spiritual sea husband returning like a drowned man to possess his faithless bride. It is a *merchild*, a 'half' creature, in the same sense that she is a *mermaid*, sharing the death-infected attributes of mortal flesh and the mysterious supranatural affinities with spirit. And its death would seem, in retrospect, to condemn Ellida as an adultress, a woman who has betrayed her sea marriage by continuing her habitation of the mundane and spiritually effete conditions of land life. Wangel, with the dim intuitive understanding of a doctor–psychiatrist, diagnoses Ellida's sexual reticence as a fear of inveigling *him* in some obscure adulterous relationship with his dead and living wives: 'You think my heart is divided between you and her. That's what's upsetting you. You see something, as it were, immoral in our relationship. That's why you can't . . . or won't live with me any more as my wife' (VII, 58). It is an ingenious suggestion, but it fails to take account of the dead child and its haunting, mysterious eyes – eyes that condemn Ellida as surely as little Eyolf's condemn Rita, eyes which to Ellida seem to change colour with the sea and which explain 'det uutsigelige' (III, 351) – 'the unspeakable' – which obsesses her:

ELLIDA [*whispers, trembling*]: The child had the eyes of the stranger.
WANGEL [*gives an involuntary cry*]: Ellida!
ELLIDA [*clasps her hands in despair about her head*]: Now you must understand why I *won't* . . . why I *daren't* ever live with you again as your wife! (VII. 68)

'Rent galt og meningløst' (III, 349) – 'Utterly crazy and senseless': this is how Ellida, at her most pragmatic, regards her relationship with the Stranger. But her image of their 'marriage' is not entirely neurotic or irrational. It has all the qualities of a carefully structured Romantic mythology, a fiction built upon strange facts and Gothic fancies, which compels even Wangel to suspend medical diagnosis and empirical judgement in the face of the 'unknowable' necessities of the psyche. He is having to grapple, as he admits, not with things as they are, but with things as Ellida imagines them to have been; and her memories, far from being static or photographic images capable of precise recall, are constantly evolving fantasies which change to suit the dynamism of her myth-making. Lyngstrand, as I have suggested, provides the raw material for her Romantic imagination to work upon – a strange blending of factual coincidence, transmuted by his own taste for the Gothic, into lurid visions of sodden corpses thrown up by the sea to accuse the living of infidelity. His sensationalism is infectious. 'What a very strange idea', says Ellida, closing her eyes all the better to share his *frisson*. 'Yes, I can visualize it so clearly' (vii, 47). And so the connections are formed, linking the crude sculptural idea to a living man's vow to return 'as a drowned man from the dark sea' (48), to the Stranger, to the exact dates of Ellida's pregnancy. And so her imagination reconstructs the past as a bricolage of disparate images, building the myth from shifting memories, and investing sudden intuitions with retroactive Romantic significance until distinctions between Romance and reality blur into literal beliefs. As in her response to the child's 'eyes. 'I assure you that was simply your imagination', Wangel tries to tell Ellida. 'The child had exactly the same eyes as other normal children' (68). But there is no withstanding the operation of the myth-making mind, which, on the slender basis of present evidence, invests the past with miraculous meanings. 'That must be another figment of her imagination which has developed in the last two days', says Wangel of Ellida's timing of her conception with the Stranger's 'drowning' (94). But how can medical science draw the line between gynaecological symptoms of a difficult pregnancy, and a Romantic *hysterica passio*? And how can reason argue against the transformations that memory effects upon reality? In *The Lady from the Sea,* Romanticism – with its demands for infinity, absolute freedom, experience of the unknown, and the completion of self in an immortal lover – stands upon the verge of mental illness, in its most recognisable modern form.

The Stranger from the Sea is no longer, in the modern scene, a dramatic enigma variously interpreted as hallucination or meta-symbol, 'endopsychic automatism' or personified thought,[15] or an expressionistic device akin to Miss Julie's distorted vision of Jean at the end of Strindberg's play. He is simply the substance of the Romantic heroine's sexual fantasies. Madame Bovary would have reconised him instantly as one of those faceless, disembodied erotic ideals – although far more elemental than her own pre-revolutionary aristocratic preferences. In the fiction of the 1970s, he is the no-longer-shocking demon lover of the liberated feminist's erotic fantasies,[16] a sexual will-o'-the-wisp pursued through a series of brief and anonymous affairs by trans-sexual Don Juans in search of the absolute. The most conscious an-

atomising of these fantasies, amounting almost to a psychoan
alysis of nineteenth-century erotic archetypes, is Erica Jong's *Fear
of Flying* – a modern counter-Romantic study of yet another
doctor's wife, saved from destructive promiscuity and the black
soundless wings by her own tough, existential self-knowledge.
Perhaps Isadora makes too fully articulate what Ibsen allows to
remain delicately understated; but her analysis of the sexual
quest clarifies Ellida's subtextual perceptions at the end of the
play:

> Perhaps the search was really a kind of ritual in which the
> process was more important than the end. Perhaps it was a
> kind of quest. Perhaps there was no man at all, but just a
> mirage conjured by our longing and emptiness. . . . Maybe the
> impossible man was nothing but a specter made of our own
> yearning. . . . Or maybe he was really death, the last lover.[17]

The whole point of Ellida's Romantic yearning, it seems to me, is
to create precisely such a mirage, which no more matches the real
man when he appears than Léon or Rodolphe incarnates Emma
Bovary's fantastic desires. The controversy over the Stranger as
spectre or substance is resolved within the context of the play
itself: he is *both* – the 'impossible man' of Ellida's paradisal
desires, and the tourist with the Scottish cap who doesn't quite
mesh with the image in Ellida's mind. Ibsen's intention, indeed,
seems manifested in the very discrepancy. For no living man can
possibly bear the god-function Ellida imposes upon their relationship; and, although the Stranger offers her exactly what she
wants – the freedom 'to come with me across the sea' (vii, 81) – it is
clear that her needs are far beyond what any mortal man can
guarantee. Her sea-voyage must be out of nature into the infinite
unknown, the dreadful and the desirable; and, although she is
drawn by the undertow of freedom projected in her lover, she is
also terrified of drowning in the freedom she demands. Absolute
freedom *is* death, 'the last lover'. And in pursuing her quest to its
limit, she must finally confront the reflection of what most
appalls her in the finite world of bourgeois marriage, mortal
imperfection, and transient joy.

There is also something Conradian about the Stranger from the
Sea: a 'sharer' of one's deepest desires in whose presence the self is
clarified, and who therefore seems somehow *symbolic* of one's

secret idenity. The ordinary 'Johnston' merges in Ellida's imagination into the symbolic 'Friman', which is another of the essentially anonymous Stranger's names – and his anti-social violation
of land values defines at least one aspect of the 'freedom' his name
suggests: a chaotic reversion to licence, which frees the ethical self
from the moral responsibilites of land life and from what Rolf
Fjelde calls 'the hard-won human order of civilization'.[18] Friman
has murdered his captain, but there are no known motives for his
act, apart from his insistence that to have done so was 'right and
proper' (VII, 63). And Ellida, utterly will-less when subjected to
his strange power, is compelled to suspend all ethical sense and so
become an accessory after the fact. Despite the Romanticism of
the sea marriage, the symbolic union of the lovers to the limitless
and the free, the implications of 'Fri-man' and 'frihet' (III. 369)
bear the dark ethical taint of Rebekka West's savage liberalism.
And the Friman who walks about with a loaded pistol to ensure
that he lives and dies a free man merely reinforces the atmosphere
of violence, death and suicide that typifies the 'last lover'.

When the Stranger actually makes his appearance, it is not as a
larger-than-life Romantic symbol, but as a rather ordinary red-
bearded traveller. '*That* man?' (VII, 78) Wangel asks when Ellida,
in panic-stricken reaction to the Stranger's surprisingly con-
ciliatory manner, points out her demon lover to her husband.
There is an ironic disjunction between the myth and the man – as
there is, more comically, in Synge's *Playboy of the Western World*
when Christy Mahon's folkloric monster father suddenly appears
in the likeness of an old tramp. Ibsen controls this disparity very
consciously and very carefully. Ellida first thinks the Stranger is
her husband and responds to his arrival with an ecstasy quite mis-
interpreted by the other man, whom she completely fails to recognise as her fantasy husband – a fact with which Wangel, later,
encourages her to come rationally to terms:

WANGEL: Well, how was it you didn't recognize him immediately?
ELLIDA [*starts*]: Didn't I?
WANGEL: No. You said yourself afterwards that to begin with you
    had absolutely no idea who the man was.
ELLIDA [*struck*]: I do believe you are right! That was strange,
    Wangel, wasn't it? Fancy my not recognizing him at once! . . .
WANGEL: Not so very strange. A new image has presented itself . . .
    Reality. And this overshadows the old one . . . so that you can

no longer see it. . . . And it overshadows your morbid fancies too. This is why it is a good thing that reality came as it did.   (vii, 96–7)

Wangel imagines, somehow, that 'virkeligheten' (iii, 367), the perception of reality, will have a therapeutic effect on Ellida and that regressive Romanticism can be healed by their combined efforts: by Ellida's confronting the real, and by his protecting her against it. His own course of action may be well-meaning, but it is pathetically inappropriate – an uxorious oversolicitousness which denies her the right to choose for herself and so merely aggravates the condition he intends to cure. He fails to understand that it is not the red-bearded traveller who is his antagonist, but the demon lover – the Romantic impulse itself; and, as Ellida points out, he is powerless to oppose forces which have no 'real' existence in the physical world: 'What is there to protect me against? There is no external power or force threatening me. This thing is much more deeply seated, Wangel! The pull is within my own mind. And what can you do about that?' (vii. 102). The doctor has tried, unsuccessfully it would seem, to administer anti-depressants; and the husband, in his anxiety to protect, has diminished even further the freedom for which she yearns. In this terrible *impasse* there seems nothing he can possibly give Ellida comparable to the 'free will' which the Stranger offers her, and no way of responding to her cry – as of one drowning – to 'Save me from myself!' (83)

What Wangel finally does, despite the fearful risk involved, is to give Ellida what she wants by offering her a freedom far more significant than the Stranger's and far less destructive than the absolute freedom that terrifies her. There are clearly gradations of freedom in the play, from the ultimate freedom of death, to licence which acknowledges no ethical responsibility, to the relinquishment of self to desire, to existential free choice, in which the self is defined by accepting the consequences of choosing in freedom. Ellida's yearning ranges along the entire scale of possibilities—the extreme romantic impulse with its terrors and its undertow held in check by the need for autonomy and self-definition in the act of freely deciding her own fate. For what most she wants is the *freedom to choose*. Without it, the self is merely determined by the limitations placed upon it and defined by decisions made by others on one's own behalf. Her plea, in modern existential terms, is for 'authenticity' – the decisive act of self-creation which transforms the passive, institutionalised *role* into a dynamic *being* whose every choice remakes the free woman. 'I don't want to dodge the issue by claiming to be another man's wife', she says. 'Nor by claiming that I have no choice. Because then it would be no real decision. . . . I must be free to choose. Choose one way or the other. I must be able to let him go away alone . . . or to go with him' (101). To Wangel, this seems a choice between sanity and madness, and he refuses to allow her the option of going with the Stranger. 'You need your husband . . . and your doctor . . .', he argues. 'To assume the authority and act on your behalf' (108). The security and safety of marriage, the protection she craves against her own anarchic drives, now begins to constrict and strangle. But, although the Stranger allows her to decide 'of her own free will' (80), his liberality is as narrow and limiting as Wangel's, without the positive corollaries of safety and security. The point is that he frees her only to decide to go with him. Failing that, he threatens to abandon her – as Wangel *never* does – turning her decision into one of those ruthless either/or choices in which the rigidity of the formulation negates its freedom. There is, as Rolf Fjelde puts it, a 'compulsive and devouring limitation'[19] about the Stranger, his inability to acknowledge Ellida's freedom to reject him (which she has already tried to do on a number of occasions), and his implicit denial of individual liberty as the right of each to liberate himself in his own way. Ellida may be intoxicated by his 'free will' formula – but the Stranger's terms qualify it drastically; and, in the final analysis, he can offer her nothing but the punitive consequences of not choosing *his* version of freedom: 'And be clear about one thing', he warns her, ' – if you don't leave with me tomorrow, that's the finish of everything. . . . I shall never come here again. You will never see me again. Never hear from me, either. I shall be as though dead and gone from you forever' (81). There is a Brand-like obsessiveness about the man, a Romantic tendency to deal only in extremes and to ignore the middle ground on which human decisions are generally made without such be-all or end-all compulsions. The Stranger's gift of 'free will' flies in the face of Ellida's yearning for freedom. He presents her with an ultimatum which, in the nature of all such choices, implies no alternative whatsoever.

Wangel's course of action, like that of the true mother in Solomon's judgment, is to relinquish out of love and concern the being whom most he loves – to free Ellida, while still providing the context of security and safety without which her decision would be terror and a potential loss of self. Paradoxically, there is no other way of saving her than by cancelling the bonds that hold her to him: 'Nu kan du altså velge din vei – i full – full frihet' (III, 380) – 'So, now you can make your choice – in complete – complete freedom.' To choose the Stranger's way is to be *lost*, not free. But Wangel's 'full frihet' implies a supportive system which remains impervious to Ellida's choice: love, nurtured during their years of living together – or, in other words, the operation of time and custom, 'accommodation' in its most life-enhancing aspect, upon a good marriage. The freedom he offers is full but not absolute. And the qualifications that delimit it make a genuine choice possible by cancelling the dread lurking beneath the limitless and infinite freedoms of Romanticism. The context of a secure marriage makes Ellida's free choice possible; and the constraint implicit in 'full frihet' – the necessary acceptance, as Wangel points out, of responsibility for one's decisions – rescues the self from drowning in oceanic freedom. It is *ansvar* – responsibility – which imposes moral limits upon absolute freedom, saves one from the loss of identity in the formless infinitude of the sea, defines selfhood in the nature of one's choices, and ensures autonomy by making man the creature of his own decisions. 'Frihet under ansvar' (ibid.) – freedom defined by responsibility: this is what finally liberates Ellida from her romantic attachment to the sea and her demon lover by showing her the potential for change inherent in creative choice. Because she is freed to reject her land marriage, she is also free – as she had not been before – to accept it as an expression of her own will, and to accept the responsibilities it entails as an extension of self rather than a restraint imposed involuntarily upon it. The alienated being returns gladly to the family, the community – not as a sudden and ineptly motivated *volte-face*, but as a satisfaction of those desires most urgently voiced throughout the play: the need to be needed, to be accepted as a mother by the children, to share in the intimacies of their family life. And by 'remarrying' Wangel as an act of free choice, by embracing responsibility, Ellida in turn liberates the others from the 'halfness' of their ambiguous and uncommitted roles within the family. She becomes the mother for which Hilde yearns. She frees Bolette to live an independent life, assured that her father will now have a 'real' wife. And she changes her sexually frustrated marriage for one remade through the power of choice. 'I am coming back to you', she tells Wangel (vII, 122); and to Hilde, watching them embrace in public, they look like a newly engaged couple.

But for many readers the *dénouement* of *The Lady from the Sea* has proved either rhetorically unconvincing or highly problematical. 'Frihet under ansvar' seems, from Brian Johnston's Hegelian perspective, a retreat of the free spirit into a mode of morality formalised by Kant's categorical imperative; and, from this point of view, Ellida's decision marks a drastic fission in modern consciousness – the confinement of Romantic aspiration in a despiritualised bourgeois world to the point where vision is finally eliminated by reality and common-sense.[20] Inga-Stina Ewbank leaves the issues more generously open; but, in comparing the play's ending to the Romantic energies of *Wuthering Heights,* or by speaking of the sense of loss when Ellida returns to domestic life, or of the 'cool British' nature of the play's exceptional close, her pointed questions would seem to imply their own answers:

> Are social adjustment and moral responsibility reconcilable with passion, creativity, with the free life of the imagination? Or, are those qualities bought at the expense of the deepest human feelings? – as they are seen to be, for example, in Charlotte Brontë's *Villette,* where Lucy Snowe in an epiphanic moment sees her own emotional register (described very much in the pre-Freudian psychological vocabulary of the 'unknown', 'nameless', 'bottomless and boundless', 'unutterable', 'unendurable', 'indescribable', etc.) as superior to the limited register of Dr John . . .[21]

Judged by Hegelian standards, or by the Romantic energies of the Brontës, Ellida may seem a rather dispirited heroine. She is a Catherine Earnshaw who suffers no loss by dismissing Heathcliff and the power of his will, an Emma Bovary who can endure reality without recourse to arsenic, and a Lucy Snowe who sees the danger of an emotional register balanced perilously on the rim of madness. Romantic heroines (so the argument would imply) should not survive suicide, insanity, or spiritual self-immolation. And, if they do, then the Romantic spirit, acclimatising itself to bourgeois domesticity, is seen to choose its own death. Those who abandon Paradise for the human world – the sea in favour of the land – must suffer the spiritual negation implicit in that choice. But Ellida, at the end of the play, defies her critics – those who demean her choice, and those who see her resolution as a trick of rhetoric, a mouthing of cold philosophies. *Ansvar* is no more a Kantian abstraction for Ellida than Rita Allmers's commitment to 'responsibility' as a criterion of ethical concern. For both, although in different ways, it is a lived-through reality experienced upon the pulse – acts of love which reaffirm the connections of the self to the world. For Ellida, those connections have always been there, unseen because unacknowledged; and, in accepting the children as her own, and Wangel as her 'real' husband, she gives human substance to abstract ideas, embracing *ansvar* as freedom from her mermaid state – but without perishing in the process, and without suffering the desiccation of spirit darkly prophesied by Hegel and parodied in Ballested's Romantic genre-painting of the mermaid exiled from the sea and dying in the brackish shallows.

In many ways, *The Lady from the Sea* is a dramatic terminus in Ibsen's work where difficult themes are temporarily resolved before seeking out new depths of complexity. Nora must slam the door on the doll's house to find her freedom, while Ellida acknowledges a form of freedom paradoxically consistent with the constraints of marriage. But, on the other hand, although Ellida discovers a way of satisfying *lengslens vei,* the yearning after freedom in the Land without Paradise, Hedda Gabler – unable to 'accommodate' her desires to a very different marriage – can find her freedom only in death. The vision is multifaceted. One woman's resolution is another's agony, and there are as many different 'freedoms' in Ibsen as there are plays – from Mrs Alving's intellectual emancipation from dead ideas to Maja's song of freedom from the valley. One fact, however, remains consistent: *frihet* in Ibsen is no glib resolution to the protagonist's dilemma, but a condition of the spirit strenuously attained – often a painful dying to the old complacent self, as in Nora's experience, to be reborn a new creature strong enough to bear the consequences of one's choices. It is always relative, often tragic in its realisation, and inevitably qualified by death itself. Ironically, those who seek freedom from death absolute – like Hedda and John Gabriel Borkman – are the least free of Ibsen's protagonists, confined in structures which incarcerate them, physically and psychically, and cut them off from life. It is the clarifying vision of *The Lady from the Sea* that reveals, all the more poignantly, the failure and destructiveness in the plays that follow. Hedda Gabler's nauseated response to love as 'det klissete ord!' (iii. 403) – 'that sickly-sweet word' – far from denying Ibsen's ability to 'place' love in the world, merely reveals the tragic gap that separates Hedda's relationships from Ellida's. Each throws into relief the other's Romantic impulses and desires, especially the desire for self-completion in the spirit life of her lover, Dionysos or the Stranger from the Sea. The Romantic heroine who demands satisfaction beyond the possibilities of the mortal world merely confirms her own incorrigible apathy – so that the desperate search for love finally becomes a self-destructive quest; 'and then we try to convince ourselves', as Isadora puts it, 'that self-annihilation is love'.²² This is the tragedy of Romanticism that Ellida transforms, in her love for Wangel and in the spirit of responsibility, into a 'celebratory comedy'²³ – the complement to Hedda Gabler which creates the wholeness and the steadiness of Ibsen's vision. If Ellida defies Romance by consigning her demon lover back to the sea from which he came, it is because the most extraordinary man turns out, in the last analysis, to be the most ordinary – the husband who frees her to complete herself and whose compassion becomes the answer to self-annihilation. Their reconstituted marriage will be a union of autonomous and independent spirits, voluntarily entered into, sexually renewed, and no more or less perfect than any other 'land' relationship. This cosmology of two is the closest Ibsen comes to responding to Nora's cry, at the end of *A Doll's House,* for a miracle.

II

If *The Lady from the Sea* provokes us into redefining 'freedom' from within the narrow confines of a carp-pond, then *Rosmersholm* – perhaps the bleakest and most depressing of Ibsen's plays – goes even further in challenging us to dredge 'joy' out of despair and revalue its substance in circumstances that would seem to negate it completely. The very language of Romanticism would seem to be rewritten here, its central values radically redefined in actions which reduce *a priori* assumptions about the nature of 'freedom', 'love' and 'joy' to 'talemåter' (iii. 322) – empty phrases – to use one of Rebekka West's dismissive terms. Indeed, an entire century of Romantic rhetoric, once fired by the spirit of revolution and the politics of a restored democratic paradise, seems to have fizzled out in *Rosmersholm,* reduced to maudlin platitudes incapable of vigorous response to a fierce reactionary backlash. Emptied of meaning, the vocabulary of spiritual liberalism has degenerated into mockery, cynicism and morbidity – the distinctive tones of Ulrik Brendel, that arch-radical and arch-Romantic pitifully run to seed. He is the spokesman, at the end of the play, of a nightmare vision of aspiration horribly defeated, of the world reduced to cosmic absurdity and nothingness – 'nichts og ingenting' (324). And, with the self-destructive impulse of an old Werther, he abandons himself to a suicidally regressive mock-Romanticism: 'Nu går jeg hjemover. . . . Jeg har fått hjemve efter det store ingenting' (323) – 'Now I'm returning homewards. . . . I am homesick for the great nothingness.' He is the dead-end of nineteenth-century liberalism and the parodist of its values: the democratic revolutionary who despises the people, the idealist incapable of transforming the alcoholic vision into sober reality, the Romantic who discredits the very words he utters. Most dangerously, however, he is a mirror who tempts others to recognise their own failures as in a distorted reflection. Dressed in Rosmer's cast-off clothing, he plays the fallen *alter ego* who seeks, like Lucifer in Byron's *Cain,* to demoralise the hero through moral infection, and paralyse through cynicism. Brendel is ultimately an incarnation of that very nihilism and nothingness in dread of which Rosmer has constructed his own abstractly conceived and ill-thought-out programme of spiritual revolution – his dream-ideal, in the face of political reaction, of an egalitarian paradise in which man will discover new modes of morality, freedom and joy. His life's mission recaptures, in peculiarly Ibsenian terms, the mood and spirit of those Romantics who struggled to contain their despair at the manifest failure of revolutionary ideals earlier in the century; and it is crucial to see the quality of strenuously defined 'joy' that Brendel, in his monstrous apathy, persuades Rosmer to relinquish.

Rosmer, who has abandoned his faith together with the conservative traditions of his family, still clings to the belief that men may be regenerated, in the fallen modern world, by their own capacities for moral transformation without recourse to God. For the lapsed Christian there is no longer the hope for a literal

Kingdom of God – but the longing remains, and with an almost desperate intensity he tries to refashion Paradise in the secular and political life of the community. Given the climate of the times, however, the dream of reordering the political structure into a recovered *social* Paradise – a Romantic 'apocalypse by revolution'[24] – seems no longer remotely possible in the Norway of 1886. The contemporary political realities lurking behind the events of the play all point to a collapse of liberal hopes: a *Storting* in conflict with the overriding will of a conservative king and his executive, a strong reactionary movement in the student community, and a general sense of revolutionary failure in a country which had declared its sovereignty and adopted a democratic constitution only seventy years before. The sense of an ending hangs heavily over the play, a tradition of energy and will destroyed in the lives of its exponents, parodied by those who once preached its values or debased by pragmatic politicians for reasons of expediency, while the forces of conformity and moral repression flourish. Rosmer's only hope, in the climate of failure and political collapse, is to create a revolution in the *spirit* of man, 'å skape det sanne folkedømme' (292) – 'to create a genuine democracy of liberated intellects' – an equality of souls comparable to Wordsworth's vision of paradise regained in the transformation of common men into seers, what M. H. Abrams calls 'apocalypse by cognition':

In the ruling two-term frame of Romantic thought, the mind of man confronts the old heaven and earth and possesses within itself the power, if it will but recognize and avail itself of the power, to transform them into a new heaven and new earth, by means of a total revolution of consciousness.[25]

The substance of that revolutionary consciousness in *Rosmersholm* may seem visionary to the point of vagueness; but its moral content is unmistakable. The aim of spiritual democracy, as Rosmer defines it, is to measure all men by their highest common denominator: by their potential for nobility, independence of thought, and the ability to choose what is right in purity of will and through the power of autonomous decision. No man can legislate for another or liberate another: the morality of freedom demands that each emancipate himself, and the fundamental assumption of the spiritual democrat is that man is the source of his own moral system. The intellectually liberated man has, as Rosmer puts it, 'a natural instinct for morality' (VI, 227) – as if to mitigate against the disappearance of God as moral absolute. His vision of man is that of the new existential Adam – a Brand-like vision of moral integrity, without the Brand-like compulsion to impose it upon all and sundry. Rosmer, on the contrary, will exemplify his revolutionary consciousness in his own conduct, utterly convinced that the free man can choose only what is 'right and proper' and utterly contemptuous of Kroll's malicious identification of free-thinking with free-love and freedom with moral laxity. For Rosmer's nobility of mind is inseparable from purity of motive, from radical innocence. And the prerequisite of both is 'joy', the source and end of Rosmer's moral system, and the central mystery of the play. It is a delicate and terribly vulnerable ideal that he constructs with Rebekka's assistance, her revolutionary energies allied to his visionary mission; and, with grim inevitability, we watch the erosion from within of Rosmer's moral idea, the collapse of a Paradise built upon his fallible belief in man's capacity to act correctly in innocence and freedom. It is from the ruins of this lost Paradise that 'joy' must finally be recovered as a supreme value of the apocalyptic vision.

There is an exchange in Act III which, given the dour and apparently joyless temperament of Rosmer, seems unintentionally ironic, perhaps even funny if read out of context:

> ROSMER: . . . Any cause that wants to win a lasting victory – must be undertaken, in joy, by a man free of guilt.
> REBEKKA: Is joy so absolutely essential for *you* Rosmer?
> ROSMER: Joy? Yes, Rebekka – it is that.
> REBEKKA: For you, who can't ever laugh?
> ROSMER: All the same. I assure you, I have a great capacity for joy.

The emphasis on 'joy' and 'joyful' – *glede* and *glad* – here and throughout the play, is insistent to the point almost of obsession; and this alone should caution one against misreading or misinterpreting the value which Rosmer assigns to the word. The man who never laughs, but insists upon his susceptibility to joy, is clearly making a profound distinction between a necessary condition of the spiritual life and the pleasures and delights of the sensuous. Translation is hazardous; but I have chosen 'joy' as the most feasible equivalent of the idea rather than the more colloquial 'happiness' or 'gladness' – not only because it relates to one of the central values of European Romanticism inherent in the play, but in order to distinguish it (if I read Ibsen's intentions correctly) from two approximate synonyms: *lykke* (*lykkelig, lykksalighet*), with its overtones of good fortune or the sort of happiness that derives from temporary pleasure, and *fryd,* which suggests delight – not as a condition of being, but as a response to the world. There are clearly gradations of joy/happiness/pleasure in the play, as there are gradations of love from the desperate infatuation of 'forelskelse' (III, 313) to the transforming power of 'den stille kjærlighet' (323). And, like so many other abstract concepts in Ibsen, the idea of *glede* is subject to a process of dynamic redefinition from scene to scene, accruing meaning by association with other interrelated values, or reciprocating meaning with conjoined ideas – as in *Ghosts,* where joy, again, becomes an indispensable quality of existence in an unremittingly joyless world. Osvald's *livsglede* is an early precedent for Rosmer's *glede,* a concept in which both 'life' and 'joy' – that most Romantic of verbal constellations[26] – constantly enhance each other in the context of related image-clusters and *Leitmotive:*

> Mor, har du lagt merke til, at alt det jeg har malt, har dreiet seg om livsgleden?. . . Der er lys og solskinn og søndagsluft, – og strålende fornøyede menneskeansikter. (III, 147)

> Mother, have you ever noticed that everything I've painted keeps returning to life's joy?. . . To light and sunshine and sensations of freedom, – and the faces of people, radiant with happiness.

The poetry is fully articulated in *Ghosts* – joy and life, irradiated by light and sun, and enveloped in the spiritual harmonies of *søndagsluft,* which, in turn, become a living experience in the artist's vision of man. Rosmer's claim to joy may be affirmed in attenuated poetry stripped of such association and reciprocation; but it refers, no less insistently than Osvald's art, to a mode of consciousness quite distinct from the pleasure principle or the amusement expressed in laughter. *Glede* obviously does not exist in absolute isolation from *lykke* or *fryd;* but, although these gradations of joy/happiness/pleasure may often inhere in a single phrase, they are no more interchangeable in their contexts than any of the many possible synonyms are interchangeable with Coleridge's vision of joy in his ode 'Dejection'.

The most distinctive quality of Rosmer's peculiar poetry is its patterning of language into constellations of value which reverberate, like major chords, until their accumulated meaning becomes an aspect of the play's central idea. They insist upon our attention, conjoining ideas in series after series: 'stille og glad og lykkelig' (III, 292) – 'calm and joyful and happy'; 'fred og glede og forsoning inn i sinnene' (ibid.) – 'peace and joy and reconciliation in the hearts and minds [of men]'; 'den stille, glade skyldfrihet' (306) – 'that quiet, joyful innocence'; 'i frihet, i fryd, i lidenskap' (307) – 'in freedom, in delight, in passionate intensity'; and so on. Rosmer may seem to speak in vague abstractions. But he is clearly making constant reference to what M. H. Abrams has called the great 'Romantic Positives',[27] however anachronistic his language may sound in a world that has lost contact with the values of a civilised order –.with Rosmersholm itself. Rosmer is a Romantic idealist; and, although we have been encouraged, ever since Shaw, to regard all such idealism as suspect and destructive, there is the great danger of eliminating its most enduring qualities by discrediting the whole. When Rosmer speaks of the spiritually ennobled society, men bound together in a vital community of joy, he speaks as one of the visionary company—members, in Abrams's words,

> of what Wordsworth called the 'One great Society . . . / The noble Living and the noble Dead,' whose mission was to assure the continuance of civilization by reinterpreting to their drastically altered condition the enduring humane values, making whatever changes were required in the theological systems by which these values had earlier been sanctioned.[28]

Rosmer the apostate is also, in a highly relevant sense, Rosmer the Romantic – a lapsed Christian who elects as his mission to transform the transcendental values of the noble dead into the living values of a new earthly life. This is his answer to nothingness, nihilism and despair; and it is phrased in the language of the old verities given new currency in the 'high Romantic words': *glede, forsoning, skyldfrihet, frihet, fred, lykksalighet.* There is no way of grasping Rosmer's full intentions, it seems to me, without the structure of meaning, the cultural contexts, and the ideological implications that lie beneath the language he speaks. His verbal constellations are analogous to the interrelated ideas of European Romanticism, even if they are not precisely identical or synonymous with them; and M. H. Abrams's synthetic definition of the 'high Romantic words' is a helpful gloss on the complexities of Rosmer's abstractions. Life, he writes, is the ground concept of all Romantic value –

> the highest good, the residence and measure of other goods, and the generator of the controlling categories of Romantic thought. Love . . . expresses the confraternity of the one life shared not only with other men but also with a milieu in which man can feel fully at home; while liberty signifies not only a political circumstance, but also the deliverance of mind and imagination from the mortmain of custom and the slavery of sense so that they may transform the dull and lifeless world into a new world instinct with the life and joy it reciprocates with the perceiving mind. Hope (with its related value, fortitude) is essential for sustaining the possibility of the triumph of life, love, and liberty. And the norm of life is joy – by which is meant not that joy is the standard state of man, but that joy is what man is born for: it is the sign that an individual, in the free exercise of all his faculties, is completely alive; it is the necessary condition for a full community of life and love; and it is both the precondition and the end of the highest art.[29]

This, surely, is the ideology behind the ringing tones of Rosmer's redemptive vision, which, even in translation, catches the echo of a familiar apocalyptic rhetoric:

> Oh, what what joy [fryd] then to be alive. No more bitter strife, only friendly rivalry. All eyes fixed on the same goal. Every mind, every will striving on and on . . . up and up . . . each by the path best suited to its nature. Happiness [lykke] for all . . . created by all.   (vi, 349)

But there are crucial gaps in Rosmer's 'high Romantic words'. He speaks of his new heaven, new earth as a paradise already lost, or beyond his personal achievement – which is to say that his vocabulary has no word for *hope* and its correlatives: 'modige vilje', 'evnen til å handle' (III, 321) – courage and will, and the power to make one's vision viable. Rebekka, of course, is the living incarnation for Rosmer of these Romantic abstractions, as she is of all his other high ideals: the 'new and living reality' (VI, 342) upon which he will build his world; the exemplar of life lived in a state of perfect, innocent friendship; his inspiration to freedom from the dead hand of moribund values; the embodiment of everything he means by 'love' and 'joy': 'denne stille, glade, begjærløse lykksalighet' (III, 311) – 'that calm and joyful contentment, free of sexual passion'. She is, in other words, his own particular analogue of Paradise; and their relationship together assumes for him the paradigmatic nature of that harmonious community of liberated minds and chastened wills which will inherit the earth:

> If we really think about it, Rebekka . . . we began our life together like two children falling sweetly and secretly in love. Making no demands, dreaming no dreams. . . . And it was this life of intimacy, *with* each other and *for* each other, we took for friendship. . . . our life together has been a spiritual marriage . . . perhaps from the very first day.   (VI, 351)

But there is a gap, again, between his vision and his expression of it. His grammatical tense begins to slip into a past conditional: a sense of what *could have been,* rather than an expectation of what *will be*; and the tone in which both he and Rebekka recall their dream of the transformed society gradually recedes into a pathetic nostalgia for lost possibilities:

> REBEKKA: . . . You wanted to grab hold of life in all its vitality – life lived intensely [*i dagens levende liv*] – so you said. You wanted to go like a messenger of liberation from house to house. Winning over their minds and wills to your purpose. To create noblemen all around you, – in wider and wider circles. Noblemen.
> ROSMER: Joyful [*glade*] noblemen.
> REBEKKA: Yes – joyful.
> ROSMER: For it is joy than ennobles the mind, Rebekka. . . . I shall never again come to enjoy that which makes life so marvellously wonderful to live.
> REBEKKA: . . . What is it you mean, Rosmer?

ROSMER [looks up at her]: That calm, joyful, innocence.
REBEKKA [takes a step back]: Yes. Innocence.

Their loss of the great Romantic positives is devastating – the
miraculously beautiful life, peace, freedom from guilt, the hope
of sustaining a noble community of love, and joy –

> Joy that ne'er was given,
> Save to the pure, and in their purest hour.[30]

For Rosmer, a loss of personal purity is synonymous with a loss of
Paradise; and his fall from innocence into ever deepening levels
of dejection and despair invokes that most characteristic of
Romantic experiences, epitomised in Coleridge's 'Dejection' ode:
a spiritual crisis in which the introspective mind submits itself to
painful self-analysis until, from the depths of despondency, it
once again envisions 'joy' as an antidote to desolation.

Rosmer has built his Paradise upon two unquestioned
assumptions: an absolute conviction of personal innocence, and a
belief in the purity and the beauty of his relationship with
Rebekka. Both assumptions are tragically belied. There is a
naïve, Rousseauist strain in Rosmer's image of man as a radically
innocent creature with a natural instinct for goodness, free of
guilt – skyldfri – as the basic condition of his existence. His naïvety,
moreover, is compounded by his believing himself to be such a
man–pure in every motive, ethically exonerated from any
implication in his late wife's suicide, and sexually chaste in his
relationship with Rebekka. To be innocent is, above all else, to be
'begjærløs' (III. 311) – free of the overt sexuality that brings death
to Paradise, that precipitates the Fall; and it is typical of Rosmer
that he should envision their incipient affection in images purged
of all eroticism, 'som en søt, lønndomsfull barneforelskelse' (ibid.)
– 'like the sweet love of small children, full of intimate secrets'.
And – despite malicious rumours, dirty minds, and Rebekka's own
initial passion for Rosmer – their relationship has been rigorously
asexual, 'innocent' almost to the point of perversely denying the
reality of desire. But to be absolutely innocent is to be free not
only of overt carnality, but also of the even more terrifying possibility of subliminal desire, which, once brought to consciousness,
immediately compromises the purity of one's every motive and
one's belief in personal integrity. Perhaps, unwittingly, his

relationship with Rebekka was grounded not in 'barneforelskelse', but in 'kjærlighetsforhold' (ibid.) – in love than encompasses desire. Perhaps, unwittingly, he had given Beate every cause for desperation. To admit an element of sexuality into their 'pure and beautiful' relationship is to restore it to its full humanity – but the cost of this admission is an inescapable implication of Rosmer in the causes of Beate's suicide. In the final analysis, there is no escaping the scrupulous moral responsibilities of the Rosmer conscience, its ruthless doomsessions over the self which erode all happiness and undermine that quest for freedom. One by one, Rosmer allows the prerequisites for the new life to slip away: innocence on which joy depends; joy that brings nobility of mind; and the dream of a true spiritual democracy based upon nobility and love.

To salvage what remains of this dream of liberal democracy, to absolve Rosmer of his burden of guilt and save him from despair, Rebekka – at great risk and at great personal cost – shoulders the entire burden of blame, as well she might. 'I want to give you back again what you need to live your life', she tells him. 'You shall have your joy and innocence back again, my dearest friend.' 'Glade skyldfrihet' (316): this is what she can restore to Rosmer only by smashing the symbol-system he has built on her integrity, by revealing the gross impurity of her motives, the vicious impulses masquerading as the liberal ideal, and 'dette ville, ubetvingelige bejær' (321) – 'that wild, unappeasable sexual passion' – sweeping away all nice considerations of ethical morality. There was, she admits, nothing at all cold-blooded in her disposing of Beate, but an ineluctable yielding to the dreadful 'thing' she never believed would happen. Her predicament is classical in its tragic implications, an experience of overmastering erotic desire which, like Phaedra's, suspends conscience in the very act of exercising it: 'I knew', says Euripides's heroine, 'that both the thing I craved, and the craving itself, was a sin . . . But this is how we should regard the matter: we know and see what is right, yet fail to carry it out. Some fail through sloth, others through valuing some pleasure more than goodness; and life offers us many pleasures. . . .'[31] Rebekka, as she admits, wants things both ways:

> I wanted to get rid of Beata, one way or another. But I never really imagined it would ever happen. Every little step I risked, every faltering advance, I seemed to hear something call out

within me: 'No further. No a step further!' . . . And yet I could
not stop. I had to venture a little bit further. . . .   (VI, 363)

And so it happens that in the name of some rationalised 'goodness' – her ideal of full and complete freedom for Rosmer – she
violates the very essence of the 'good' and the 'free'. Behind the
disinterested idealism of the liberal democracy there is the lust
that drives her to fight Beate to the death; and Rosmer's belief
that the free agent, ennobled in intellect, will choose only what is
right and proper is appallingly belied. The rational mind is not
always independent of passionate impulse; and the liberated
intellect does not, in itself, guarantee responsibility of conduct.
Guilty of what Strindberg called *själamörd*[32] – psychic murder –
Rebekka reduces the high Romantic concept of liberty to the
squalid licence of the Stranger from the Sea.

And so it is with all the other Romantic positives she embodies.
But Rebekka is more than a counter-Romantic exercise in exposing the naïvety of a value-system based on love, hope, joy and
innocence. Like Hedda, she experiences the tragedy of Romanticism itself – not only as a collapse of private or esoteric myths,
but as the disintegration of its most widely acknowledged beliefs;
and, like Hedda, she struggles to restore those values – not only in
her own consciousness, but in their relevance to the world of
ethical behaviour. Hedda is a Romantic aesthete for whom life is
meaningless without beauty, ecstasy and life's poetry – Rebekka, a
Romantic moralist for whom life is equally meaningless without nobility and the profound joy of reordering the world by
recovering one's own capacity for responsible action. The loss of
'pleasure' to 'goodness' may be incalculable; but tragedy, in
Yeats's brilliantly compressed definition of its form, is inseparable
from the sense of terrible dissolution before that moment of
redemptive clarity:

All men have aimed at, found, and lost;
Blackout; Heaven blazing into the head:
Tragedy wrought to its uttermost.[33]

In *Rosmersholm* all the Romantic positives are found, lost again,
and then redefined in a dramatic rhythm where collapse and
reintegration become simultaneous processes – as they are in
Oedipus, for example, where the dying of the former self is co-

extensive with the birth of the new. There is one superb dramatic moment where all the phases of the tragic form cohere – triumph, despair and revelation – in a single incoherent utterance. Rosmer, at the end of Act II, asks Rebekka to become his wife; and, after a moment of speechlessness, '*Rebekka skriker opp i glede*' (III. 307) – a 'shriek of joy' which, in its tonal ironies, recalls Clytemnestra's ambivalent yell as she welcomes home her husband to the bath, the jacket and the axe. It is a cry so intense and so abhorrent in its triumph that Rebekka, as if responding to its echo, hears despair in the very throat of joy. Motives stand revealed in such shocking clarity that, in her next breath, she immediately cancels all hope of freedom, joy, and passion by refusing her most ardently sought-after goal. 'It's even more impossible for me to become your wife', she tells Rosmer. 'Never in this world can I be that' (VI, 343). It is one of those supremely challenging moments to the Ibsen actress, where meaning inheres beneath the level of utterance in the unspoken and the unspeakable. But, however varied and complex the reasons for her refusal, and whatever explanations Rebekka later adduces for her reaction, the sub-text should convey an instant of momentous self-revelation – 'Heaven blazing into the head' as a sudden leap forward of the moral conscience in the process of its own evaluation. The impossibility of becoming Rosmer's wife in this world – despite the Freudian reasons given for this *volte-face*[34] – has its basis, here, in the gradual redefinition of *joy* from the scream of amoral triumph to the act of ethical justice joyfully performed at the close of the play. The unspoken revelation, to which her shriek alerts her, is surely that the spiritually ennobled are forbidden by conscience and morality to profit in any way from their crimes. And her behaviour, to the end, is consistent with this rediscovery of value from the great nothingness of Romantic failure.

Rebekka's primary experience, however, expresses itself as a litany of irrecoverable loss. Her free spirit, with its once boundless vitality, is forced to confront the limitations imposed on personal freedoms – not only in the sphere of public morality, but in her own conviction of untainted selfhood free of the forces of determinism. Kroll, whose cunning lies in his smashing of the illusions of innocence and happiness on which the liberal democracy depends, insinuates a case-history for Rebekka which – true or not – undermines her own belief in radical innocence. 'But there's always some little thing or other that sticks and you can't shake yourself free of it', she admits (365) – and, when that 'thing' turns out to be the possibility of an unwittingly incestuous relationship with the man she thought to be her stepfather, she experiences the primal trauma that Freud has so carefully detailed in his analysis of Rebekka. The liberal spirit, however free its pretensions, is not emancipated psychically from the revulsion of violated taboo; and Dr West's exercise of absolute sexual freedom has left her appallingly 'unfree' in her loss of integrity. And so continues that long process of *sparagmos*, analogous to Rosmer's: the falling apart of the innocent self under the scrutiny of all past conviction, the disintegration of every value – passion, will, courage, hope and freedom – which once gave substance to Rebekka's Romantic image of her essential selfhood. It is a process already half-completed by the time the play begins with its image of Rebekka, subject to the forces of Rosmersholm, crocheting her large white shawl. She is not the woman she was, and it takes Rosmer's proposal of marriage to bring fully to consciousness the truth of her transformed nature. Marriage with Rosmer can no longer initiate the liberal democracy or confer a new and living reality upon life, freedom, joy and passion – not as *she* understands those values, at any rate, and not as *he* enacts them in his daily life. Her vision, suddenly, is one of hopelessness – 'håpløs' (iii. 326), as she now defines her love for Rosmer and his inability to reciprocate it. And this spirit of hopelessness – of fortitude, strength and energy drained away – permeates the final act of the play in images of devastation, paralysis, disease, and enslavement:

Rosmersholm has broken me. . . . Completely and utterly broken me. When I first came here, I had some spirit; I wasn't afraid to do things. Now I feel crushed by a tradition quite foreign to me. I feel after this as though I hadn't any courage left for anything. (vi, 369)

Rosmersholm has paralysed me. My will-power has been sapped, my spirit crippled. . . . I have lost the power to act. (370)

It is the Rosmer philosophy of life . . . that has infected my will. . . . And made it sick. Made it a slave to laws that meant nothing to me before.   (371)

She has lost liberty – enslaved by Rosmersholm and compromised by her past. She has lost hope and its correlatives – 'fredige vilje', 'makt' (III, 322). And, as the climax of her long threnody of loss, she mourns the end of all life's happiness:

> The Rosmer philosophy of life ennobles all right. But . . . it
> kills happiness. . . . Yes, Johannes . . . that is the terrible thing
> . . . the very moment when I am being offered all the
> happiness in life I could wish for . . . it's now I see my own past
> confronting me like a barrier.   (VI, 371–2)

'Det rosmerske livssyn adler. Men . . . det dreper lykken, du, (III, 322). Her words are chosen with the sort of meticulous care that one would expect of a woman recasting the contents of her moral being; and one must assume that Ibsen's emphasis on *lykke,* in both references to 'happiness', is deliberate and significant. It is not 'joy', not *glede,* that Rosmersholm destroys, but 'pleasure' – as if, to adapt Phaedra's formulation of the moralist's tragedy, the demands of 'goodness' will ultimately take their toll in gratification and delight. But to experience 'goodness' itself, to value it above personal satisfaction, is to experience the meaning of 'joy'; and it is part of the tragic rhythm of the play – the simultaneity of loss and recovery, collapse and reintegration, *sparagmos* and *anagnorisis* – that Rebekka should forfeit *lykke* to regain *glede.* Rosmersholm, which has crushed her, has also made her whole again. The Rosmer way of life, which frustrates the assertion of amoral will and which inhibits the freedom of energies dissociated from ethical goodness, restores to Rebekka the courage and the will and the power to act in the name of justice and nobility. It is not a broken or a paralysed woman who demonstrates, at the end of the play, the lost values of *modige vilje* and *makt* – 'courageous will' and 'self-confidence' – redefined in the spirit of joy. Ennoblement destroys only to restructure. It is a principle of dynamic change which tempers the revolutionary impulse with the conservative values of a humane past, which transforms chaotic energy into the peaceful order of civilisation – as in Rebekka's experience of savage and murderous lust, 'et vilt, ubetvingelig bejær' (321), subsiding into the tranquillity of gentle love and affection, 'den stille kjærlighet' (323):

But when I began living here with you . . . in peace . . . in
solitude . . . when without any kind of reserve you shared all
your thoughts with me . . . all your feelings just as they came,
so delicate and fine . . . *then* I felt the great transformation
taking place. Gradually, you understand. Almost imperceptibly
. . . but overwhelmingly in the end, and reaching right to the
very depths of my soul. . . . All the rest . . . this horrible,
sensual passion . . . faded far, far away. My restless agitation
subsided in peace and quiet. A feeling of tranquillity came
over me . . . a stillness like that which comes over a colony of
sea-birds on the Northern coast under the midnight sun. . . . I
felt that this was the beginning of love . . . a great and selfless
love that was content with being together as we *have* been
together.   (VI, 370–1)

Eros which destroys Paradise is transformed by Rosmersholm into
agape – 'den store forsakende kjærlighet' (322) – upon which Paradise is built. And all that this great and selfless love requires to
make it fully human is the sexual gesture, the embrace, which
Rosmer and Rebekka, in fear and renunciation, have scrupu-
lously avoided.

A more symbolic way of coming to terms with Rebekka's
transformation is to say that she has seen the White Horse of
Rosmersholm – a mysterious irruption of consciousness which
frustrates attempts at precise analysis. It is a device which, in
Inga-Stina Ewbank's description of similar metaphors in Ibsen,
'holds meanings in suspension, rather than clarifies and clinches
them';[35] and, not only does its significance evolve dynamically
within the individual consciousness, but different people perceive
it in different ways. Mrs Helseth sees the Horse as a folkloric
horror, returning from the dead to claim the living; Rosmer sees
it as the power of the past, rushing in out of the darkness, to
disturb with doubt and fear and scruple; and Rebekka, at first
dismissing the Horse as a morbid fantasy, gradually succumbs
to it as the Rosmer conscience operating through the loss of
skyldfrihet – 'innocence'. It becomes for her the spirit of remorse –
not in images of Gothic malignancy battening on the human
soul, but as a creature of extraordinary power, purity and beauty.
For, if it is death, the pale horse of Revelation, it may also connote, as Inga-Stina Ewbank points out,[36] the White Horse of
the Apocalypse on whose back rides the power of faithfulness

and truth, the warrior for justice who judges with integrity (Revelation 19: 11–12). And unremitting self-judgement, the perception and acknowledgment of guilt which destroys one's sense of innocence, is also the origin of conscience which restores value to the world. With Byron's Cain, Rebekka discovers that atonement in remorse and guilt establishes personal criteria of morality which, in turn, withstand the Luciferian temptation to see creation as an ethical void, meaningless and empty.[37] The supreme challenge that Rebekka must face at the end of the play is to convince Rosmer of her ennoblement, the living proof of their vision of spiritual democracy, and so strengthen him against the appalling negation of Brendel's seductive cynicism.

But how does one *prove* a condition of spirit, an alteration of consciousness? And how does one *convince* when language itself has lost all credibility? Rosmer's attempts to console Rebekka, and hers to reassure him of the ennobling power of his influence are all reduced to 'talemåter' (III, 372) – empty phrases. 'How *can* I believe you,' he asks, 'after the furtive way you have gone on here!' (VI, 373) And, even when he finally concedes his willingness, at the end, to believe in her ennoblement *on her bare word alone*, it is Rebekka who insists on the futility of words which she has herself emptied of substance. Indeed, the whole play has been a brilliant explication of the semantics of deception – not merely in Rebekka's deliberate lie about her age but in unconscious self-deceptions, unwitting suppressions of truth or the intentional speaking of half-truths to distract attention from the horror of the unspoken other half. 'Talemåter', she responds to Rosmer (III, 326) – 'Empty phrases, Johannes. No easy way out now, my dear, no running away. How can you ever take my word for things after today?' (VI, 379). The *impasse* is paradoxically resolved by the return of Brendel, who, in the very attempt to pervert and undermine their vision, suggests the appropriate course of action, though for grotesquely wrong reasons – which is in the nature of all such diabolical temptations. As I have already suggested,[38] Brendel's role is analogous to other Romantic tempters to negation, nihilism and despair – Lucifer or Mephisto – in whom the hero will either see the reflection of his own failure, or against whom he will struggle to assert his spiritual autonomy. In Byron's play, as Terry Otten suggests,[39] Lucifer's intention is to gain possession of Cain's will by confronting him with the nothingness of existence, man's ultimate despair in the face of death. And this is precisely what Brendel, in the spirit of defeat, tempts Rosmer to acknowledge: a vision of moral bankruptcy where idealism is sacrificed to expediency – the dust and ashes of liberal aspiration finally succumbing to the great nothingness of all humane value. The master-stroke of his cynicism, however, is to insinuate a remedy for Rosmer's failed project of the spirit, and a way out of the dilemma of unproven and unconvincing ennoblement:

> His success is assured. But . . . I would have you know . . . on one inescapable condition. . . . That the woman who loves him goes out into the kitchen and gladly chops off her dainty, pink and white little-finger . . . *here,* just here near the middle joint. Furthermore, that the aforesaid woman in love . . . equally gladly . . . cuts off her incomparably formed left ear. (vi, 376)

'. . . Gladelig . . . gladelig' (iii, 324) he keeps insisting. But the very idea of joy has become *talemåten* on his lips – a mutilation of the body, in a meaningless pseudo-Christian sacrifice, to pleasure soul. It is a gross exaggeration of Rosmer's own inability to conceive of spiritual transformation without the expurgation of the sexual, and a temptation to Rebekka to immolate herself in the spirit of the late Beate – to perform a neurotic action in the name of love. To follow Brendel's scheme is to enact a madness, a rite of mere perversity. But, just as Lucifer's counsel of despair challenges Cain to assert morality and meaning in the void, so Brendel's negation contains the positive solution to Rosmer and Rebekka's dilemma: the abandonment of words for a form of symbolic action, the declaration in deed of what can no longer be spoken, and the discovery of joy in its performance. The implications of what must be done so terrify Rosmer that, impelling him to speak against his will, Rebekka is forced to demand such knowledge as her right. There is no question of his goading her to destruction. Rebekka's death is a voluntary undertaking, neither psychic murder nor absurdity, but a recovery of all the qualities of the free spirit – 'mot', vilje', 'glede' (326) – now redefined by the moral conscience. And it will restore to Rosmer his dream of the liberal democracy:

> REBEKKA: But supposing I did have the courage? If I did dare, and gladly. What then?

ROSMER: Then I should have to believe you. Then surely I would
get back my faith again in the cause . . . faith in my power to
bring nobility to the minds of men . . . faith in man's power
to achieve that nobility of mind. (VI, 378)

But Rosmer cannot trust his own motives for allowing her to enact
conviction, and he fears the horrible fascination of her proof.
He speaks not with determination, but in fear and trembling,
finally restraining her from the 'vanvidd' (III, 326) – the possibility
of Brendelian "madness' that lurks beneath her purpose. And,
again, it is Rebekka who assures him of the purity of motive in the
act she must perform – an affirmative gesture of courage, will and
joy, neither mad nor despairing nor an admission of failure. It is
an assurance conveyed, as it must be now, through the eloquence
of dramatic gesture as Rebekka throws the long white shawl over
her head as the preliminary assertion of her purified intention.
For any comparable sense of spiritual preparation in an act of
symbolic robing, on must turn to the ritual articulated in
Cleopatra's death-scene:

> Give me my robe, put on my crown; I have
> Immortal longings in me. . . .
>   husband, I come:
> Now to that name my courage prove my title!
> I am fire and air; my other elements
> I give to baser life.
> (*Antony and Cleopatra*, v. ii. 279–89)

Her white shawl is not only, like Cleopatra's robe, the wedding-
garment in which she will marry Rosmer, nor is it merely the
shroud of her immolation. It is also the emblem of her nobility,
the 'fire and air' of the purified moral conscience, the will and
strength of innocence recovered. Nothing could be further from
the parody of Brendel's notion of sacrifice, or from the 'neurotic
imitation'[40] of Beate's way that Mrs Helseth sees at the end of the
play. Rebekka makes this clear:

ROSMER: . . . You are not like Beata. You are not in the power of
some twisted view of life.
REBEKKA: But I am in the power of the Rosmersholm view of life
. . . *now*. Where I have sinned . . . it is right that I should

atone.   (vi. 379)

She may repeat Beate's way, but she denies Beate's meaning. In
dying, she will free herself from the guilt of Beate's death and free
Rosmer. It will be an act of justice, confirming man's ethical
conduct in a world emptied of moral positives. It will not be a
religious rite. And Rosmer acknowledges this existential redefinition of the unfettered life as a complex of moral responsibilities
and moral judgments on the self: 'Well then,' he tells her, 'I give
my loyalty to our emancipated view of life. There is no judge over
us. Therefore we must see to it that we judge ourselves' (ibid.).
They may be free agents, but freedom is not synonymous with the
idea that everything is permitted. Existential freedom – man's
awful autonomy in the absence of God – confers upon him the
responsibility of right and proper action; and Rosmer and Rebekka enact their doom in the absence of all positives, and so
create value out of nothingness. They die for the right reasons:
not to affirm the power of a dead past or the tenacity of Beate,
but to reassert the moral will, to free their love of guilt, and to
establish once again the primacy of human values in the world of
ordinary experience. They die in joy, in that complete fulfilment
and realisation of self in the love of the other which, in the
language of an earlier dispensation, would be synonymous with
blessedness or grace.

'If you go,' says Rosmer, 'I go with you' (ibid.). He must die,
not because he is a criminal, nor to punish himself for acquiescing
in Rebekka's death. He must die because he can no longer live
without Rebekka, just as it is the destiny of Milton's Adam to eat
the apple so that he may be judged with Eve:[41]

> with thee
> Certain my resolution is to Die;
> How can I live without thee, how forgoe
> Thy sweet Converse and Love so dearly joind.[42]

This is precisely what Rosmer cannot *say*, for words of love, like
all other verbal reassurances, are merely *talemåter*. And just as
Rebekka cannot restore hope to Rosmer 'på blotte og bare ord'
(iii, 326) – 'in plain and simple language' – so Rosmer, unable even
to step on the bridge from which his wife hurled herself, cannot
possibly convince her of a love now free from the entangling guilt

of Beate's suicide. Like Rebekka, he too must abandon language
for a form of symbolic action; and in the rites of marriage he
transforms the hopelessness of her love for him – 'det var det som
gjorde min kjærlighet håpløs' (326) – into an amalgam of hope,
love, and joy:

> ROSMER: Rebekka . . . now I lay my hand on your head . . . [*does
> so*] and take you to be my truly wedded wife.
> REBEKKA [*takes both his hands and puts her head on his breast*]:
> Thank you, Johannes. [*Lets go.*] And now I go gladly.
> (VI. 380)

'Og nu går jeg – gladelig.' She will repeat this affirmation of joy as
her final line in the play, but with a change in pronoun that seals
their commitment to each other and defines the nature of their
marriage: 'Så går vi gladelig' (III. 327) – 'Then *we* will go, joyfully.'
And so they move from expiation and self-judgement to joy,
restoring order to the moral universe and rediscovering in each
other the Romantic positives in a world barely able to compre-
hend them. For the duration of the play there had been exhort-
ations – from Kroll and Mortensgaard, and even by Rosmer – for
them to marry, in the sense of conferring bourgeois respectability
on a sexually suspect union. Now they will marry for the right
reasons, as they will die for the right reasons: to affirm love and
joy in the meeting of two independent spirits, neither dominating
the other, neither submitting to the demands of the other, neither
dying as a sacrificial lure to the other. They will die as a fusion of
autonomous spiritual powers, a single consciousness, a genuine
cosmology of two. 'Is it you who goes with me, or I with you?'
Rebekka asks; and Rosmer replies, 'We go together, Rebekka. I
with you, you with me. . . . For now we two are one.' If there is a
synthesis in their ceremonious rite with its curious liturgy, it is
not, I think, that synthesis of abstractions that Ibsen envisions as
the Third Empire of *Emperor and Galilean*: neither Christianity
and paganism, nor orthodoxy and enlightenment. There is a
joining of two human beings in a union, both real and symbolic,
which dramatises joy as that process of atonement, both secular
and divine, endemic to the greatest traditions of love poetry:

> The phoenix riddle hath more wit
> By us: we two being one, are it.[43]

For nu er vi to *ett.* . . . Nu er vi *ett.*   (iii. 327)

It is not outlandish to yoke Donne and Ibsen together in this way.
Both are searching for analogues of grace in the secular would,
for the idea of joy in human experience commensurate with the
blessedness of the soul's union with God. And Christ's prayer for
the atonement of all mankind in Him and His atonement in
God – the echo that John Northam detects beneath the bare,
monosyllabic words of Rosmer and Rebekka –[44] may indeed
provide the source for all those images of diversity resolved in
unity, and alienation in reconciliation, which extend from the
Metaphysicals to the Romantics:

> May they all be one.
> Father, may they be one in us,
> as you are in me and I am in you. . . .
> I have given them the glory you gave to me,
> that they may be one as we are one.
> With me in them and you in me,
> may they be so completely one
> that the world will realise that it was you
>   who sent me. . . .   (John 17: 21–3)

But, whereas Donne's canonised lovers derive their mystery from
the values of a wittily intensified faith, the Romantic lovers must
redefine joy in a world without God.

It is difficult to find precise analogues in Romantic literature
for Ibsen's peculiar *glede.* 'Joy', as Abrams points out, may be a
central, recurrent term in the vocabulary of Romanticism; but it
often has a specialised meaning for the individual poet.[45]
Coleridge's vision of the secular apocalypse, of paradise recovered
in the spirit of joy, recaptures some of Ibsen's dramatic
metaphors –

> Joy, Lady! is the spirit and the power
> Which, wedding Nature to us, gives in dower
>   A new Earth and new Heaven[46]

– but Rosmer's paradise is not dependent upon an abstract
marriage of man's perceiving mind to the natural universe. Joy, in
Ibsen, is the spirit and the power of moral perception – the

restoration of value to the desolate world, even at the cost of life and happiness. It is the exhilarating flood of light at the end of *Ghosts*, 'Heaven blazing into the head', the tragic revelation which restores reality and freedom and wholeness to life. Neither Coleridge, nor Schiller's 'An die Freude', nor Beethoven's joyous tonalities are appropriate to Ibsen's idea. And for any comparable sense of the sombre joy in which Rosmer and Rebekka go to their consummation and their death, one must turn to Mahler's setting of Nietzsche – 'The Song of the Midnight Bell', with its dark celebration of a joy more strenuous and challenging than despair:

> Die Welt ist tief,
> Und tiefer als der Tag gedacht.
> Tief ist ihr Weh –,
> Lust – tiefer noch als Herzeleid;
> Weh spricht: Vergeh!
> Doch alle Lust will Ewigkeit –,
> – will tiefe, tiefe Ewigkeit![47]

> The world is deep,
> And deeper than day had thought.
> Deep is its woe –,
> Joy – even deeper than agony;
> Woe counsels: Give up!
> But all joy wants eternal life –
> wants deep, deep eternal life!

'Sorrow', writes Morse Peckham, 'is a sentimental lust for finality; joy is the penetration beyond that sentimentality into the value-lessness of reality, into its freedom, the achievement of which is inevitably its loss. Joy is the eternal recurrence of the same problem, forever solved and forever unsolvable.'[48] It is, in other words, a relinquishment of the self to process, to *Ewigkeit*, to what Nietzsche calls 'the eternal joy of becoming, beyond all terror and pity – that joy which includes even joy in destroying'.[49] For to create value in the void, and to embody that value in existential action is to affirm one's self even in the process of losing that self – as the Buttonmoulder enigmatically puts it to Peer Gynt:

BUTTONMOULDER: To be one's self is to kill one's self.
I doubt if that answer means anything to you.
So we'll put it this way: to show unmistakably
The Master's intention whatever you're doing.
PEER: But what if a man has never discovered
What the Master intended?
BUTTONMOULDER: Then he must sense it.   (III. 411)

And if there is no master, then one must act as if there were, if necessary become one's own master, whatever the risk, and place the self at the disposal of those values which infuse meaning into nothingness. Joy derives from asserting, even in death, what can be asserted in no other way: love free of guilt, and a paradigm of moral justice which recreates the universe in the image of man's heroic choices. To create a 'new Heaven and a new Earth' out of nothing, order out of emptiness, selfhood out of moral responsibility, is to experience that paradox of a joy deeper even than sorrow. And this, it seems to me, is the closest approximation, in the literature of Romantic joy, to that spirit of *glede* in which Rosmer and Rebekka choose their course of action and so create their liberal democratic paradise as an earthly possibility.

Little wonder that Mrs Helseth can make nothing of their deaths. Our vision of the *dénouement* of *Rosmersholm* is reduced to the limited perception of a Northern Mrs Grundy first hemming in her disapproval of the nocturnal goings-on, and then openly voicing her condemnation of a couple she clearly believes to be an adulterer and his concubine. She embodies a form of petty-bourgeois mean-spiritedness which perceives no value in momentous action, and which substitutes self-righteousness for the far more difficult effort of comprehension. Like Brendel, she tempts us to see in Rosmer and Rebekka nothing more than a contemporary sense of pathetic existential failure.[50] At the same time, however, Mrs Helseth's eyewitness account of what happens offstage provides us with sufficient information to resist the interpretation she forces upon us. Indeed, the irony begins to operate only when we dissociate ourselves from her cries of censure, and acknowledge a meaning she is incapable of grasping. Her superstitious mind sees only the White Horse of retribution claiming its victims – not the perfected conscience, of which Rebekka's shawl in the emblem; and her cry of outrage, 'God forgive the sinful creatures! Putting their arms round each other!'

(vi, 381), deflects attention from the triumph of the gesture. For the first time in the play, Rosmer is able to walk freely onto the bridge from which Beate flung herself into the millrace, no longer a prisoner to her memory or to his self-lacerating guilt. And for the first time in the play Rosmer and Rebekka are able to transcend the powerful inhibitions and the fears of sexuality in a gesture of love which defies the dead woman who haunts them. Mrs Helseth's puritanism *tempts* us to see them as depraved capitulants to the vengeful power of the past. Ibsen *challenges* us to recognise in them the operation of a stringent moral conscience which finds, even in the act of death, those forces of passion and joy which make it fully human. That their deaths may be a delusion, a yielding to the White Horse, Rosmer freely admits; and yet he takes the risk of committing himself to uncertainty and mystery.

> Thus the Romantic once more enters into history and human life, for to create is to choose, without ever knowing whether or not the choice is the right choice, for the act of choice changes the world.[51]

This, for Peckham, is the triumph of Romanticism; and he locates the resolution of the Romantic dilemma – the search for value in a world without meaning – in the work of Nietzsche and his discovery of the way to encompass the paradoxes and the irreconcilable antinomies of life. Ibsen, it seems to me, shares in that triumph, in perceiving value as process – even as the tragic process of eternal discovery and loss, of perpetual disintegration and reintegration – which is the basis of reality and life and joy.

It is a difficult vision to grasp, enfolded as it is in layer within layer of irony, its affirmations channelled – as in Mrs Helseth's curtain speech or the final platitudes of Brack and Tesman – through cries of negation, misrepresentation and error. But to yield to the choral voices, to deny freedom in Ellida's choice or joy in the fate of Rosmer and Rebekka, is to demonstrate the habitual recourse of our age to an easy cynicism and hasten the advent of a world in which the moral conscience and the liberal ideal degenerate into political pragmatism, and in which survival becomes synonymous with the philosophy of the troll: 'To thine own self be – all-sufficient' (iii, 295). Brendel sees it all with horrifying clarity and, in the glib pessimism of his own defeated ideal-

ism, hails Mortensgaard as the harbinger of the twentieth
century:

> Peter Mortensgaard is lord and master of the future. Never
> have I been in a more august presence. Peter Mortensgaard
> possesses the secret of omnipotence. He can do whatever he
> wants. . . . Because Peter Mortensgaard never wants to do
> more than he *can*. Peter Mortensgaard is quite capable of
> living his life without ideals. And it is precisely *that*, don't you
> see, that is the secret of practical success. It is the sum of all the
> world's wisdom. (VI, 375)

To the man of the future, Rosmer and Rebekka will seem mere
irrelevant failures, Romantic idealists whose language is no
longer understood, and whose positive philosophy the pragmatist
cannot take seriously. Instead of the poetry of Romanticism, in all
its fallibility and triumph, we are persuaded to see only that
cynicism which is the fashionable modern vision. But to make
Ibsen our contemporary, in the sense that Jan Kott has conferred
modernity on Shakespeare, is to reduce his stature as a great
tragedian and a celebrant, however paradoxical and renegade, of
Romanticism as a constructive and life-affirming vision.

Notes

1. Rolf Fjelde, 'The Lady from the Sea: Ibsen's Positive World-View in a
   Topographic Figure', *Modern Drama*, XXI (1978) 379.
2. McFarlane, Introduction to *The Oxford Ibsen*, VIII, 31.
3. Wilson Knight, *Ibsen*, pp. 96–7.
4. Ibid., p. 98.
5. Fjelde, in *Modern Drama*, XXI, 379.
6. Bradbrook, *Ibsen the Norwegian*, p. 109.
7. Cf. Brian Johnston's Hegelian discussion of *The Lady from the Sea* and the
   disastrous implications of Ellida's decision, in *The Ibsen Cycle*, pp. 111ff.
8. Francis Fergusson, '*The Lady From the Sea*', in Haakonsen, *Contemporary
   Approaches to Ibsen*, I; repr. in McFarlane, *Ibsen: A Critical Anthology*, p.
   410.
9. George Steiner, *In Bluebeard's Castle*, p. 24.
10. Sainte-Beuve's review of *Madame Bovary*, 4 May 1857; repr. in Gustave
    Flaubert, *Madame Bovary*, ed. Paul de Man (New York, 1965) p. 331.
11. Erica Jong, *Fear of Flying* (New York, 1973) p. 11.
12. Auden, *The Enchafèd Flood*, p. 68.
13. Fjelde, in *Modern Drama*, XXI, 384.

14. Ibid., p. 389; James McFarlane, 'Meaning and Evidence in Ibsen's Drama', in Haakonsen, *Contemporary Approaches to Ibsen*, I, 49.
15. Cf. Richard Schechner, 'The Unexpected Visitor in Ibsen's Late Plays', *Educational Theatre Journal*, XIV (1962) 120.
16. See, for instance, Rachel's sexual fantasies in Margaret Laurence's *A Jest of God* (Toronto, 1966).
17. Jong, *Fear of Flying*, p. 110.
18. Fjelde, in *Modern Drama*, XXI, 384.
19. Ibid., p. 388.
20. Johnston, *The Ibsen Cycle*, esp. pp. 122–5.
21. Inga-Stina Ewbank, 'Shakespeare, Ibsen and the Unspeakable: An Inaugural Lecture' (Bedford College, London, 1975) p. 24.
22. Jong, *Fear of Flying*, p. 328.
23. Fjelde, in *Modern Drama*, XXI, 388.
24. The terminology and the history of the various forms of Romantic apocalypse are fully dealt with by M. H. Abrams in *Natural Supernaturalism*, and 'English Romanticism: The Spirit of the Age', in Frye, *Romanticism Reconsidered*.
25. Abrams, *Natural Supernaturalism*, p. 334.
26. Cf. 'The World's Song of Life and Joy', ibid., pp. 431–7.
27. Cf. 'The Romantic Positives', ibid., pp. 427–31.
28. Ibid., pp. 430–1.
29. Ibid., p. 431.
30. S. T. Coleridge, 'Dejection: An Ode', stanza V.
31. *Hippolytus*, in *Euripides: 'Alcestis' and Other Plays*, trs. Philip Vellacott (Harmondsworth, 1965) p. 39. I have slightly rearranged the lines.
32. 'Själamörd (apropos *Rosmersholm*)', trs. Rolf Fjelde in the *Tulane Drama Review*, XIII (1968) 113–8.
33. W. B. Yeats, 'Lapis Lazuli', in *Collected Poems*, p. 338.
34. Cf. Freud's analysis of Rebekka West in 'Some Character-Types met with in Psychoanalytic Work', in McFarlane, *Ibsen: A Critical Anthology*, pp. 392–9.
35. Ewbank, in Haakonsen, *Contemporary Approaches to Ibsen*, I, 105.
36. Ibid., II, 78.
37. Cf. Terry Otten's discussion of *Cain* in *The Deserted Stage*, pp. 60–6.
38. For a detailed discussion of the priest–Devil alliance in Ibsen, see Brian Johnston, 'The Dialectic of *Rosmersholm*', *Drama Survey*, VI (1967) 205.
39. Otten, *The Deserted Stage*, pp. 60–1.
40. Cf. Marvin Carlson's acquiescence in the Helseth point of view in 'Patterns of Structure and Character in Ibsen's *Rosmersholm*', *Modern Drama*, XVII (1974) 274.
41. Cf. Bradbrook, *Ibsen the Norwegian*, p. 113.
42. John Milton, *Paradise Lost*, IX. 915–18.
43. John Donne, 'The Canonization'.
44. John Northam, 'On a Firm Foundation – The Translation of Ibsen's Prose', and 'A Note on the Language of *Rosmersholm*', *Ibsenårbok* (Oslo) 1977.
45. Abrams, *Natural Supernaturalism*, p. 276.
46. Coleridge, 'Dejection', stanza V.
47. From Nietzsche's, *Also sprach Zarathustra*, III (1884). Mahler's setting of

Nietzsche forms the fourth movement of his Third Symphony.
48. Peckham, *Romanticism*, p. 33. There is a more detailed discussion of Nietzsche's poem in ch. 20 of Peckham's *Beyond The Tragic Vision*, pp. 364–72.
49. Quoted ibid., p. 368.
50. I have discussed, at far greater length, the idea of 'temptation' as an aspect of dramtic form in 'The Temptation to Err: The Dénouement of *Rosmersholm'*, *Educational Theatre Journal*, xxix (1977).
51. Peckham, *Romanticism*, p. 33.

7 Conclusion: 'All of Paradise that We Shall Know'

Whether we be young or old,
Our destiny, our being's heart and home,
Is with infinitude, and only there;
With hope it is, hope that can never die,
Effort, and expectation, and desire,
And something evermore about to be.[1]

The dramatic context of this most Romantic of Wordsworthian revelations is tinged with undertones of peculiarly Ibsenian irony. Following an Alpine track's 'Conspicuous invitation to ascend / A lofty mountain', and inspired by 'hopes that pointed to the clouds', the poet and his companion quite inadvertently cross the Alps. Infinitude suddenly becomes finite – their only direction now is downwards. Momentarily depressed by the reduction of marvellous sublimity to the ridiculously mundane, Wordsworth soon fortifies himself with the consolations of his insight into Romantic psychology: his vision of a spiritual striving *beyond* the satisfactions of what is merely possible, the boundlessness of human aspiration, the immortality of unrequited hope, and man's strenuous reaching after potential rather than actuality. It is an image analogous to what Inga-Stina Ewbank, in a different context, has called 'the expression of the vertical drive in Ibsen's plays'[2] – which, she argues, makes Ibsen peculiarly 'alien' to the English imagination. But that same drive which impels Solness to the top of his tower and Irene and Rubek up the Peak of Promise also makes them kin to the familiar figure of the Romantic, dedicated to his *Streben nach dem Unendlichen* – Faust's aspiration after Eternal Womanhood, or Wordsworth's vision of man's 'home' as infinitude. Which leads me back to E. M. Forster's essay, 'Ibsen the Romantic'.

198

To compare Ibsen with Wordsworth [he writes] is to scandalize the faithful in either camp, yet they had one important point in common: they were both of them haunted until the end of their lives by the romantic possibilities of scenery. Wordsworth fell into the residential fallacy; he continued to look at the gods direct, and to pin with decreasing success his precepts to the flanks of Helvellyn. Ibsen, wiser and greater, sank and smashed the Dovrëfjeld in the depths of the sea, the depths of the sea.[3]

The contrasting Romantic visions of the two mountain poets grow typically impressionistic in the opacity of Forster's prose until all that remains is a vague sense of Ibsen's anomalous romanticism, an 'otherness' which Forster simply calls 'wiser and greater'. This, in the final analysis, is the Romantic Ibsen who demands to be accounted for.

Part of that greater wisdom, I have been arguing, is the conscious awareness that the upward drive towards epiphany on the heights is a movement towards the inhuman, a sacrifice of the living 'something' that *is* to a 'something' evermore *about to be.* What distinguishes the Romantic temperament, moreover, is its inability to conceive of an alternative to infinitude which is not tainted by gross imperfection, by what Hedda in her anguish calls 'det latterlige og det lave' (iii. 432) – 'the ridiculous and the soiled'. Ecstasy or despair, Paradise or the abyss, are the polarities of experience on the vertical drive. But the genuinely human dimension, the mid-point between the ideal and its brutal negation, stands in danger of being overwhelmed or engulfed. This upwards–downwards thrust, the extremities of Romanticism, is perfectly caught in a moment at the end of *Little Eyolf* where transcendentalism and cynicism struggle to define man's place within this existential geography:

RITA: . . . A change *is* taking place in me. I can feel the pain of it. . . . Almost like giving birth.

ALLMERS: That's what it is. Or a resurrection. A transition to a higher life.

RITA [*stares dispiritedly ahead*]: Yes . . . and with it the loss of all life's happiness.

ALLMERS: In that loss is our gain.

RITA [*vehemently*]: Empty phrases! In God's name, we are still human. Creatures of the earth.

ALLMERS: But with some kinship to sea and sky, too, Rita.   (VIII,
        99)

"Jordmennesker' (515) – earth-folk, mortal beings – must finally
accommodate themselves to the bounded and the finite, not by
abandoning the vertical structure which satisfies their aspirations
towards infinitude, but by discovering those points of horizontal
contact with other beings subject to the same processes of
mutability and change. They talk, at the end of the play, of
looking upwards to the mountains, and beyond the mountains to
the stars, and beyond the stars to the vast silence of infinitude.
But their hands are stretched out to each other. And in these
brief moments of vertical and horizontal intersection Ibsen
intimates the only paradise that *jordmennesker* shall know.

The more conventional Romantic paradise – Wordsworth's or
Coleridge's, for example – lies in the imaginative capacities of
mind operating upon and interacting with the natural universe
until the real is transformed into the Edenic:

> For the discerning intellect of Man,
> When wedded to this goodly universe
> In love and holy passion, shall find [Paradise]
> A simple produce of the common day.[4]

The divinity of mind finds its analogue in the divinity of nature;
and in their 'great consummation',[5] man rediscovers integrity and
redeems himself from death. This association of man and deity is
an aspect of Wordsworth's revelation on Mount Snowdon which
transforms the landscape into an emblem of majestic intellect:

> a mind sustained
> By recognitions of transcendent power,
> In sense conducting to ideal form,
> In soul of more than mortal privilege.[6]

The creative power of the human imagination, in turn, associates
man's mind with that which 'feeds upon infinity'; and, in an act
of radical identification, self in communion with nature, the
merely human is raised from earth to heaven and becomes divine.
At the risk, again, of scandalising the faithful in either camp, I
would suggest that Wordsworth's Paradisal intimations on Mount

Snowdon find their precise counter-Romantic equivalents in John
Gabriel Borkman's visions on the wild slopes and ridges of his
mountain Kingdom. For him, the invisible subterranean world of
nature has always been instinct with enormous pent-up energies,
with latent powers in which his own psychic nature seeks affinity.
Down in the mines he hears the song of the ore, and it sounds like
a cry of release and joy which echoes the harmonies of his own
spiritual music. If only he could free the sleeping spirits of gold,
control the unleashed powers hidden in earth and mountains,
master the energies of forest and sea and so create his empire of
humanism. Like Wordsworth, he experiences a sense of 'Kindred
mutations' in which nature and human nature reciprocate a
'like existence'; and this identification of self and nature in
'interchangeable supremacy'[7] finally confers a more than mortal
privilege on the Borkmanian soul. 'The romantic quality of his
identification with nature', as Charles Lyons points out, 'is very
important – not because the play in any way uses that identification romantically, but because the play works to show that
romantic identification as false and destructive in several subtle
ways.'[8] This is the Ibsen of whom Forster takes too little account –
not the mountain poet haunted by the Romantic possibilities of
landscape, but the counter-Romantic whose vision penetrates
beneath the goodly surface of the universe to the cold, inanimate
region of imperishable forms. Its harmonies are the rhythms of
the *danse macabre,* and the breath of inspiration that blows
across this frozen Kingdom is the icy blast of death. 'To me it is
the breath of life', cries Borkman. And with outstretched arms he
strains after a final consummating union with the subterranean
forces of the inorganic world.

As Ibsen's destructive winter landscape exposes the fallacy of
what Forster calls 'the romantic possibilities of scenery', so
Borkman-as-Romantic belies the basic assumption of Wordsworthian romanticism: that man's creative imagination may
transform the natural world into a recovered paradise. Torn
between a sympathetic identification with nature's power and an
appropriating need to possess and harness its forces, terrified of
natural process and attracted only to what is hard and ironlike,
Borkman finally locates his Eden *out* of nature in a realm of static
forms. The apocalyptic marriage of mind and nature, the 'great
consummation' which 'gives in dower, / A new Earth and new
Heaven',[9] is dramatised by Ibsen as a tragic displacement of those

erotic energies which Borkman lavishes on rock and ore. Out of the very 'types and symbols of Eternity'[10] in which Wordsworth rediscovers Paradise, Ibsen reveals the anti-Eden to which the quest for infinitude may lead. And here, perhaps, he is the greater and the wiser poet. For it is not so much the destructive force of nature which Wordsworth fails, ultimately, to confront, as the potentially dangerous implications of the vertical drive itself, the fallacies of Romantic psychology.

'And shall the earth / Seem all of paradise that we shall know?'[11] Ibsen's response to the central, insistent question of Romanticism would seem to be that Paradise inheres neither in the infinitude of idealism nor in the mundane regions of earth-life, neither in Romantic impossibility nor in the realistically possible, but at the point where aspiration and limitation meet to *enhance* each other, where (in Wallace Stevens's phrase)

> we ourselves
> Stand at the centre of ideal time,
> The inhuman making choice of a human self.[12]

There is a compelling magnificence in the Romantic demand of Solness or Hedda for 'more than mortal privilege', and for this reason we cannot reject the idealist in Ibsen who craves the satisfaction of a deep psychic need for Paradise. But those who finally experience the miracle are not those who seek it on the heights. The 'more than mortal' spirit which accommodates itself to mortality, which is rescued from the inhuman by reaching out into a human dimension, recovers, if not Paradise itself, at least the *condition* of Paradise as 'a simple produce of the common day': the joy of Rosmer and Rebekka in enacting their moral choice, the compassion for each other which redeems Rita and Allmers from the dark night of absurdity and alienation, the sanity and wholeness that Ellida finds in tempering Romantic freedom with the constraints of human responsibility. Vertical and horizontal intersect at the centre of ideal time; and the dramatic figure of that intersection is a 'marriage' – an analogue of the soul's Paradisal union with Christ which radiates behind the wedding of Rosmer and Rebekka and which the Romantic poets envision as a marriage of the creative mind and nature. But there is nothing abstract about Ibsen's marriages or those acts of restoration and rededication that conclude *Little Eyolf* and *The*

Lady from the Sea. Paradise is regained in an act of human love – not the imperishable bliss on the Peak of Promise nor the carnality in the abyss, but an affirmation of self in the selfhood of the other which finally assuages the terrors of sexuality and the perverse sublimations of romantic eroticism. In this sense – in his definition of *menneskeliv* as the living process that unites men and women, permeates all human connections, and reveals itself most delicately in the presence of the child – Ibsen the Romantic shares in and shapes the most fundamental vision of Romanticism: the affirmation of life, the celebration, as M. H. Abrams puts it, 'of that which lives, moves, and evolves by an internal energy, over what is lifeless, inert, and unchanging.'[13]

There is a fleeting image of Ibsen as a character – a type of fictional reality – in a short story by Isak Dinesen called 'The Pearls'. The heroine, a romantic young Danish girl, encounters him in a Norwegian mountain village (where she delights in standing recklessly on the edge of precipices); and, seeing her come from the local shoemaker's shop, Ibsen asks with a smile, 'You have not lost your sole in the mountains?' Quite impervious to his mischievous pun, she tells him that she has just taken her pearls to the man to be restrung, and the conversation turns to this strange shoemaker – a collector of children's tales and national folklore, who once dreamed of being a poet before destiny drove him to the cobbler's last.

After a pause he said: 'I have been told that you and your husband come from Denmark, on your wedding trip. This is an unusual thing to do; these mountains are high and dangerous. Who of you two was it who desired to come here? Was it you?' 'Yes,' said she. 'Yes,' said the stranger. 'I thought so. That he might be the bird, which upward soars, and you the breeze which carries him along. Do you know that quotation? Does it tell you anything?' 'Yes,' said she, somewhat bewildered. 'Upwards,' said he, and sat back, silent, with his hands upon his walking-stick. And after a little he went on: 'The summits! Who knows? We two are pitying the shoemaker for his bad luck, that he had to give up his dreams of being a poet, of fame and a great name. How do we know but that he has had the best of luck? Greatness, the applause of the masses! Indeed, my young lady, perhaps they are better left alone. Perhaps in

common trade they cannot reasonably purchase a shoemaker's
sign board, and the knowledge of soling. One may do well in
getting rid of them at cost price. What do you think, Madam?'
'I think you are right,' she said slowly. He gave her a sharp
glance from a pair of ice-blue eyes.
  'Indeed,' said he. 'Is that your advice, on this fair summer
day? Cobbler, stay by your last. One should do better, you
think, in making up pills and draughts for the sick human
beings, and cattle, of this world?' He chuckled a little. 'It is a
very good jest. In a hundred years it will be written in a book: A
little lady from Denmark gave him the advice to stay by his last.
Unfortunately he did not follow it. Good-bye, Madam, good-
bye.'[14]

The spiritual landscape of Romanticism is beautifully encom-
passed in Isak Dinesen's parable, Ibsen the Romantic caught up
in the same conflict of aspiration and limitation that so obsesses
his protagonists: the avocational calling that leads the poet upwards to the summit, and the vocation that confines the apothe-
cary's apprentice to the business of the world. The intellect of
man, as always in Ibsen, is forced to choose between the sublime
and the mundane. And Ibsen himself, however ambiguously
attracted to the common trade, in a final *galskap* betrays the very
advice that he persuades the romantic young lady to articulate.
But, in the final analysis, it is paradoxically not Dinesen's image
of Ibsen that exemplifies the Ibsenist position, but Ibsen's own
parable of the shoemaker – the man who strings pearls, and who
has at his disposal a whole store of treasures ('pearls if you like',
says Ibsen) which are perfectly consistent with his symbolic
profession. This shoemaker is a cripple. He has no feet – which
means that he can no longer ascend the summits of his dreaming,
but neither is he bound to walking only on the earth. This
strange, expressionistic image of the poet–artist and sage,
mender of souls and custodian of his nation's heritage, exists at
that peculiarly Ibsenian point where the vertical drive of poetic
aspiration and the horizontal tension of cobbling intersect in his
'knowledge of soling'. He embodies my sense of 'Ibsen the
Romantic'.

Notes

1. Wordsworth, *The Prelude,* vi. 603–8 (1850 text).
2. Ewbank, in Durbach, *Ibsen and the Theatre,* p. 37.
3. Forster, in McFarlane, *Ibsen: A Critical Anthology,* p. 235.
4. Wordsworth, 'Prospectus for "The Recluse"', ll. 52–5.
5. Ibid., l. 58.
6. Wordsworth, *The Prelude.* xiv. 74–7 (1850 text).
7. Ibid., ll. 94–5, 84.
8. Lyons, in *Scandinavian Studies,* xlv, 296.
9. Coleridge, 'Dejection', ll. 68–9.
10. Wordsworth, *The Prelude,* vi. 639 (1850 text).
11. Stevens, 'Sunday Morning', stanza iii.
12. Wallace Stevens, 'Of Ideal Time and Choice', concluding lines.
13. Abrams, *Natural Supernaturalism,* p. 431.
14. Isak Dinesen, 'The Pearls', *Winter's Tales* (New York, 1961) pp. 116–7.

Select Bibliography

Abrams, M. H., 'English Romanticism: The Spirit of the Age', in Frye, *Romanticism Reconsidered.*

——, *Natural Supernaturalism: Tradition and Revolution in Romantic Literature* (New York, 1971).

Auden, W. H., *The Enchafèd Flood: or The Romantic Iconography of the Sea* (New York, 1967; first published 1950).

Becker, Ernest, *The Denial of Death* (New York, 1973).

Bradbrook, Muriel, 'Ibsen and the Past Imperfect', in Haakonsen, *Contemporary Approaches to Ibsen,* II.

——, *Ibsen the Norwegian,* new edn (Hamden, Conn., 1966).

Brontë, Emily, *Wuthering Heights* (1847), ed. David Daiches (Harmondsworth, 1966).

Buckley, Jerome, 'Symbols of Eternity: The Victorian Escape from Time', in Warren D. Anderson and Thomas D. Clareson (eds), *Victorian Essays: A Symposium* (Kent, Ohio, 1967).

Byron, George Gordon, 6th Baron, *Selected Verse and Prose Works,* ed. Peter Quennell (London, 1959).

——, *Lord Byron's 'Cain': Twelve Essays and a Text with Variants and Annotations,* ed. Truman Steffan (Austin, Tex., 1968).

Camus, Albert, *'The Myth of Sisyphus' and Other Essays,* trs. Justin O'Brien (New York, 1955).

Carlson, Marvin, 'Patterns of Structure and Character in Ibsen's *Rosmersholm'*, *Modern Drama,* XVII (1974).

Coveney, Peter, *Poor Monkey* (1957); repr. as *The Image of Childhood: The Individual and Society: A Study of the Theme in English Literature* (Harmondsworth, 1967).

Dinesen, Isak, *Winter's Tales* (New York, 1961).

Dostoievski, Feodor, *Crime and Punishment* (1866), trs. Constance Garnett (London, 1967).

Downs, Brian, *Ibsen: The Intellectual Background* (Cambridge, 1946).

——, *Modern Norwegian Literature 1860–1918* (Cambridge, 1966).

Durbach, Errol (ed.), *Ibsen and the Theatre* (London, 1980).

Ewbank, Inga-Stina, 'Ibsen and "The Far More Difficult Art" of Prose', in Haakonsen, *Contemporary Approaches to Ibsen.* II.

——, 'Ibsen's Dramatic Language as a Link between his "Realism" and his "Symbolism"', in Haakonsen, *Contemporary Approaches to Ibsen,* I.

——, 'Ibsen on the English Stage: "The Proof of the Pudding is in the Eating"', in Durbach, *Ibsen and the Theatre.*

——, 'Shakespeare, Ibsen and the Unspeakable: An Inaugural Lecture'

(Bedford College, London, 1975).

Fergusson, Francis, 'The Lady from the Sea', in Haakonsen, *Contemporary Approaches to Ibsen*, I; repr. in McFarlane, *Ibsen: A Critical Anthology*.

Fjelde, Rolf (ed.), *Ibsen: A Collection of Critical Essays* (Englewood Cliffs, NJ, 1965).

_____, 'The Lady from the Sea*: Ibsen's Positive World-View in a Topographic Figure', *Modern Drama*, XXI (1978).

Forster, E. M., 'Ibsen the Romantic' (1928), in McFarlane, *Ibsen: A Critical Anthology*.

Freud, Sigmund, 'Some Character-Types met with in Psychoanalytic Work' (1916), in McFarlane, *Ibsen: A Critical Anthology*.

Frye, Northrop, 'The Drunken Boat: The Revolutionary Element in Romanticism', in Frye (ed.), *Romanticism Reconsidered* (New York and London, 1963).

Furst, Lilian, *Romanticism in Perspective* (London, 1969).

Haakonsen, Daniel (ed.), *Contemporary Approaches to Ibsen*, I (Oslo, 1965) and II (Oslo, 1971). Vol. III (Oslo, 1977) is ed. Harald Noreng *et al.*

Halstead, J. B., *Romanticism* (New York, 1969).

Hofmannsthal, Hugo von, 'Die Menschen in Ibsens Drama' (1891), in McFarlane, *Ibsen: A Critical Anthology*.

Holtan, Orley, *Mythic Patterns in Ibsen's Last Plays* (Minneapolis, 1970).

Hurt, James, *Catiline's Dream: An Essay on Ibsen's Plays* (Urbana, Ill. 1972).

Ibsen, Henrik, *Ibsen: Letters and Speeches*, ed. Evert Sprinchorn (New York, 1974).

Johnston, Brian, 'The Dialectic of *Rosmersholm*', *Drama Survey*, VI (1967).

_____, The Ibsen Cycle: The Design of the Plays from 'Pillars of Society' to 'When We Dead Awaken'* (Boston, Mass., 1975).

Jong, Erica, *Fear of Flying* (New York, 1973).

Joyce, James, 'When We Dead Awaken', *Fortrightly Review*, LXXIII, (1900); repr. in McFarlane *Henrik Ibsen: A Critical Anthology*.

Kerans, James, 'Kindermord* and Will in *Little Eyolf*', in Travis Bogard and William Oliver (eds), *Modern Drama: Essays in Criticism* (New York, 1965).

Kierkegaard, Søren, *Fear and Trembling* (1857), trs. Robert Payne (London, 1939).

Knight, G. Wilson, *Ibsen* (Edinburgh and London, 1962).

Lawrence, D. H., *Phoenix: The Posthumous Papers of D. H. Lawrence* (London, 1961).

Lowenthal, Leo, *Literature and the Image of Man* (Boston, Mass., 1957).

Lyons, Charles, 'The Function of Dream and Reality in *John Gabriel Borkman*', *Scandinavian Studies*, XLV (1973).

_____, Henrik Ibsen: The Divided Consciousness* (Carbondale and Edwardsville, Ill., 1972).

_____, 'Some Variations of *Kindermord* as Dramatic Archetype', *Comparative Drama*, I (1967).

McCarthy, Mary, 'The Will and Testament of Ibsen', *Partisan Review*, 1956; repr. in McFarlane, *Ibsen: A Critical Anthology*.

McFarlane, James, Introductions to *The Oxford Ibsen*, I–VIII (London, 1960–77).

_____, *Henrik Ibsen: A Critical Anthology* (Harmondsworth, 1970).

_____, 'Meaning and Evidence in Ibsen's Drama', in Haakonsen, *Contemporary Approaches to Ibsen*, I.

_____, 'The Structured World of Ibsen's Late Dramas', in Durbach, *Ibsen and the Theatre*.

Mann, Thomas, 'Disorder and Early Sorrow', in Lionel Trilling (ed.), *The Experience of Literature* (New York, 1967).

Meyer, Michael, translation of *Hedda Gabler* (London, 1962).

Miller, J. Hillis, *The Disappearance of God* (Cambridge, Mass., 1963).

Northam, John, *Ibsen: A Critical Study* (Cambridge, 1973).

_____, 'A Note on the Language of *Rosmersholm*', *Ibsenårbok* (Oslo) 1977.

_____, 'Ibsen–Romantic, Realist or Symbolist?', in Harald Noreng *et al.* (eds), *Contemporary Approaches to Ibsen*, III (Oslo, 1977).

_____, "On a Firm Foundation–The Translation of Ibsen's Prose', *Ibsenårbok*, 1977.

Nietzsche, Friedrich, *'The Birth of Tragedy' and 'The Genealogy of Morals'*, trs. Francis Golffing (New York, 1956).

Otten, Terry, *The Deserted Stage: The Search for Dramatic Form in Nineteenth-Century England* (Athens, Ohio, 1972).

Peckham, Morse, *Beyond the Tragic Vision: The Quest for Identity in the Nineteenth Century* (New York, 1972).

_____, *Romanticism: The Culture of the Nineteenth Century* (New York, 1965).

_____, 'Towards a Theory of Romanticism', *PMLA*, LXVI (1951).

Popperwell, Ronald, *Norway* (New York, 1972).

Praz, Mario, *The Romantic Agony* (London, 1970).

Rank, Otto, *Das Inzest-Motiv in Dichtung und Sage* (Leipzig, 1925).

Raphael, Robert, 'From *Hedda Gabler* to *When We Dead Awaken*: the Quest for Self-realization', *Scandinavian Studies*, XXXVI (1964).

_____, 'Illusion and the Self in *The Wild Duck, Rosmersholm*, and *The Lady from the Sea*', *Scandinavian Studies*, XXXV (1963).

Šaari, Sandra, 'Of Madness or Fame: Ibsen's *Bygmester Solness*', *Scandinavian Studies*, L (1978).

Schechner, Richard, 'The Unexpected Visitor in Ibsen's Late Plays', *Educational Theatre Journal*, XIV (1962).

Shaw, G. B., *Shaw and Ibsen: Bernard Shaw's 'The Quintessence of Ibsenism' and Related Writings*, ed. J. L. Wisenthal (Toronto, 1979).

Solomon, Eric, 'The Incest Theme in *Wuthering Heights*', *Nineteenth Century Fiction*, XIV (1959).

Spengler, Oswald, *The Decline of the West* (Eng. trs. 1926–9), quoted in Richard Ellmann and Charles Feidelson (eds), *The Modern Tradition* (New York, 1965).

Steiner, George, *In Bluebeard's Castle* (London, 1971).

_____, *Nostalgia for the Absolute* (Toronto, 1974).

Stevens, Wallace, *The Palm at the end of the Mind* (New York, 1971).

Strindberg, August, *Six Plays by Strindberg*, trs. Elizabeth Sprigge (Garden City, NY, 1955).

_____, *'Själamörd* (apropos *Rosmersholm*)', trs. Rolf Fjelde, *Tulane Drama Review*, XIII (1968).

Suzman, Janet, '*Hedda Gabler*: The Play in Performance', in Durbach, *Ibsen and the Theatre.*

Valency, Maurice, *The Flower and the Castle* (New York, 1963).

Van Ghent, Dorothy, *The English Novel: Form and Function* (New York, 1953).

Wordsworth, William, *The Poetical Works,* ed. Thomas Hutchinson and Ernest de Selincourt (London, 1959).

Weigand, Hermann, *The Modern Ibsen* (New York, 1925).

Yeats, W. B., *Collected Poems* (London, 1958).

Index

Index